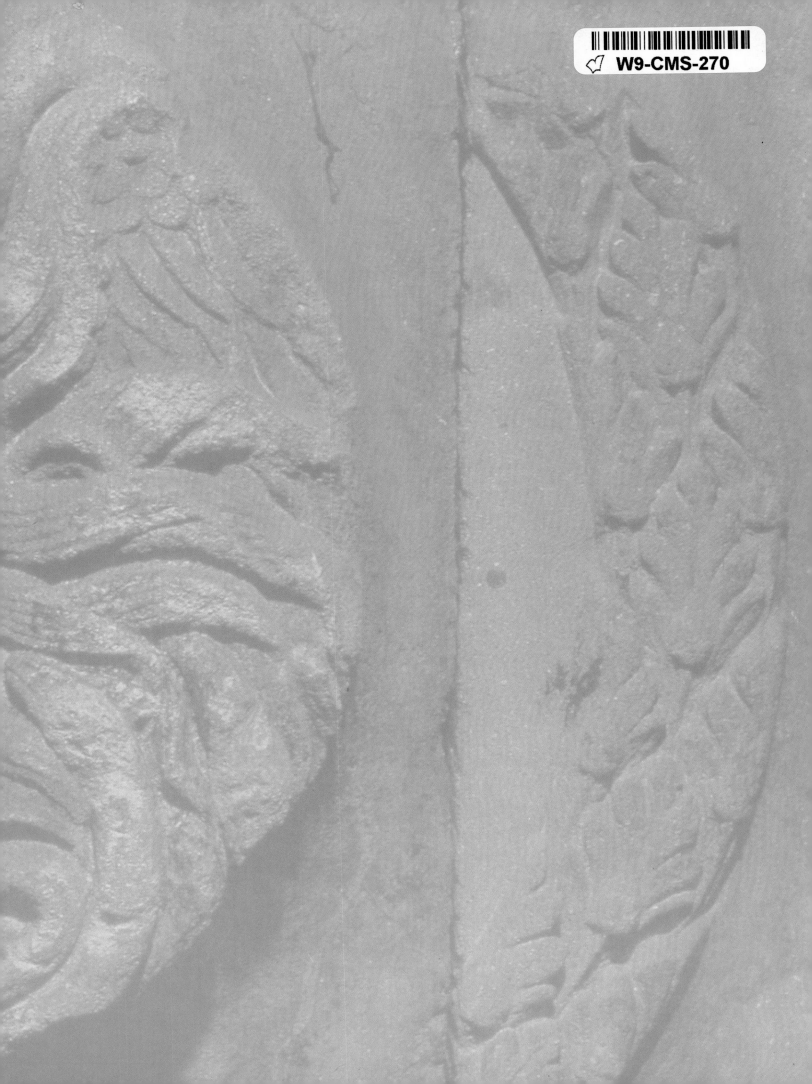

HISTORY OF ANCIENT

Rome

HISTORY OF ANCIENT
Rome

NATHANIEL HARRIS

hamlyn

Executive Editor: Julian Brown
Project Editor: Katey Day
Editor: Anne Crane
Creative Director: Keith Martin
Senior Designer: Claire Harvey
Designer: Marc Burville-Riley
Picture Research: Christine Junemann
Production Controller: Lee Sargent

First published in Great Britain in 2000
by Hamlyn, an imprint of
Octopus Publishing Group Limited
2–4 Heron Quays, Docklands,
London, E14 4JP

Copyright © 2000
Octopus Publishing Group Limited

ISBN 0 600 59809 8

Distributed in the United States and
Canada by
Sterling Publishing Co., Inc.
387 Park Avenue South
New York, NY 10016-8810

A catalogue record for this book is available
from the British Library

Produced by Toppan
Printed in China

CONTENTS

INTRODUCTION

NO ACCOUNT OF OUR OWN CIVILIZATION CAN GET VERY FAR WITHOUT INVOKING THE NAME OF ROME, WHETHER THE SUBJECT IS LAW, POLITICS, RELIGION, WAR OR LITERATURE. THE SPECTACULAR REMAINS OF ROMAN CIVILIZATION ARE SCATTERED OVER THREE CONTINENTS, AND IMAGES FROM ITS HISTORY – OF SENATORS IN TOGAS, BLOODSHED IN THE ARENA, TRIUMPHANT LEGIONS – ARE PART OF EVERYONE'S MENTAL FURNITURE.

Simply as a narrative, the history of Rome is astonishing and thrilling. Beginning as a little group of settlements on the River Tiber in Central Italy, with neighbours and rivals established only a few kilometres away, Rome took over the entire peninsula, destroyed the North African power of Carthage, and pursued a career of conquest that would make the Mediterranean Sea a 'Roman lake' and bring Gaul (France) and Britain within the circle of Roman civilization. Even more impressively, Rome began at an early date to extend citizenship to the subjected peoples. Unheard of in the ancient world, this policy ensured that the conquered would become reconciled to Roman rule, and that the Empire would be populated, and upheld, by peoples of many different races and religions.

Meanwhile it became more and more difficult for Rome's republican institutions to cope with the administration of a vast empire and the ambitions of politicians and military men. The Roman world was ravaged by a series of life-and-death struggles, between Marius and Sulla, Julius Caesar and Pompey, and Octavian and the lovers Antony and Cleopatra, which have all the fascination of high drama (and have in fact provided subjects for Shakespeare and other playwrights). Octavian emerged victorious and under a new title, Augustus, became the first Roman emperor: although appearances were kept up, the Republic gave way to a system of rule by one man.

Much depended on the character of that one man, and the efforts of 'good' emperors such as Augustus and Trajan were offset by the murders and enforced suicides inflicted by bloodthirsty, half-mad tyrants like Caligula and Nero. But in spite of occasional periods of turmoil, mainly affecting Rome itself, the Empire flourished mightily for two centuries. New cities were founded and old ones improved. A network of straight roads linked every part of the Empire. Magnificent feats of engineering brought water supplies and sewers to the cities. Splendid public buildings proclaimed the supremacy of the distinctive Roman way of life: forum and temples, public baths, the theatre, the circus for chariot-racing and, the greatest blot on Roman civilization, the amphitheatre in which gladiators fought and men and beasts were massacred. Although the poor in Rome were crammed into tenements, the town house and country villa provided elegant and pleasant surroundings for their betters. Culture flourished, and even if much of it was imported from Greece, the Romans made respectable contributions of their own to architecture, the arts, literature and philosophy.

From the 3rd century AD the peace of the Empire was increasingly broken by conflicts between rival emperors, and the legions struggled to defend the all-too-long imperial borders against the pressure of 'barbarian' peoples engaged in great folk migrations. The vicissitudes of Rome's political history tend to obscure the continued vitality of the Empire; it survived while undergoing tremendous changes, of which the most far-reaching was the adoption of Christianity as its state, and eventually its exclusive, religion. In the 5th century the Empire fragmented and there was a total collapse in the West, completed in AD 476 with the abdication of the last emperor; in the East, the Empire lasted another thousand years, albeit in a very different Greek and 'medieval' (Byzantine) form. But, as the final chapter of the book explains, this was by no means the end of Rome's influence upon the history of civilization.

1 REPUBLIC AND EMPIRE

Below: Aeneas is treated for a wound while comforting his weeping son Ascanius. The founders of Rome, Romulus and Remus, were said to be descended from the mythical Trojan hero. Pompeian wall painting, 1st century AD.

ROME'S RISE TO EMPIRE WAS SLOW BUT SPECTACULAR. EARLY IN HER HISTORY THE ROMANS DROVE OUT THEIR KINGS, AND IT WAS UNDER THE REPUBLIC THAT THE GREATEST ROMAN CONQUESTS TOOK PLACE. ITALY WAS SUBDUED; THE DEFEAT OF CARTHAGE MADE ROME MISTRESS OF THE WESTERN MEDITERRANEAN; A SERIES OF CAMPAIGNS TURNED GREECE, THE NEAR EAST AND EGYPT INTO ROMAN PROVINCES; AND THE EXPLOITS OF JULIUS CAESAR EXTENDED ROMAN RULE BEYOND THE MEDITERRANEAN INTO NORTH-WEST EUROPE. ALL THIS TOOK SOME FIVE HUNDRED YEARS, AND OWED AS MUCH TO ROMAN TENACITY AS TO THE MILITARY MIGHT OF THE LEGIONS. ROME WAS TRANSFORMED INTO A SUPERPOWER, BUT HER REPUBLICAN INSTITUTIONS FAILED TO COPE WITH THE CONSEQUENCES, AND A SERIES OF VICIOUS CIVIL WARS CULMINATED IN RULE BY ONE MAN, AUGUSTUS, THE FIRST OF THE ROMAN EMPERORS. DESPITE ERRATIC PERSONALITIES AND OFTEN SANGUINARY EVENTS AT THE CENTRE OF POWER, THE EMPIRE FARED REMARKABLY WELL, ITS LAWS AND CITY- AND VILLA-BASED CULTURE HOLDING SWAY FROM YORK TO PALMYRA. BUT FROM THE 3RD CENTURY AD IT CAME INCREASINGLY UNDER PRESSURE. IN THE 4TH CENTURY CHRISTIANITY WAS ESTABLISHED AS THE STATE RELIGION, BUT THE STRAINS ON THE EMPIRE BECAME INTOLERABLE AFTER GERMANIC TRIBES CROSSED INTO ITS TERRITORIES AND RAN WILD. IN THE WEST THE EMPIRE ENDED IN 476, WHEN THE LAST EMPEROR, LITTLE MORE THAN A PUPPET, ABDICATED; THE GREEK-SPEAKING EAST, HOWEVER, SUPPORTED A MORE OR LESS ROMAN STATE FOR ALMOST A THOUSAND YEARS MORE.

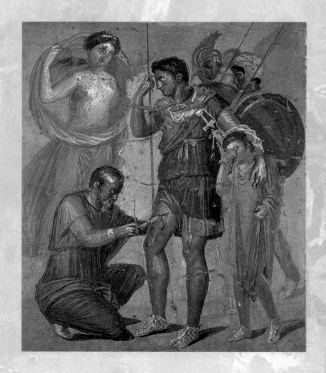

ORIGINS, REAL AND MYTHICAL

Rome began as a group of hilltop villages, easily defensible against intruders who might venture into the marshy lowlands through which the River Tiber ran down to the sea. The sites, later the famous Seven Hills, proved to have other advantages: they controlled the most convenient north-south route across the Tiber and, situated only 27 km (16¾ miles) from the sea, were in a position to control trade with Central Italy. Settlement on the Roman hills seems to have begun in the 10th century BC, when Latin-speaking peoples moved in after occupying Latium, the area south of the Tiber. By the 7th century BC the villages had joined forces and the Forum, a valley between the Palatine and Esquiline Hills, was being drained and laid out as a civic centre.

Roman tradition dated the foundation of the city to 753 BC and credited it to two brothers, Romulus and Remus, who had been left to die in the wilderness but were suckled by a she-wolf. Romulus founded Rome and peopled it with fugitives and outlaws; then he acquired women for the community by stealing them from the neighbouring Sabines, an episode known as 'the rape of the Sabine women'. Though the legend has a certain low-life plausibility, it appears to have been suggested by Greek myths, which powerfully influenced Roman thinking. A later legend attached Rome directly to the mythical past of the Greeks and gave Romulus a distinguished human ancestor (he was, in any case, a son of the war god Mars). The Greeks believed that in some past age they had besieged the city of Troy for ten years, until the Trojans were tricked into hauling a large wooden horse into their city; at night the Greek warriors hidden in it emerged and opened the gates to their army. The Trojans were slaughtered and their city levelled, but in Roman legend one of their princes, Aeneas, escaped and made his way to Italy, where he married the daughter of King Latinus and became the ancestor of the Romans. (The poet Virgil composed a narrative on the subject, the *Aeneid*, which became the Roman national epic.)

The Greek elements in these stories are not surprising, since the Greeks established themselves in Italy during the 8th century and strongly influenced the Etruscans, whose city-states dominated north-central Italy. Among other things the Etruscans acquired the alphabet and writing from the Greeks, passing it on to the Romans. In the late 7th century an Etruscan, Tarquinius Priscinus, is said to have become king of Rome, and over the following century there were Etruscan or Etruscan-related rulers. During this period Rome became the leading city-state in Latium, capturing its main rival, Alba Longa, in about 600 BC. The city's Etruscan kings also seem to have introduced the earliest of the civic amenities for which Rome was to become famous: a system of public sewers including the Cloaca Maxima, and the Temple of Jupiter, Juno and Minerva (known as the Capitol) on the Capitoline Hill.

Both structures have been credited to the last king of Rome, Tarquinius Superbus ('Tarquin the Proud', traditional reign dates 535–510 BC), although some authorities believe that he is a mythical figure, created to symbolize the evils of monarchy. As such he was depicted as a tyrant who was finally brought down when his son Sextus raped the Roman matron Lucretia; this is said to have provoked a revolt led by Lucius Junius Brutus that drove Tarquinius from Rome. As a consequence, in or around 510 BC Rome was simultaneously freed from Etruscan control and became a republic.

The power of myth. This bronze statue, the Capitoline Wolf, is Etruscan, c. 500 BC. The figures of the children were added during the Renaissance; they converted it into a now famous image of Romulus and Remus being suckled by a wolf.

THE CONQUEST OF ITALY

In the two and a half centuries that followed the expulsion of King Tarquinius, Rome was almost constantly at war. At the same time, fundamental institutions were being forged that would serve the state for the rest of its history. Initially the Roman Republic was created by and for the upper class of patricians, who alone served as public officials. The chief executive power was vested in two consuls, who were elected every year by the *comitia*, an assembly largely controlled by the patricians and their clients. In dire emergencies a special officer was chosen, the dictator, who held absolute power for the duration of the emergency and was expected to lay it down the moment the crisis was over. Legislation and leisurely pondered advice was the business of a senate of elders (*patres*), already established under the monarchy.

The patricians probably originated as the wealthy class, but if so they had hardened into an aristocratic caste by republican times, unwilling to admit even the richest members of the lower or plebeian class (*plebs*) into their ranks. During the next two hundred years the plebeians forced one concession after another from the patricians, who were dependent on their inferiors for military manpower. The struggle was conducted in a remarkably peaceful fashion. The main weapon of the plebeians, and a very compelling one, was

The ruins of the Forum Romanum, the oldest of the great *fora* , or squares, of ancient Rome. Once a market place between two of Rome's seven hills, it later became a splendid city centre.

secession – literally withdrawing themselves *en masse* from the city, which apparently happened several times from 494 BC onwards. Plebeian equivalents to patrician institutions were devised, notably elected tribunes and a plebeian assembly; the patricians were forced to accept their integration into the political system, giving the tribunes the power to veto most decisions while the plebeian Assembly of the People (*concilium plebis*) could pass resolutions (*plebiscites*) that had the force of law. In time plebeians gained admittance to all the chief offices and a plebeian element appeared in the Senate.

In theory Rome had become a state in which the people ruled; in practice the wealthy and well-born continued to dominate politics. Only the richer plebeians had much time for political life, and they soon joined forces with the patricians in a more broadly based ruling class. Popular resentments needed to be defused, but this was achieved through the shrewdness of the ruling class and the growing success of Rome. Reforms of the harsh laws penalizing debtors, and new land made available by conquest or colonization, did a good deal to alleviate the discontent of the poorer plebeians, and in the crises of the following few centuries the Romans proved to be an impressively united people.

This unity was maintained during long wars that were far from being unbroken triumphs. Following the establishment of the Republic, Rome was unable to maintain her predominance in Latium and had to accept the other cities of the region as equal partners in a Latin League. The Romans gradually acquired the upper hand in the course of the 5th century BC, concurrently warding off common enemies of the Latins such as the interloping Volsci and Acqui; meanwhile they came close to disaster before conquering and absorbing the neighbouring Sabines in 460–449 BC.

Grim local struggles continued into the 4th century. In 396 the neighbouring Etruscan city of Veii was besieged and destroyed; this was a significant victory, since Veii, only 19 km (12 miles) from Rome, had long been a serious military threat and commercial rival. Etruscan power was by now in decline, and the inability of the Etruscan city-states to work together allowed the

Romans to destroy them piecemeal. But the immediate aftermath of the success at Veii was a near-fatal setback in 390, when a horde of Gauls – Celtic invaders sweeping down from the north – defeated a Roman army and captured and sacked the city itself; the Capitol held out, but the Gauls left only after they had been paid off.

The city had to be rebuilt, yet within a few years Rome reasserted her leadership of the Latin League and began to turn her partners into subordinate allies; this was not accomplished without resistance, but the Romans emerged victorious from the final Latin War of 340–338 BC. Another half a century of warfare was needed to subdue the fierce Samnite tribes of the southern Apennines, who were doughty mountain fighters and surprisingly adept at creating alliances with Etruscan, Gaulish and other peoples, so that at times the

Republican hero. The subject of this strong-featured bronze bust has traditionally been identified as Lucius Junius Brutus, leader of the revolt that drove out the last king of Rome; 3rd century BC.

The Chimaera, one of the stranger hybrid beasts of mythology, with the head and body of a lion, a snake's tail, and a goat's head in the centre of its back. Etruscan bronze, 4th century BC. The Etruscans' culture deeply influenced early Rome.

very existence of Rome seemed threatened. Once more a Roman army sustained a humiliating defeat – in 321 at the Caudine Forks, where it allowed itself to be trapped in a narrow defile and was forced to surrender; and once again Rome fought on and proved successful. In 312, even before bringing the Second Samnite War to a victorious conclusion (in 302), the Romans began to build the first of their great strategic roads, the Appian Way (Via Appia); during this period it ran south as far as Capua, strengthening Roman control over the fertile region of Campania. Final victory in the Third Samnite War (298–290 BC) enabled the Romans to secure Campania and also to push north, bringing Etruscans and some of the Gauls to heel and planting colonies among them.

Gauls and Samnites had humiliated the Romans without halting their expansion. It was Rome's power of endurance and recovery, more than her military strength, that made her seem irresistible. Other peoples might win victories; the Romans won wars. Later writers looked back on the early centuries of the Republic as a golden age of sternly virtuous patriots, spartan in habits and selflessly devoted to duty: men such as Cincinnatus, who was called from the plough during an emergency to become dictator, saved the state in 16 days, and then went straight back to his farm. Another important factor in the long-

term success of Rome was her relatively generous treatment of initially unwilling allies and conquered enemies. From as early as the 380s BC Rome was extending citizenship rights to at least some of these, increasing the numbers of Romans and giving her victories a permanence unknown to most ancient empire-builders. (However, the alternative Roman practice was to be merciless, massacring or enslaving the defeated so that they never again posed a threat.) New territories were further secured by planting colonies of Roman and Latin settlers at strategic points, ensuring that there were loyal elements even among defeated peoples who remained hostile. The policy of reconciliation was not applied as consistently or quickly as it might have been, but the fact that it was done at all is a tribute to Roman foresight. Its value was to be proved by the loyalty shown by Rome's Italian allies during her long wars against Carthage, the great Phoenician power of North Africa.

In the early 3rd century BC the Carthaginians were not yet enemies, and when the Romans' expansion to the south brought them up against the Greeks of Southern Italy, common interests brought Rome and Carthage together. As a great maritime trading power Carthage had for centuries been in competition with the Greeks in the western Mediterranean, and the Carthaginians had earlier found allies among the Etruscans to help them restrain Greek ambitions. Centuries of struggles in Sicily had ended in a stalemate, leaving Carthage in control of the western and the Greeks of the eastern half of the island.

The situation in Southern Italy was complicated by rivalries between the Greek cities situated along the coast, the anti-Greek activities of the Lucanians and other inland tribes, and the growing suspicions of Roman encroachments felt by the most important of the Greek states, Tarentum. In 282 the Greek city of Thurii, menaced by the Lucanians, appealed to Rome, which sent a force that was installed as a garrison. The Tarentines were alarmed enough to drive it out, sink a Roman fleet and hire a restless military adventurer, Pyrrhus, King of Epirus (north-west Greece), to take the offensive. Pyrrhus arrived with a professional army of 25,000 men and 20 elephants, a war weapon familiar to the Greeks since the Indian campaigns of Alexander the Great in 327–325 BC but unknown to the Romans. He twice defeated Roman armies, but his forces suffered such heavy losses that he retired to Sicily; his famous remark 'Another such victory and I shall be ruined' gave rise to the phrase 'pyrrhic victory'. The Romans refused Pyrrhus' peace offers and allied with the Carthaginians, whose

Sicilian possessions were under attack from Pyrrhus. In spite of his earlier experiences the king returned to the mainland for one more attempt to conquer the Romans; beaten at Beneventum and having lost two-thirds of his army, he sailed away and left the Tarentines to their fate. By 270 Rome was mistress of the Italian peninsula from the River Arno in the north down to the Straits of Messina separating the mainland from Sicily.

Hades, lord of the underworld, and his wife Persephone; vase painting by a Greek artist from Southern Italy. Roman expansion brought contacts – and wars – with the long-established Greek cities in Italy. Greek culture profoundly influenced the Roman way of life.

THE STRUGGLE AGAINST CARTHAGE

Control of the Straits of Messina was the issue that brought Rome and Carthage into conflict. But war was probably inevitable, given Rome's new position as a Mediterranean power. Messina itself (then known as Messana) was controlled by the Mamertines, Italian mercenaries who had seized the city after being brought to Sicily by Pyrrhus. When they were attacked by the leading Greek state, Syracuse, different factions of the Mamertines appealed to Carthage and Rome respectively, creating a situation in which the two great powers became embroiled in a war.

One of the Roman adjectives meaning 'Carthaginian' was *punicus*, and the Roman-Carthaginian conflicts are generally known as the Punic wars. The First Punic War was a hard-fought affair that lasted for 23 years (264–241 BC). Rome's citizen armies performed well against the mercenaries employed by Carthage, but Rome had to become a naval power to win; she built several fleets and developed new boarding tactics involving grapnels that enabled the legionaries to make their prowess felt. After its first surprise victory at Mylae, in 260, the Roman navy suffered some serious reverses; an expedition to attack Carthage itself turned into a disaster; and though the Carthaginians were pushed back in Sicily, the Romans failed to achieve a decisive result. Finally the Roman navy won command of the seas with a victory off the Aegates Islands and the two exhausted combatants made peace. Carthage ceded her Sicilian possessions to Rome and paid a war indemnity of 3,200 talents. Three years later, taking advantage of a mercenary revolt that had paralyzed Carthage, the Romans used the excuse of an appeal by some of the mercenaries to seize Sardinia and Corsica; when the Carthaginians protested against this blatant aggression the Romans added insult to injury by extorting another large indemnity from them.

Syracuse had switched to the Roman side early in the war and, though now a client state, retained

The Temple of Concord at Agrigento in Sicily. This famous Greek temple was built in the mid-5th century BC and survived the centuries-long wars between Carthaginians, Greeks and Romans. The nearby Temple of Zeus was less fortunate: built by Carthaginian prisoners, it was later destroyed by a vengeful Carthaginian army.

its independence; but the rest of Sicily passed directly to the Romans and was organized as a province, distinct from the now-extensive mainland territories that made up 'Rome'. The existence of overseas possessions led to the first 'imperial' administrative measures a few years later, when two extra magistrates were appointed, one to take charge of Roman Sicily, the other to administer Sardinia and Corsica. The creation of a 'republican empire' had begun.

The Carthaginians reacted energetically to their reverses, building up a new empire in Spain under Hamilcar Barca, his son-in-law Hasdrubal, and Hamilcar's son Hannibal. This Barca family represented the Carthaginian 'hawks', bent on expansion and revenge on Rome. There was also a peace party, led by a senator called Hanno, which argued that Carthage's future lay in Africa; but their influence seems to have prevailed only at the most unfortunate moments, when their lack of enthusiasm hampered military operations without stopping them or conciliating the Romans.

Beyond this, little is known of life at Carthage, although the bare facts about her oligarchic city-state constitution have been preserved. Her religion certainly involved human sacrifices to Baal and other gods; her art was imitated from the Greeks; and in Roman eyes the only Carthaginian book worth translating was an encyclopaedic treatise on farming. This may or may not have been true: like the Roman phrase 'Punic faith' (meaning treachery), the supposed cultural barrenness of Carthage may reflect nothing more than the extent of Roman prejudice, through which most of our information has been filtered.

The forward policy of the Barcas in Spain brought on the war that was to decide the fate of the Mediterranean. According to a Roman-Carthaginian agreement of 226 BC, Spain south of the River Ebro was recognized as the Carthaginian sphere of influence. But like most such agreements it left opportunities for discord if the parties to it were in the mood. In this instance the opportunity for disagreement lay in

Episodes from the story of Queen Dido of Carthage and the Trojan Aeneas are shown on this mosaic pavement from a Roman villa at Lowham in Britain, c. AD 350. The Roman ancestor-figure Aeneas abandoned Dido to pursue his destiny – one reason, in legend, for the 'eternal' hostility between Carthage and Rome.

the existence of a Roman ally, the city of Saguntum, on the Spanish coast south of the Ebro. Hannibal tried to bring Saguntum under Carthaginian control; Saguntum refused and resisted; Hannibal besieged and captured the city; and the Romans declared war. Evidently both sides were spoiling for a fight.

Hannibal was one of history's greatest generals, and certainly the most dangerous opponent

Fragments of a broken culture: a Carthaginian votive stele (upright stone) carved to represent a gable-like structure, with images of a presiding goddess and the prow of a ship from the city's once formidable navy.

that Rome ever had to face; while he was still a boy, his father, Hamilcar, had made him vow undying enmity towards the Romans. His power to command loyal service is all the more striking in that the majority of his men were mercenaries with no permanent commitment to the Carthaginian cause; they were also of many nationalities (Numidians, Spaniards, Celts), each fighting in its native fashion and posing difficult problems of coordination. Hannibal mastered these and won victory after victory over the Roman legions, despite their advantage in being a citizen militia, raised from a single community and trained to fight together. Like most great generals, Hannibal moved fast and kept the initiative by doing the unexpected.

All this became apparent during his early campaigns. The Romans equipped armies to invade Spain and Africa, confident in their naval superiority and huge reserves of manpower; but instead of letting them choose their own ground, Hannibal decided to strike into Italy and raise the subject-cities of Rome against their masters, and by doing so reverse the balance of manpower. The Carthaginians marched through Spain and southern France, gave the slip to a Roman army based on Marseilles, and crossed the Alps – an epic feat until modern engineers tamed the mountains with roads and tunnels; bringing an army over them was still heroic when it was done by Napoleon Bonaparte two thousand years later. Early autumn snows made Hannibal's task even more difficult, and he came down into Italy with a force of only 26,000 men (about half the original number) and a much depleted train of elephants with which to disorganize and terrorize the elephantless Romans.

The benefits of Hannibal's daring were rapidly felt. The Celtic inhabitants of the Po Valley, subdued by the Romans only a few years before, began to go over to the Carthaginians; and the Roman army in Sicily, on the point of sailing for Africa, had to be recalled to face the invader. When it joined the existing Roman forces in the north and attacked Hannibal in December 218 – only eight months after he had set out from Spain – he outmanoeuvred, ambushed and routed it at the battle of Trebbia.

An exceptionally severe winter gave Rome a breathing-space in which to raise fresh armies. But in May 217 Hannibal crossed the Apennines into Central Italy; and at the battle of Lake Trasimene a pursuing Roman army allowed itself to be pinned between the hills and the lake and was driven into the water with huge losses.

In spite of this brilliant success, the cities of Etruria and Latium remained loyal to Rome – the first setback for Hannibal's strategy and one of the fruits of Rome's relatively enlightened policies towards subjects and allies. Hannibal therefore pushed on into Southern Italy, where he hoped to find support among the less-reconciled Samnites and Greeks. The Romans appointed as dictator one of their elder statesmen, Fabius, who was so impressed by Hannibal's victories that he decided to avoid a pitched battle and try to buy time for a Roman recovery and wear down the Carthaginians. The Romans nicknamed the dictator Fabius Cunctator ('Delayer'), and 'fabian tactics' has passed into English to describe 'masterly inactivity'. Though he was later considered to have saved the state, Fabius' policies seemed dubious to many of his contemporaries, who argued that they left the Carthaginians free to march all over Campania and Apulia, looting and burning at will, and apparently demonstrated the impotence of Rome to her allies. In 216, when Fabius had served the six-month maximum term as dictator, he was replaced by two newly elected consuls, Paullus and Varro, who collected a large army and moved directly against the invaders.

At Cannae in Apulia, Hannibal's army, though outnumbered, won the greatest of its victories and the Romans suffered their greatest-ever disaster. The legions forced back the Carthaginians in the centre, but Hannibal's African pikemen held the wings and his Spanish and Celtic horsemen drove off the Roman cavalry. The specially reinforced Carthaginian centre did not break; the Africans closed in from the sides; and the Spaniards and Celts completed the encirclement by attacking from the rear. The Romans were slaughtered, and one of the consuls, Paullus, fell. Soon afterwards, Capua and many other southern Italian towns declared for Hannibal, and Rome's situation appeared to be desperate.

This proved to be the high point of Hannibal's fortunes. Rome raised new legions, accepting even criminals into the ranks; but her leaders returned to Fabius' policy of avoiding battle. Instead, Roman troops engaged the Carthaginians and their allies wherever Hannibal was *not* present. Capua, Syracuse, Tarentum and other pro-Carthaginian cities were besieged and taken; Hannibal's brother, Hasdrubal, was defeated and killed when he attempted to bring reinforcements

Hannibal, the Carthaginian general who campaigned in Italy for 16 years and won many victories over the Romans – without, however, breaking their spirit; marble Roman bust, found at Capua in Southern Italy.

Conqueror of Hannibal: bronze bust of Scipio Africanus. In it, he is evidently much older than when, as a 35-year-old general, he invaded North Africa and ended the war against Carthage in 202 BC with a decisive victory over Hannibal at the battle of Zama.

from Spain; and a new young Roman general of genius, Publius Cornelius Scipio, invaded Spain and eventually drove the Carthaginians out of the peninsula. With steadily declining manpower, Hannibal was forced back to Bruttium, in the toe of Italy. When Scipio invaded Africa and his victories threatened Carthage itself, Hannibal was recalled; he left Italy after 16 years' campaigning, having out-generalled his enemies time after time without managing to break the Romans' resolve or take their city.

In Scipio, Hannibal met his match. At the battle of Zama in 202 BC, there was no successful ambush or out-flanking, but a straight fight between the two armies – Hannibal's almost certainly without his veterans, most of whom were probably impossible to transport from Italy to Africa, while the Romans were strengthened by the presence of Carthage's former Numidian allies, who had prudently changed sides. The outcome was decided by Scipio's Roman and Numidian cavalry, who broke their opponents' ranks and then fell on the Carthaginian rear. Hannibal's army was destroyed, although himself managed to escape. After this crushing defeat Carthage sued for peace, agreeing to dismantle her navy, give up all claims to Spain and pay an enormous war indemnity. Rome emerged from the war in full control of Sicily, where the destruction of Syracuse in 211 had eliminated the Greeks as a political force; and Carthage gave up all her possessions on the east coast of Spain, although almost two centuries would pass before the Romans managed to subdue the entire peninsula. In recognition of his victory at Zama, Scipio was given the honorary title 'Africanus', and he is known to history as Scipio Africanus.

Although Carthage was now no more than a dependent ally of Rome, suspicion of her had become ingrained in the Roman mind. When Hannibal began to reform the Carthaginian government and economy, the Romans willingly believed the reports of his opponents in the city, who accused him of plotting a war of revenge with the Seleucid kings of western Asia. Hannibal was forced to flee from court to court, seeking shelter from enemies or doubtful friends of Rome; when, in about 182, the king of Bithynia in Asia Minor (present-day Turkey) decided to give him up to the Romans, he poisoned himself to avoid a more degrading and painful fate. Carthage survived untouched until 150 BC, although her renewed commercial prosperity made the Romans uneasy and caused the fanatical Cato to end his every speech in the Roman Senate, whatever the subject, with the words *Carthago delenda est*: 'Carthage must be destroyed.' And destroyed it was, by a series of deliberately contrived incidents that finally provoked the Carthaginians into attacking one of Rome's allies. The Romans intervened and in 146, after a three-year blockade, razed the city. The Senate grimly decreed that neither house nor crop should again rise on the site, which was ploughed and sown with salt; however, Carthage was so well situated as a port and entrepôt for the African hinterland that she did rise again a hundred years later, becoming one of the most prosperous Roman cities in the Mediterranean.

The ruins of old Carthage: remains of a graveyard. The Romans' hatred of their foes was so intense that their destruction of Carthage in 146 BC obliterated almost all evidence of the Carthaginian way of life and cultural achievements.

VICTORIES AND VIOLENCE

The Romans now controlled the entire western Mediterranean. With so much new territory to organize, they were reluctant to become involved in Eastern affairs, even though they had a score to settle with Philip V of Macedon, who had fought against them as an ally of Hannibal. Macedon was one of the great powers of the eastern Mediterranean and the Near East, along with the Seleucid empire in western Asia and Ptolemaic Egypt. All three were ruled by Greek dynasties which had established themselves when the vast Greco-Macedonian empire of Alexander the Great broke up following his death in 323 BC; lesser powers included Pergamum in Asia Minor and the city-states of Greece, among them Athens, which had immense prestige because of its glorious past, but maintained only a qualified independence in the shadow of Macedon to the north. The entire region, including Egypt, was wealthy, filled with great cities, and politically and culturally Greek; both its powers and its culture are consequently described as 'Hellenistic'.

Rome was probably bound to become involved in the East sooner or later; what could not have been predicted was that it would be sooner, and that the great powers there, which had been fighting one another for over a century without a definite outcome, would go down relatively quickly before the Romans. When Rhodes, Pergamum and other Greek states appealed for help against Philip V's ambitions, Rome intervened and in 197 BC won a decisive victory; but though Macedon was stripped of her conquests, her fleet and 1,000 talents, Rome proclaimed the liberation of the Greek city-states and actually withdrew her forces. The result was to create a power vacuum that the Seleucid king Antiochus attempted to fill. When he invaded Greece the Romans returned, defeated him at Thermopylae (191), and then drove his forces out of Asia Minor. The nominal beneficiaries were Rhodes and Pergamum, for Rome, though very much the protecting power, still held back from making direct territorial gains. But after another war against Macedon and a series of Greek intrigues and squabbles, Macedon was turned into a Roman province along with the rest of Greece, which was cowed by the complete destruction in 146 of the historic city of Corinth. Thirteen years later Attalus of Pergamum died, bequeathing his kingdom to his Roman allies, and the province of Asia (rather smaller than it sounds) was formed. Meanwhile, the tribes along the coasts of southern France and Dalmatia had been subdued. With Egypt friendly and Seleucid Syria visibly in decline, the Mediterranean was taking on the appearance of a Roman lake.

The acquisition of such an enormous empire within a few generations put a terrible strain on the Roman political system and the Roman way of life. As in other rapidly enriched societies, there was irresponsible luxury, women were allowed more freedom in practice if not in theory, and the young became harder to control. 'Culture' acquired a separate and prestigious existence. The conquest of Greece led to a Greek counter-conquest of Rome in the spheres of religion, philosophy, literature and the plastic arts: like parvenus everywhere, the Romans paid cash down for statues, paintings and lessons in philosophy and rhetoric; and like most impoverished artists and intellectuals, the Greeks willingly sold.

Conservatives inevitably complained that the new sophistication was incompatible with the ploughman virtue of Cincinnatus and that luxury was enervating; but there were deeper causes for the upheavals that shook and finally destroyed the Republic in the space of a century. In practice the old Roman system had been run by the Senate, although both magistrates and the plebeian institutions – the tribunate and popular assembly – had wide powers that were never brought into play. With the growth of empire there was discontent at home on several fronts. The new-rich businessmen and capitalists resented their exclusion from power by the aristocracy controlling the Senate. An ever-growing mass of landless proletarians crowded into the tenement blocks of Rome, mutely threatening the security of the possessing classes; they found themselves redundant

Opposite: The Temple of Vesta in Rome, still on its site after 3,000 years; its round-hut form was preserved through many rebuildings. Vesta was the Roman goddess of the hearth, and the Vestal Virgins ensured that a flame was kept constantly burning on her altar.

in a world where the peasant could not compete against the products of mass slave labour on large estates. Many Italian cities had not yet been admitted to the privileges and profits of Roman citizenship, and began to grow restive. And the provinces of Rome's young Empire felt that they were being fleeced by their governors and tax-gatherers, appointed by an administration that was still adapted only to governing a city-state. The provincial's best hope was to be protected by a Roman general with larger ambitions than self-enrichment; and the troops too developed a more personal loyalty, looking to their general for protection against sharp businessmen and other exploiters when their service was over and they had been settled on the land.

In the light of all this, the confused and violent history of the late Republic becomes easier to follow; what remains astonishing is that Rome survived when she was so often simultaneously torn by civil war and engaged in testing conflicts with foreign enemies. The first crisis occurred in 133–132 BC, when the tribune Tiberius Gracchus proposed a drastic agrarian reform that would have limited the size of estates and ensured that the surplus was used to re-create a class of small farmers. Since the conservative Senate opposed the measure, Gracchus persuaded the Assembly of the People to pass it – thus invoking the dormant sovereignty of the people but (in conservative eyes) violating the conventions of the constitution. When he sought re-election as tribune, a group of senators and their followers assassinated him on the Capitol; whether they acted through self-interest, or genuine fear that Gracchus was aiming to become a tyrant, remains an open question. The murder of Gracchus was the first act of violence in Roman political life, foreshadowing the epidemic slaughter of later decades.

Ten years later Tiberius' younger brother, Gaius Gracchus, was elected to the tribunate and took up the reform programme again. He was even more radical than Tiberius, proposing measures to keep the price of wheat low, to begin redistribution of the land, and to tackle unemployment by a programme of public works and the establishment of colonies in Italy and abroad. Since these were designed to help the poor, the Assembly of the People readily passed them, while the Senate short-sightedly disapproved. But when Gaius sensibly proposed to extend Roman citizenship to the Latins and give the other Italian allies new rights, the people were easily persuaded not to share their privileges. Gaius failed in a bid to be re-elected, and shortly afterwards the Senate issued an emergency decree (*senatus consultum ultimum*) authorizing the consuls to take whatever measures were necessary 'to save the state'. The result was a massacre of Gaius' followers; and Gaius himself committed suicide to avoid capture.

The Gracchi can be viewed as revolutionaries or reformers, or simply as faction leaders: they were, after all, members of the aristocracy, like most later chiefs of the *Populares*, or popular party, and were arguably impelled to manipulate popular assemblies because they were unable to control the Senate, where their conservative opponents, the *Optimates* (the best men), were in the majority. If the policies advocated by the Gracchi seem too idealistic – and too risky – to have been motivated by pure self-interest, the same cannot be said of their successors. Roman party politics soon became on both sides more a matter of personal ambition, political machinery and horse-trading than of genuine conviction. In time party machines developed, run by powerful families and staffed by their clients (dependants), with an executive arm drawn from more disreputable elements including street gangs; these fought and intrigued against each other in the city unless (or until) the army intervened.

All this lay in the not very distant future. For a decade or so following the death of Gaius Gracchus the *Optimates* ruled unchallenged. But their position was weakened by the incompetent handling of a war against Jugurtha, king of Numidia, that dragged on for years. Finally, against the wishes of the Senate, the command was given to Gaius Marius, an officer of relatively humble birth who reached the top at an advanced age (he was about 48). Marius created a new kind of paid professional Roman army, largely raised from the urban proletariat, which in the event would prove more loyal to its leaders than to the state. Jugurtha was defeated, captured after

Opposite: Roman luxury; painted panel from a villa at Boscoreale, near Pompeii in Southern Italy, where it decorated the bedroom of Publius Fannius Synistor. The painting, one of several from the villa, suggests the Romans' wealth, their appetite for culture, and their large-scale architectural ambitions.

The dictator as portrayed by a near-contemporary. This portrait bust of Sulla was carved in the mid-1st century BC, and impresses as an image of force and cruel violence. Though he won supreme power, Sulla failed in his attempt to put the clock back.

negotiations skilfully conducted by Marius' able young lieutenant, Lucius Cornelius Sulla, and executed. Then, in 102–101 BC, Marius won two bloody victories over the Cimbri and Teutones, Germanic tribes whose ferocity and early successes in invading Italy had shaken the Romans. Marius was now a power in the state, with an enormous personal following of which the most important elements were the veteran soldiers for whom he had obtained land grants. Securing these involved him in politics, although he had few other political aims other than satisfying his vanity by holding numerous consulships; and when his clumsy manoeuvres upset both *Optimates* and *Populares*, he prudently retired.

In Rome, violence broke out again in 91 BC with the murder of Drusus, another tribune who had proposed extending the franchise. This time the Italian allies reacted vigorously to the disappointment of their hopes: they rose in arms, proclaimed a separate Italian republic, and fought so effectively that Rome was able to win the war only by conceding citizenship to all who were prepared to stop fighting. In effect, all free Italians became citizens.

This, the Social War, confirmed the military talents of Sulla, who emerged as the rival of his former commander Marius; Sulla's aristocratic background made him more congenial to the *Optimates* and ensured that Marius became associated with the *Populares*. As consul for the year 88 BC Sulla was given command of the army against Mithridates VI of Pontus, who had invaded Roman Asia and had received an enthusiastic welcome from a provincial population disillusioned by Roman exactions. Marius, who wanted the command for himself, allied with the tribune Sulpicius and was named by the plebeian assembly to replace Sulla.

Instead of giving up his command, Sulla simply marched on Rome, took it, executed Sulpicius, and 'rectified' the political situation. This assault on Rome itself marked a new stage in the decline of respect for constitutional forms, and makes Sulla something of an enigma: he was the conservative champion of the Senate, bent on restoring the old ways, yet lawless and murderous in the means he used to do so. Leaving a precarious situation in Rome, he marched east to deal with Mithridates. While he was gone Marius, who had fled to Africa, returned; finding the Romans already at odds with one another, he allied himself with the dissident consul Cornelius Cinna, and besieged and captured Rome. Once in control he indulged in a five-day orgy of revenge on all who had offended him; now about 70 years old, he died before he could set off for the East and meet Sulla on the battlefield.

Sulla, technically an outlaw while his enemies controlled Rome, defeated Mithridates but made peace with him in return for money and supplies. Having looted the cities of Roman Asia, he invaded Italy, crushed the Marians, and by 82 BC found himself master of the Roman state.

There followed another round of bloodletting. Sulla acquired a quasi-legal authority by having himself appointed dictator 'to restore the state'; like so many of his 'traditionalist' measures it was essentially fraudulent, since the dictatorship had been legally abolished over a century before and its revived form omitted the liberty-preserving six-month limit on holding the office. Meanwhile Sulla conducted a reign of terror and wiped out every trace of opposition, posting up list after list of those proscribed (named as outlaws, to be killed on sight) for a fearful citizenry to scrutinize. He also enacted a complete programme of reforms that made the Senate more representative (of the possessing classes), broke the power of the tribunes, and protected the state against the ambitions of generals – such as Sulla. While he lived, and could call upon his veterans, comfortably settled on confiscated lands, Sulla's constitution worked, even after his retirement in 80 BC; but most of his measures were scrapped within ten years of his death in 79.

Since his power was absolute with or without a constitution, Sulla must have been sincere in his traditionalism. Curiously, he failed to realize that using violence against the state – whether the object was to reform, rule or ruin it – was bound to subvert, not preserve, its traditions. More than most saviours, Sulla was a harbinger of the doom he sought to avert.

Cicero the statesman: an imperial-period copy of a bust made soon after Cicero's death in 43 BC. In his political life he stood for moderate policies and tried in vain to uphold the republic against the factional and military forces that destroyed it.

THE TRIUMVIRS

The Senate's authority had been restored by Sulla, but it soon became clear that the old order was incapable of managing a huge empire and coping with political and social problems at home. Moreover the attempt to do so brought new dangers by increasing the dependence of the state on self-interested military men.

Sulla's settlement was under threat almost from the first. As early as 78 BC one of the consuls who sympathized with the popular party, Marcus Aemilius Lepidus, attempted to restore the tribunate by force of arms, but was defeated. A more serious challenge was posed by Sertorius, a follower of Marius who turned Spain into a formidable independent republic which he led from 80–72 BC; luckily for the Romans he was assassinated by an ambitious but less able subordinate who was disposed of rapidly. In both these instances the military *coup de grâce* was delivered by a young Roman general who was not a member of the Senate, Pompey (Gnaeus Pompeius), who had been one of Sulla's lieutenants.

Pompey and another of Sulla's followers, Marcus Licinius Crassus, were to be responsible for sweeping away their former chief's constitution. They probably had no intention of overthrowing the state, but the Senate's suspicion of successful soldiers restricted their influence and encouraged them to align themselves with subversive forces that would ultimately destroy the Republic.

Another result of senatorial hostility was that Crassus and Pompey, though rivals, were more than once compelled to work together to achieve their political aims. Crassus had the smaller military reputation, but more money: he had exploited his position under Sulla to become rich, and a series of later investments turned him into a multimillionaire. His military services to Rome were actually as valuable as Pompey's, for he defeated a slave revolt that threatened the very basis of Rome's existence. Its leader was Spartacus, a Thracian who led a break-out from the gladiators' school at Capua (gladiators were held in virtual imprisonment), and gathered an army of runaway slaves. For three years (73–71 BC) they plundered Italy and defeated Roman armies; if Spartacus' advice had been taken they would have marched right out of Roman territory to freedom, creating a precedent deeply disturbing to the Roman ruling class. Instead, Spartacus' forces were trapped in Southern Italy by Crassus' troops and destroyed; prisoners were crucified all the way along the Via Appia as far as Capua, where the revolt had begun.

Pompey's military career was wider-ranging and more spectacular. As a young man he won victories in Africa that caused Sulla to award him the title 'the Great' (Pompeius Magnus), although with dry humour the all-powerful Sulla was content to style himself 'the Lucky' (Sulla Felix). Pompey was involved in operations against Lepidus and in Spain, returning to Italy in time to steal some of Crassus' credit for defeating Spartacus. But instead of falling out, the two generals used their joint influence to become consuls in the year 70 BC; Pompey's election was quite illegal, since he had not held one of the series of lesser positions that qualified a Roman for the

British two-horned bronze helmet. It was intended for ceremonial, not military use – perhaps as an offering to a god, since it was found in the River Thames. Caesar's expeditions to exotic Britain brought prestige rather than solid benefits.

consulship. Once in office, Pompey and Crassus dismantled Sulla's settlement, restoring the power of the tribunes and removing the Senate's exclusive control of the law courts. Whatever the merits of these measures in the abstract, their practical effect in the not very long run was to revive earlier conflicts between the Senate and the tribunes and the Assembly of the People, with the generals waiting in the wings.

The immediate outcome was less dramatic. At the end of his year of office Pompey simply retired into private life. His motives were obscure to his contemporaries and have been much discussed since; his later career suggests that he had no very definite political aims beyond being the man of the hour whenever a crisis occurred – which he may have been shrewd enough to realize would from now on be all too often. In the event he fared much better than Crassus, who had few opportunities to see action and spent the next decade trying without much success to build up a political following. In 67 it was Pompey who received a special commission to clear the Mediterranean of

pirates, at that time so numerous and confident that they were sacking cities and threatening the grain supplies to Rome itself. Furnished with extraordinary powers, Pompey took only three months to accomplish what was arguably his greatest feat, driving the pirates from one sector after another and finally destroying their power completely. In the following year he was sent to the East and crowned his career with a victorious campaign against Mithridates VI of Pontus, followed by the official incorporation of Syria into the Empire and a thoroughgoing reorganization of the East. Still only 42 years old, Pompey returned from the East in 62 BC. Possibly to the surprise of the Senate, he dutifully disbanded his army and travelled to Rome in modest style, presumably confident that his services would receive ample recognition.

Meanwhile Roman politics had become more tangled than ever. One of the most influential figures in the Senate was Cato, great-grandson of the Cato who had inspired the final destruction of Carthage; he imitated his ancestor's conservatism, and his rigid outlook made it more difficult to achieve compromises between the Senate and powerful individuals such as Pompey and Crassus. A more moderate figure was Cicero, the greatest of all Roman orators: by birth a 'new man' like Marius, he nonetheless worked to save the state by bringing together the Senate and the equestrians in a centre party that stood for unity, law and order against over-mighty individuals. (The *equites*, or equestrians, were the class of wealthy non-aristocrats; they had been given a measure of political and judicial influence by Gaius Gracchus.) Cicero's great moment came during his consulship in 63 BC, when his defeated opponent in the election, Catiline, began plotting to seize power. Although lacking definite proof of Catiline's intentions, Cicero excoriated him so effectively in the Senate that all those sitting near him began to move away, finally leaving him in guilty isolation. Eventually Catiline fled to join his supporters in Etruria while Cicero acted vigorously in the city, arresting Catiline's fellow-conspirators and persuading the Senate to sanction their immediate execution. Catiline was defeated and killed in battle, and Cicero was hailed as the saviour of the state. He later made a habit of reminding Rome of the fact on every possible occasion; which did not, however, increase his political influence.

Another political force was Gaius Julius Caesar, who as a young man had narrowly escaped execution by Sulla because of his connections with the popular party (his aunt had married Marius). These connections served him well in his chequered career as a machine politician of dubious aims and methods; for much of the time he worked with Crassus, whose money oiled the machine while also helping to finance Caesar's extravagant personal and political lifestyle.

After Pompey's return from the East the Senate proved reluctant to allot land to his veterans or ratify his Asiatic settlement, measures that would have sustained Pompey's influence by creating an extensive network of patronage. Having too confidently laid down his military command, Pompey was forced into a new alliance with Crassus; Caesar acted as 'honest broker', thereby achieving near equality with Pompey and Crassus for the first time. An irresistible combination of political and financial strengths, this informal alliance – the First Triumvirate – was able to impose its will on the republic: Caesar became consul in 59, used his power to satisfy his partners, and then took up a five-year command based on the Roman provinces on either side of the Alps.

As a politician-turned-soldier, the middle-aged Julius Caesar surprised the Roman world by proving himself a military genius. He rapidly conquered Gaul from the Atlantic to the Rhine, adding vast new non-Mediterranean territories to the Empire. When the situation in Rome deteriorated and the accord between Pompey and Crassus began to show signs of strain, Caesar brought them together for a conference at Lucca, where new arrangements were made: Pompey and Crassus were to become consuls for the year 55 BC and then to have commands in Spain and the East; Caesar's commission was to be extended for five years. During the next two years Caesar became the first Roman general to bridge the Rhine and penetrate the great forests of Germany, and the first to cross the Channel and fight the blue-painted Celts of damp and foggy Britain, who submitted to him for the duration of his visit. Then a series of Gallic revolts began, culminating in a coalition under an able leader, Vercingetorix, that stretched Caesar's resources of manpower and genius to the limit. Vercingetorix was finally besieged and captured at Alesia in 52, and by the end of the following year the last Gallic resistance had been broken.

Siege weaponry: a modern model of a javelin-firing Roman catapult. The Romans took over the siege tactics and machinery developed in the Greek East, improving on them and applying them with the unparalleled tenacity that made Roman armies so formidable.

Master of Rome: a sesterce (bronze coin) with an image of Julius Caesar and an inscription proclaiming his status as dictator. Although this was an official title, by Caesar's time it was not granted freely by the Senate but extorted from it.

THE CIVIL WARS

In the meantime the balance of power within the Republic had been upset. In Syria, Crassus went into action against the Parthians, a semi-nomadic people based in Iran and Mesopotamia. Their tactics were unusual – fighting as archers on horseback, leading the enemy on but always staying out of range; and in 53 BC the over-eager Crassus fell into a trap at Carrhae (Harran) and was killed along with most of his men. Caesar and Pompey were left, potentially in direct confrontation; their personal ties had already been weakened by the death of Julia, Caesar's daughter and Pompey's wife, the year before. Pompey remained at Rome (he was an absentee commander in Spain), where he gradually drifted towards the senatorial party; whether he was motivated more by jealousy of Caesar's military achievements or fear of their consequences is uncertain. He now began to present himself as the champion of tradition and legality – somewhat belatedly, since he as well as Caesar had acted illegally on numerous occasions.

Indeed, respect for the law had never been the same in Rome since the Sullan era, and great men like Pompey and Caesar openly took up illegal consulships or ignored the vetoes of their colleagues. Smaller fry were equally insolent when backed by street gangs, and even during the most successful period of the First Triumvirate there were political gangsters like the infamous, erratic Publius Clodius, who might serve Caesar but were liable to get out of control. During his relatively brief career Clodius created a scandal by disguising himself as a woman and mingling with the Vestal Virgins; pursued a vendetta against Cicero, forcing him into exile for a time; and as tribune bid for popularity by distributions of grain to the citizens of Rome, who were rapidly turning into a dole-hungry mob. Clodius' exploits were abruptly terminated in January 52 BC, when he was killed by the street thugs of a rival faction leader. In the ensuing disorders the senate house was burned down and the situation became so confused that no consuls were elected. The Senate still distrusted Pompey too much to appoint him dictator, but for six months in 52 he served as sole consul and restored order.

After this the rapprochement between Pompey and the Senate was quickly effected. Now, taking a legal but disloyal course, Pompey had his own command renewed but did nothing to prevent his partner Caesar from being recalled, although the tribunes supported Caesar, making the Senate's proceedings less obviously legitimate. Contemporaries recognized that a crisis was imminent, and moderates such as Cicero gloomily prophesied that the Republic was doomed whatever the outcome. Cicero himself summed up the situation: 'Pompey is determined that Caesar shall not become consul unless he hands over his army and provinces; Caesar is convinced that he will never be safe if he relinquishes his army.' The Senate remained unyielding in its attitude towards Caesar, passing a *senatus consultum ultimum*, the kind of emergency decree that had been used in the past to authorize the execution without trial of Gaius Gracchus, Catiline and others. Caesar was left with little choice. Rather than enter Italy powerless, he broke the law by bringing his army with him; at the crucial moment, ordering his troops across the Rubicon (the river dividing Gaul from Italy), Caesar is said to have uttered his famous remark, *'Alea iacta est'* – 'The die is cast'.

The civil wars of the next 19 years (49–30 BC) ended by destroying the Republic. Caesar's advance into Italy took Pompey by surprise; he had only two legions in the peninsula, although he and his allies had ample forces in Spain, and other parts of the Empire were almost all controlled by the senatorial party. Caesar advanced rapidly and Pompey only just managed to escape to the East, where his past triumphs had enabled him to create a wide network of supporters. Having overrun Italy, Caesar defeated the

Marcus Porcius Cato was regarded by contemporaries as the embodiment of republican integrity and austerity. He joined Pompey on the outbreak of the civil war, and after holding out at Utica in North Africa, killed himself rather than submit to Caesar.

Pompeians in Spain before crossing the Adriatic and facing Pompey himself. Caesar's attempt to blockade Dyrrhachium, on the Dalmatian coast, was repulsed, and the situation began to look serious until Pompey unwisely decided to give battle at Pharsalus in northern Greece on 6 June 48; though outnumbered, Caesar's veterans were battle-hardened by ten years in Gaul, and they utterly destroyed Pompey's forces.

Pompey fled to Egypt, only to be murdered as he stepped ashore by soldiers and politicians eager to ingratiate themselves with the winning side. Caesar disembarked at Alexandria in hot pursuit, became involved in an Egyptian dynastic conflict, and finally placed one of the claimants, the 21-year-old Cleopatra, on the throne; their relations were personal as well as political, since Cleopatra became his mistress and bore a son, Caesarion, whom she claimed was Caesar's. On his way back to Italy Caesar routed Pharnaces of Pontus (son of Mithridates VI) at the battle of Zela, a victory so easy that Caesar summed it up as 'Came: saw: conquered.' Then he crossed from Italy into Africa and overcame a force of surviving Pompeians at Thapsus. One of the defeated was Cato, who committed suicide rather than be captured; the noble stoicism of his conduct during the death-throes of the Republic made a great impression on posterity, quoted whenever similar situations occurred and still a popular subject in the early 18th century, when Addison's tragedy *Cato* credited him with the famous lines: 'Tis not in mortals to command success; But we'll do more, Sempronius, we'll deserve it.'

In 45 BC Caesar came close to defeat during the last of his battles, which was also the last stand of the Pompeians, at Munda in Spain. But the sheer tenacity of his legionaries carried the day against Pompey's sons and his own sometime lieutenant Labienus. In four years Caesar had conquered the Roman world, intermittently returning to the capital to enact reforms: reducing the burdens of debtors; founding new colonies for his veterans and also for the urban poor; setting up a tax system designed to reduce the exploitation of the provinces; limiting the use of slaves in agriculture; and introducing the 365-day 'Julian' calendar.

He had also accumulated as much power as (legally) the Roman system could confer. Though republican forms were not tampered with, Caesar went much further than Sulla in self-aggrandizement: he was voted dictator for life, his portrait appeared on Roman coins, he wore a purple robe and other quasi-royal emblems, a month (July) was named after him, and the possibility arose that he aspired to divinity (something common among Greek rulers from Alexander the Great onwards) when he allowed a temple to be dedicated to him. Contemporaries seem to have believed that in him Rome had finally found a new and permanent master, different in kind from men like Marius, Pompey, and even Sulla, whose long-term aims had not gone beyond *auctoritas*, a preponderant influence in the state based on prestige, wealth and a network of Roman and provincial clients. Caesar himself never touched the formal structure of the republic and in 44 BC refused the title king, detested by Romans ever since the reign of Tarquinius Superbus; but his style of government was increasingly autocratic, and prompted the conspiracy that led to his assassination, at the age of 56, on the Ides of March, 44.

Opposite: Cleopatra of Egypt belonged to a long-established Greek dynasty but also adopted the trappings of the pharaohs. This relief retains traces of the grid used as an aid by the artist, and was probably a trial piece.

Mark Antony, ruler of the Roman East. Whatever its romantic content, Antony's partnership with Cleopatra made good political sense, ensuring access to the wealth of Egypt; but it alienated Antony's support in Rome itself.

A Roman warship. As this relief suggests, war at sea was as much a military as a naval affair. The relief is believed to have been part of a monument to Mark Antony – ironically, since it was the sea battle at Actium that doomed him.

One of Caesar's most attractive qualities was his magnanimity: he generally spared captured opponents during the civil war, and often took them into his service. (This much-lauded clemency seems to have applied only to Romans: large numbers of defeated Gauls lost their right hands for resisting Caesar, and Vercingetorix, like Jugurtha, was strangled and flung down from the Tarpeian Rock below the Capitol). In the event it was Caesar's virtues, even more than his ambitions, that led to his death: the chief assassins, Brutus and Cassius, were ex-Pompeians whom Caesar had pardoned. Crowding round him as if they were petitioners, they stabbed him to death as he was about to attend a meeting of the Senate. At the time he was preparing to embark on a new campaign in the East, against the Parthians; although his death has sometimes been said to have prevented Caesar from bringing about a golden age of good government, this fact suggests that he was above all a compulsive conqueror.

Caesar's death settled nothing, for the Republic was too far gone to be saved. Despite the version of history made familiar by Shakespeare in *Julius Caesar*, the Caesarean party made no immediate attempt to avenge their chief's death; the dictator's principal lieutenant, Mark Antony (Marcus Antonius), agreed to amnesty the assassins, and it was the anger of the citizens that drove Brutus and Cassius from Rome. Matters were further complicated by the appearance of Caesar's nephew and heir, the 18-year-old Octavian, who was at one point at war with fellow-Caesarian Mark Antony. However, they realized that by pooling their military resources they could overawe the Senate, a course of action all the more appealing since Brutus and Cassius had begun to take control of the East. In 43 Antony and Octavian formed the Second Triumvirate, bringing in Lepidus, a follower of Caesar's who controlled parts of Gaul and Spain. Unlike the First Triumvirate, this new combination acquired an official status as a five-year, three-man dictatorship, legally sanctioned by the now-subservient Senate. The Triumvirs proscribed and murdered their enemies, including the 63-year-old Cicero, who had prematurely cheered Caesar's assassination and denounced Antony. In 42 BC Brutus and Cassius were defeated near Philippi, after which both committed suicide.

In the subsequent division of the Roman world, Octavian took the West; by 36 BC he had managed to defeat Pompey's son, Sextus Pompeius, who had been holding out in Sicily, and to take Africa from Lepidus. (Lepidus was a lucky loser in a blood-soaked age: he was allowed to withdraw into private life.) With the elimination of other contenders, Octavian and Antony were probably fated to fight for supremacy in the Roman world, but conflict was several times deferred by conferences and new arrangements, despite Antony's increasingly un-Roman behaviour. Though he had married his rival's sister Octavia, he became more and more closely involved with Cleopatra, Queen of Egypt and Caesar's former mistress. She bore him three children, and their liaison has often been represented as a love story. Whether or not this was so, their famous union had solid political benefits; it was put on a permanent basis in 36, after Antony had undertaken a disastrous campaign against the Parthians, perhaps because he now believed that Egypt's rich resources were indispensable to his political survival. Moreover Cleopatra was the last of the independent Greek rulers, and as such commanded a good deal of loyalty in the Hellenized East as well as Egypt – loyalty that the partners tried to exploit by identifying themselves as Dionysus-Osiris and Aphrodite-Isis, composite Greek-Egyptian divinities.

On the other hand Antony's unconventional conduct – pointed up by territorial concessions to Egypt and the award of provinces to his Romano-Egyptian children – was bound to alienate his supporters in Italy and the army, and may therefore have cost him his life. Since Caesar had been deified, his adopted son Octavian could style himself *divi filius*, 'son of the god', but without forfeiting his credentials as a defender of Roman values. His propaganda made much of the orien-

tal decadence into which Antony had been enticed, and when he declared war in 31 BC it was, shrewdly, on the foreign temptress Cleopatra. The belligerents met in northern Greece, where Octavian's general, Agrippa, outmanoeuvred and hemmed in the enemy forces; Antony's desperate attempt to break out by sea at Actium met with disaster. He and Cleopatra fled to Egypt where, deserted by his allies and followers, he killed himself as Octavian approached Alexandria. Rather than decorate Octavian's triumph, Cleopatra too chose to die, according to legend by allowing a poisonous asp to bite her.

In the immediate post-war settlement, Egypt was annexed; significantly, it became the personal property of the all-powerful Octavian, not a province belonging to Rome. Some of the legions were disbanded, and the Empire was at last peaceful and united again. Despite the bloodshed, the most important victim of the wars was the sovereignty of 'the Roman Senate and People'; and though Romans politely continued to pretend otherwise, the Republic was now dead.

Celebrating in appropriately aquatic style: sardonyx cameo commemorating the naval victory of Octavian's forces over Antony and Cleopatra at Actium in 30 BC. The battle decided the fate of the Roman world.

Augustus, the former Octavian, appears in his full glory – armoured, but also barefoot like a god, and with Cupid riding a dolphin beside him. The reliefs on his breastplate celebrate Augustus' achievements.

AUGUSTUS AND THE EMPIRE

Octavian was probably the most level-headed and clear-sighted leader in Roman history. He had climbed to greatness over the bodies of his opponents, like Sulla and Caesar before him; but once he held power he used it moderately, presenting himself as a guardian of tradition and capitalizing on the universal longing for peace and order after generations of turmoil. He also had a gift often lacking in great leaders: the gift for discovering able and loyal lieutenants. Since he could not be everywhere, Octavian employed Gaius Maecenas as his political man-of-all-work and diplomatic troubleshooter; and, being no general himself, he found a first-class one in Marcus Agrippa, who was mainly responsible for the great naval victories over Sextus Pompeius and Mark Antony.

Having restored order and reformed the state, Octavian formally handed back control to the Senate and People in 27 BC: the Senate would function as before, elected consuls would carry out its wishes, and the people would be represented by their tribunes. Octavian did not assume the dictatorship, contenting himself with a recognized pre-eminence (*auctoritas*); as well as bearing the honorary title of *princeps*, 'the chief', he was now to be officially distinguished from other citizens as 'Augustus' (the name by which he has become best known) and given special responsibilities and powers to assist in the ordering of the state. In reality this restoration of the Republic was a sham, though perhaps a beneficent one that eased an inevitable transition. Augustus possessed the overwhelming military force, wealth and prestige that made his word law; and like his uncle he was becoming the object of religious cults. By accumulating offices he was able with perfect legality to remove recalcitrant senators, to appoint new members, and to prevent trouble-

Marcus Agrippa was Augustus' friend from his youth onwards. He won the decisive sea battle at Actium that made Augustus master of the Roman world, and subsequently became the Emperor's son-in-law and right-hand man.

makers from ever reaching the Senate. He was granted a permanent tribunician power (including an absolute veto), so that even the weapons of the popular party were made to serve the new absolutism; and as supreme commander of the armed forces he controlled the provinces in which they were stationed (Spain, Gaul, Cyprus, Syria, Cilicia), ruling through legates directly appointed by him instead of governors nominated by the Senate. Eventually he even became *pontifex maximus*, the religious head of state.

In the wake of the civil wars, Romans seem to have been content with these arrangements. Augustus' reign was one of harmony between ruler and ruled, in which the question of an appeal to ultimate authority or force scarcely arose; but he is rightly described not as the restorer of the Republic but as the first of the

Roman emperors. The permanence of the new system was ensured by Augustus' ability, by the tact with which he handled the Senate and respected traditional forms, and by the accident of longevity which gave the Roman world a single master for over 40 years, so that by the time of his death in AD 14 the old institutions had long before lost the habit of asserting themselves.

Under Augustus the Empire enjoyed peace, order and prosperity. A proper civil service was created to run it, giving good government to the provinces as well as to Rome. New roads and colonies encouraged industry and commerce. Devolution of authority (albeit mainly in routine matters) breathed fresh life into the cities. And

The Theatre of Marcellus. Augustus boasted that he had found Rome brick and left her marble, but few of his buildings survive. The theatre was designed to hold 20,000 spectators; it is still in use – as a huge apartment house.

Augustus gradually eliminated the army as a political force by greatly reducing its numbers and distributing it all through the frontier provinces; in Italy, the few thousand men of the Praetorian Guard, an elite corps created by Augustus for his personal protection, constituted the sole military presence. Rome itself was transformed into a worthy capital for a universal empire: Augustus boasted that he had found it a city of brick and left it a city of marble. He also left it efficiently supplied with water and food, minimizing the risk of political discontent: two hundred thousand people received a free corn dole and were entertained by ever more extravagant public spectacles – the celebrated policy of keeping the people happy with 'bread and circuses'.

The Empire continued to expand. Julius Caesar had conquered western Europe as far as the Rhine; under Augustus the conquest of an area roughly corresponding to modern Austria and Hungary brought the Roman frontier in eastern Europe to the Danube. The Rhine and the Danube were to remain the frontiers in Europe for another hundred years; Augustus' intention to push on to the Elbe was abandoned near the end of his reign, in AD 9, when three legions under the legate Varus – perhaps fifteen thousand men – were ambushed and wiped out in the Teutoburg Forest. This was the greatest catastrophe of his reign, and it was said that Augustus left his hair and beard untrimmed for months afterwards and often beat his head against a door, crying out 'Quinctilius Varus, give me back my legions!' As if infected with permanent bad luck, the three legions were never reconstituted. Augustus' advice to his successors was to attempt no further expansion. However, despite this setback the frontiers had been stabilized in Africa and the East as well as Europe, and honour was satisfied without recourse to war when the Parthians agreed to return the Roman standards they had captured in defeating Crassus at Carrhae.

Augustus was fortunate even in the literary history of his reign, which produced the poets Virgil and Horace and the historian Livy. All three were encouraged and generously funded by Maecenas, whose name is still often used in English to characterize the wealthy and enlightened patron.

However genuine his appreciation of talent, Maecenas also used patronage as a way of securing politically acceptable views of the state of the Empire and the role of Augustus. Virgil, in the *Aeneid*, the greatest of Roman epics, inserted laudatory references to 'Caesar Augustus, son of a god', and to Rome's splendid imperial destiny, into his account of the Romans' mythical ancestor. By contrast, the other great poet of the Augustan age was a younger man, Ovid, the author of elegantly worldly verses; whether for this reason or as punishment for some other offence, he ended his life in exile.

Ovid's playfully amoral outlook was certainly not to Augustus' taste. The emperor's traditionalism was genuine enough in most respects (although not where the tradition of liberty was concerned). He circulated ostentatiously pious images of himself, restored religious rites that had been neglected in favour of Greek and Oriental practices, and tried to revive the old Roman virtues by decree. The luxuries of the upper classes were rebuked and legislated against; marriage and paternity were encouraged; and Augustus even exiled his own daughter Julia when he found out about her lurid sex life. Like most such endeavours, this policy showed few positive results.

But the most serious of Augustus' family troubles was the succession. He and his wife Livia had no children, although Livia's son by an earlier marriage, Tiberius, became one of the mainstays of the Roman state, both as an administrator and an able and tireless campaigner. The younger men whom Augustus groomed to succeed him died in such abnormal numbers that even in antiquity there were rumours pointing to Livia as an arch-murderess on Tiberius' behalf; whether they were more than malicious gossip is another matter, despite the ingenuities of Robert Graves's famous novel *I, Claudius*. In any event Augustus was finally compelled to name Tiberius as his successor; when he died in AD 14, there was no serious possibility of a restoration of the Republic, although the 56-year-old Tiberius for a time resisted, with real or assumed vigour, the Senate's invitation to carry on the principate. Augustus' final apotheosis was a literal one – to be recognized and worshipped as a god, giving his political system the ultimate sanction of religious endorsement.

The reign of Tiberius (AD 14–37) was in most respects a conservative continuation of the

Battling the barbarians. Germanic tribes inflicted the worst disaster of Augustus' reign, and for centuries they intermittently troubled the Empire. This scene of furious activity comes from a sarcophagus of the 3rd century AD.

Augustan period: the administration of the provinces was, if anything, improved; there was little military activity; and the frontiers remained the same apart from the continuation of a process begun under Augustus, the absorption of the client-kingdoms of Asia Minor and the East. Though able, Tiberius seems to have been an unsympathetic personality, and in the early years of his reign he was far less popular than his nephew Germanicus, who appears to have culti-vated a personal following in Rome. When Germanicus died while on a special mission at Antioch, rumours circulated that Tiberius had had him poisoned; the rumours may have been unfounded, but suggest that the atmosphere of intrigue and suspicion, characteristic of autocra-cies, had begun to thicken.

In time the dangers inherent in autocracy became still clearer. After AD 23 the emperor delegated wide powers to Sejanus, the prefect (commander) of the Praetorian Guard, who car-ried out many judicial murders in pursuit of his

Imperial high noon, shown on an onyx cameo, the Gemma Augustea. Augustus sits, godlike, with an eagle at his feet. His stepson Tiberius leaves his chariot while, below, soldiers celebrate his victories over the Germans.

own ambitions and may have done away with Tiberius' own son Drusus. In 26 Tiberius retired permanently to the island of Capri, where he is said to have indulged in infamous orgies; but since the stories, like many accounts of the emperors, come from gossip-loving or nostalgically republican writers, they may be exaggerated or even false: Tiberius' residence on Capri, and his feeble or indifferent reaction to the string of treason trials that disfigured his reign, are just as likely to have been the result of old age, since he was 68 in the year 26. Sejanus' plotting or the emperor's fears (legitimate or otherwise) were responsible for the executions of Agrippina, the wife of Germanicus, and two of her children, even though they were Tiberius' heirs. But the aged emperor could still act decisively when he felt threatened, as he showed by summarily executing Sejanus in 31 and instituting a long series of treason trials that eliminated the fallen favourite's supporters and possibly many innocent victims. Tiberius' death in 37 was greeted with a joy and relief that proved to be premature.

There are fewer doubts about the character of Tiberius' successor Gaius, nicknamed Caligula ('Little Boot') by the soldiers of his father Germanicus: he was insane, arbitrary and cruel, and the 'republican' institutions of Rome proved helpless to restrain him. Parading about in the deluded belief that he was already a god, he forced senators to commit suicide, tortured and put to death equestrians, soldiers and actors with crazy impartiality, executed any wealthy man who did not make him his heir, and ensured that his fall would be greeted with universal pleasure by raising heavy taxes on every imaginable commodity to make good the effects of his reckless spending. Among Caligula's caprices was the appointment of his horse as a senator and the building of a huge bridge of boats, moored end to end, across the Bay of Baiae because a would-be prophet had once predicted that he was no more likely to become emperor than to ride dry-shod across the bay; every boat in Italy is said to have been requisitioned to construct the 'bridge', causing economic chaos while Caligula rode his horse from side to side of the bay over the planks that had been laid across the vessels.

Legally there was no way of resisting Caligula. The principate was revealed for the despotism it was, with the inescapable weakness of all despotisms – that there was no way of guaranteeing the benevolence, intelligence or even sanity of the despot. Caligula was murdered by conspirators in 41, after a four-year reign of terror. His successor Claudius was – ominously – the choice of the Praetorians (although as Caligula's uncle he was also next in line for the succession, since the principate was now effectively a hereditary monarchy). The view that the twitching, stammering Claudius was simple-minded – current even in antiquity – hardly fits the facts. His undiagnosed ailments made a public career impossible under Augustus and Tiberius, since people in antiquity ridiculed physical disadvantages and equated them with stupidity or worse. On the other hand Claudius' disabilities may well have saved his life when Tiberius and Caligula were jealously cutting down their more presentable relations; and it has been suggested that Claudius was shrewd enough to exaggerate his lack of presentability in order to be passed over as harmless.

In the event Claudius' reign (AD 41–54) was fairly successful, and there seems no reason to deprive him of the credit for its achievements. Though no soldier himself, he was generous in recognizing good service, including that of

Evil emperor: the head of Caligula on a gold aureus. Attempts have been made to rehabilitate some Roman emperors, but Caligula's four-year reign does seem to have been one of cruel and more or less insane despotism.

Family group: the Gemma Claudia, a sardonyx cameo with contemporary portraits of the brothers Claudius and Germanicus and their wives. Germanicus died young, and the less obviously gifted Claudius eventually became emperor.

Aulus Plautius, conqueror of Britain. The invasion of this remote island took place in 43, and Claudius arrived in time to take part in the storming of the British capital, Colchester. Eventually the 'lowland zone' of Britain – roughly modern England – was conquered and Romanized, while the highland areas (Scotland and part of Wales) remained Celtic strongholds.

In the Empire, Claudius encouraged the extension of Roman citizenship, mainly through the foundation of colonies and the admission of Gallic nobles to the Roman Senate. The civil service was improved by Claudius' practice of employing freedmen, although other Romans deplored their excessive influence: between them, Claudius' freedmen and his wives ruled him, if ancient authors are to be believed. The charge has a certain credibility. Even after the spectacular sexual antics of his young wife Messalina were revealed and paid for with her life, Claudius, almost 60, married again. His new empress, Agrippina, then persuaded him to adopt her son Nero as his heir; and four years later Claudius died – conveniently, since Nero, not yet 17, was old enough to inherit the throne (unlike his step-brother, Claudius and Messalina's son Britannicus) but still young enough to let himself be ruled by his mother. Rumour had it that the uxorious Claudius

expired after partaking from a wifely dish of poisoned mushrooms. After his demise Claudius was deified; Nero, in a flash of black humour, is said to have called mushrooms 'the food of the gods'.

Nero, if not quite mad, proved to be recklessly cruel and blindly vain. At first under the influence of his mother, whose head even appeared with Nero's on coins, he soon put himself under the tutelage of the philosopher Seneca and the praetorian prefect Burrus, who ruled competently in his name. But after this deceptively quiet start Nero increasingly took over the reins. He did away with Britannicus and his overweening mother; treason trials were revived to raise money from the victims' estates; and when this led to the formation of a genuine conspiracy, its discovery set Nero off on a paranoid round of executions in which any popular soldier or administrator was likely to be killed or ordered to take his own life. The disastrous fire which destroyed part of Rome in 64 has been blamed on Nero, possibly unjustly, although the emperor chose to accuse the small, obscure sect of Christians and, instead of replacing the destroyed tenements and temples, erected a vast palace-complex, the Golden House (*Domus Aurea*), on the site.

The charge that Nero 'fiddled while Rome burned' (actually that he sang 'The Fall of Troy', accompanying himself on the lyre) may only be gossip but is absolutely in character: he had a mania for art, and went in for extremes of temperament and self-dramatization. He shocked the Romans by making public appearances on the stage, and preferred spending his time in Greece, where he carried off a string of prizes as a lyrist and charioteer. The judges were presumably biased – as biased as the historian Suetonius (in the opposite direction) when he claims that during Nero's performances no one was permitted to leave the theatre, and consequently women gave birth there and men who were dying of boredom pretended to die in earnest so that they would be carried outside.

The performance had to end. Gaul, Spain and Africa rose against Nero, who could think of no remedy except singing them into submission. The Praetorians deserted him, and after an ineffective flight he killed himself in June 68.

The Emperor Nero in a relatively flattering posthumous portrait. Whatever the private and political excesses of Augustus' successors, most of the empire remained prosperous and peaceful during the 1st century AD.

Triumphal procession celebrating the crushing of the Jewish revolt in AD 70 by Titus; prominent among the spoils is the *menorah*, or seven-branched lamp-holder from the Temple at Jerusalem. Relief from the Arch of Titus in Rome.

COLLAPSE AND RECOVERY

The scandalous doings of the Caesars, which have almost certainly been exaggerated, had little effect on life in the provinces. The political classes at Rome were sometimes thinned, but over most of the period between Augustus and Nero the Empire was prosperous, well governed and at peace. The *Pax Romana* (Roman peace) became the most widely recognized benefit conferred by the Empire and a prime justification for the Romans' subjugation of other peoples; an outbreak such as the savage revolt of the Iceni under Boudicca (Boadicea) was unlikely except in a recently conquered province such as Britain.

But the events following the death of Nero did affect wide areas of the Empire, temporarily destroying its peace. Nero was the last of the

Julio-Claudians, the dynasty formed by the Julian family, represented by Caesar and Augustus, and the Claudians, relatives of Augustus' stepson Tiberius. There was now no obvious heir, and the throne was at the disposal of the Praetorian Guard – or of the legions in the provinces, who entered politics for the first time. AD 69 was 'the year of the four emperors', and re-introduced the Empire to the miseries of civil war. The aged Galba, governor of one of the Spanish provinces, was raised to the purple, only to be murdered and replaced by his colleague Otho. But when the Rhine army marched on behalf of Vitellius, Otho found himself deserted and committed suicide. Finally the Eastern legions proclaimed Vespasian (Titus Flavius Vespasianus), a tough and highly successful commander who was engaged at the time in suppressing a major Jewish rebellion; his forces overcame those of Vitellius, who was killed.

These serial blood-lettings demonstrated the danger of allowing the army back into politics. They also confirmed that the Republic was beyond revival, even when the candidates for the imperial throne were unable to claim the most distant relationship to Caesar and Augustus. Furthermore local and tribal outbreaks in Gaul and on the Rhine indicated that the stability of the Empire itself might be at risk as soon as the central power faltered. Fortunately Vespasian proved to be the strong leader the state required. Being of relatively humble birth he adopted the pose of a plain, blunt man while taking a conciliatory line with the Senate; but he left them in no doubt that his family, the Flavians, were to be the new ruling dynasty, and he implicitly dismissed the Senate's endorsement by dating his reign from his proclamation by the troops. Mindful of the way in which he had attained power, Vespasian carefully controlled the army, and his son Titus became captain of the Praetorian Guard. Civic privileges and membership of the Senate were extended, and the taxes remitted by weaker emperors to win themselves a short-lived popularity were rigorously collected. In 70 Titus ended the Jewish revolt by destroying Jerusalem and the Temple, events so calamitous that for centuries pious Jews refused to pass under the Arch of Titus, built to celebrate his victory. Vespasian died in 79 and was immediately deified; he evidently foresaw his elevation, making a final deathbed joke: 'Damn it – I can feel myself turning into a god.'

The brief reign of Titus (AD 79–81) was notable for the completion of a vast arena for gladiatorial shows and animal hunts, the Colosseum (originally known as the Flavian Amphitheatre), and for the eruption of Vesuvius in AD 79 which smothered the seaside resorts of Pompeii and Herculaneum in the Bay of Naples; layers of ash and pumice choked the citizens and buried the towns, preserving a pitiable but fascinating record of the Roman way of life. Titus was succeeded by his brother Domitian (81–96), who campaigned effectively and governed well for a few years before he gave way to fears for his own safety (perhaps not unjustified) and set in motion another epidemic of treason trials. Finally, when no one could feel safe, even Domitian's wife turned against him and joined a group of conspirators whose agent stabbed the emperor to death.

Final agony. In time, the bodies buried under volcanic ash at Pompeii and nearby sites decomposed. Modern excavators poured plaster into the voids left behind in the ash, making casts of the victims in their last moments.

THE AGE OF THE ANTONINES

Opposite: the Emperor Trajan, one of the 'Five Good Emperors'; his reign has often been seen as the summit of Roman prosperity. Some of his ambitious Eastern conquests were abandoned by his successor, Hadrian.

Withstanding an attack by Dacian warriors: one of many vivid scenes from Trajan's Column, raised in AD 113 to celebrate the emperor's conquests beyond the Danube. Dacia remained a Roman province until it was abandoned in the 270s.

The childless Domitian was the last of the Flavians, but this time the transition from one dynasty to the next was managed without an interval of bloodshed. The Senate nominated Nerva, an elderly member of their own order who had managed to remain respectable while conforming under emperors of widely different characters from Nero onwards. Nerva kept the confidence of the Senate by promising to deal fairly with it and never to execute one of its members – a promise he kept even when a senator was implicated in a conspiracy against him. Nerva was also shrewd enough to adopt an experienced general, Trajan, as his son and successor. The emperor's motive was probably to hold in check the army, and particularly the Praetorian Guard, who had admired Domitian and resented his removal. But the adoption brought such obviously beneficial results that it became something of a custom, and was followed by Trajan and his successors. (At any rate it seems unlikely to have been an accident that each childless ruler should have ensured that the adoption principle should continue by selecting a childless successor.) The result was the succession of the 'Five Good Emperors' who, linked by ability, and not by blood, gave the Empire the most efficient and humane government it had ever had. The period is often described as the age of the Antonines, although strictly speaking the term should only apply to the fourth emperor, Antoninus Pius, and his successors.

Nerva's reign was brief (AD 96–98), but Trajan had a long and energetic imperial career (98–117). Despite his Spanish birth, Trajan (Marcus Ulpius Traianus) was a ruler very much to the Roman taste, taking command personally on the frontiers. When the Dacians beyond the Danube frontier, already punished by Domitian, sought their revenge, Trajan undertook a series of campaigns in 101–106 that culminated in the death of the Dacian king, the addition to the Empire of a large, mineral-rich province (roughly corresponding to modern Romania), and loot on a scale that had not been seen for decades. Back in Rome, Trajan behaved as a model emperor, maintaining good relations with the Senate, paying close attention to administrative business, and arranging for cheap loans to farmers, the payment of subsidies to the Italian poor, and other welfare measures. He also embarked on an ambitious building programme, giving Rome one of her finest squares, the Forum Traianum, and Trajan's Market, an innovative complex best described as a multi-level shopping mall; in the Forum Traianum stood the most impressive of the emperor's surviving monuments, Trajan's Column, with a vivid bronze frieze picturing his campaigns against the Dacians. Understandably enthusiastic, the Senate awarded Trajan the official title *'Optimus Princeps'* – 'Best of Leaders'.

In the last years of his reign Trajan won substantial victories in the East against the Parthians, creating two new provinces from his conquests,

Hadrian's Villa at Tivoli, outside Rome. The 'villa' was really a vast estate filled with buildings inspired by Hadrian's travels around the empire. The photograph shows the remains of the Canopus, named after a city in Egypt.

Opposite: the interior of the Pantheon, a huge domed edifice, built under Hadrian and dedicated to all the gods. The photo shows the dome and its 8 m (27 ft) wide *oculus*, or eye, which admits natural light into the interior.

Armenia and Mesopotamia (the relatively small northern part of the region), and then pressing on as far as the Persian Gulf. However, his ambitions outran his strength and he died in the East. His successor Hadrian (117–138) took a very different view of the general situation, and his policies made it abundantly obvious that he believed the Empire was dangerously overextended. At the end of Trajan's life there were widespread revolts in his eastern conquests, and Hadrian quickly relinquished them. He spent most of his reign touring the Empire, supervising provincial administrators, overhauling the armies and tirelessly strengthening fortifications and recruiting on the frontiers. One familiar result of this activity was 'Hadrian's Wall' in northern Britain, a defensive structure that ran for 117 km (73 miles) across the narrow neck of land between the Solway and the Tyne; forts and signalling turrets positioned all along the wall were intended to prevent a successful surprise attack by the unconquered Celts of the far north. As was increasingly

becoming the case on the frontiers, defence was no longer the business of the legions but of auxiliaries who were often recruited locally.

Although his policies were essentially defensive, Hadrian was popular with the army and provincials because he was energetic and seemed to be omnipresent; the most serious internal disturbance during his reign was the protracted but ruthlessly repressed Jewish revolt of 131–135, provoked by his plan to build a new city, with a temple dedicated to Jupiter, on the site of Jerusalem. In Italy his buildings included the Pantheon and his mausoleum (now the Castel Sant' Angelo) at Rome, and a magnificent villa (really a palace complex) at the popular resort of Tibur (modern Tivoli), filled with architectural reproductions of the wonders he had seen on his travels. Many other cities in the Empire benefited from Hadrian's passion for building or from generous government funding for their own projects. One of the emperor's more unusual foundations was the city of Antinoöpolis on the Nile, commemorating

The Mausoleum of Hadrian, built to house the emperor's remains; the bridge that leads to it across the Tiber also dates from Hadrian's reign. Later the mausoleum was converted into a papal fortress, the Castel Sant' Angelo.

the drowning in the river of his young favourite, Antinous, during an imperial tour of Egypt. The grief-stricken emperor decreed that divine honours should be paid to Antinous, and cult statues of the young man, identified as various gods, were raised all over the Empire.

After Hadrian's death the Senate was slow to deify him; relations between emperor and Senate had never been very cordial since early in his reign, when Hadrian was establishing his claim to the imperial throne and four senators were executed in obscure circumstances. Hadrian's adopted son and chosen successor, Antoninus, threatened to refuse the purple unless the Senate acted appropriately – a filial stance that earned him the name Antoninus Pius. The fact that the Senate gave way illustrates the extent to which emperors now seemed indispensable, even in the eyes of the former masters of the Republic. In the heart of the Empire the reign of Antoninus Pius (138–161) was blissfully uneventful, and later generations looked back on it as a golden age. Troublesome outbreaks on the fringes (Africa, the East, the Danube, Britain) were for the moment easily contained, and in Britain the frontier was even advanced for a time to the Forth-Clyde line with the building of the Antonine Wall.

Antoninus' successor, Marcus Aurelius (161–180), was less fortunate: made for peace, he spent most of his reign with the armies in the East or in the Danube region; and the Empire itself experienced a number of calamities. Becoming emperor within a few weeks of his 40th birthday, Marcus had been groomed for office by Hadrian, and during Antoninus' lifetime he had acquired a wealth of administrative experience. On his accession Marcus chose not to reign alone, but appointed co-emperor, Lucius Verus – the first indication that the burden of empire might be becoming too heavy for a single man in any but the most favourable circumstances; however, after Verus' death in 169 the experiment was suspended. In the campaigns of 162–165 Verus repelled the Parthians and recaptured the province of Mesopotamia. Unfortunately his victorious army brought back from the East a plague that swept through the Empire and inflicted serious damage on its population, economy and morale – just how serious is impossible to quantify, although some historians have speculated that Rome may never have completely recovered from it. Meanwhile the Marcommani, the Quadi and other fierce German tribes poured across the Danube and even penetrated northern Italy and the Balkans. After more than a decade of hard campaigning, interrupted by a revolt in Syria and other worries, Marcus defeated the Germanic tribes so thoroughly that Rome seemed on the point of acquiring a large new German province when Marcus died.

Marcus' warlike career was not one that he would have chosen: paradoxically, he was the only Roman emperor who was also a philosopher. He adhered to the Stoic school, which emphasized self-sufficient virtue, the endurance of necessary evils and the fulfilment of worldly duties – principles that doubtless strengthened his resolve to remain at his post. Marcus Aurelius' notebook, published as his *Meditations*, is a classic account of a mind striving to reconcile itself to the conditions of existence. But Marcus had a son; and his philosophy did not prevent him from violating the Antonine principle of selecting the best man for the job: instead, he chose as his successor his son Commodus, who was quite possibly the worst man. Even less admirable than Nero, Commodus (180–192) was obsessed with gladiatorial displays and himself fought regularly in the arena. At the beginning of his reign, anxious to return to Rome, he made a hasty peace with the German tribes. Subsequently peace was maintained in the

Empire, but life at Rome reverted to the familiar pattern of treason trials engendering conspiracies that engendered more treason trials – until Commodus was strangled by an athlete hired for the purpose by his own inner circle.

'If a man were called to fix the period in the history of the world, during which the condition of the human race was most happy and prosperous, he would, without hesitation, name that which elapsed from the death of Domitian to the accession of Commodus.' So wrote Edward Gibbon, author of the monumental, enduring *Decline and Fall of the Roman Empire*, published between 1776 and 1788. There is still something to be said in favour of his opinion, provided 'the human race' is assumed to consist of affluent citizens, excluding (among others) slaves and barbarians. Whatever happened on the frontiers, most of the Empire was at peace. Towns flourished and civic amenities became ever more generous. An efficient system of roads drew the provinces together. Agriculture and industry prospered everywhere. Taxation was light. The number of citizens was greatly increased throughout the Empire, and the admission of provincials to the Senate made it far more representative than in the past; consequently many of the inhabitants of the Empire were beginning to think of it as a commonwealth rather than an aggregation of Rome-conquered territories. The civil service was staffed by the senatorial and equestrian classes, whose career opportunities reconciled them to the loss of their old political and judicial functions. And there was even a cultural revival – notably a 'silver age' of literature, not quite comparable with the Augustan golden age but still able to nurture such figures as the poets Juvenal and Martial, the romance-writer Apuleius, the historians Tacitus and Suetonius, the elegant letter-writer Pliny the Younger, and Greek authors like the biographer Plutarch and the satirist Lucian of Samosata.

Gibbon identified the deepest flaw in the Antonine scheme of things: 'the instability of a happiness which depended on the character of a single man'. But there were others too, less obvious, which came to light as soon as the 'single man' lost his power or his sanity. Despite state assistance, the Italian smallholders were being driven to the wall by the large slave-operated estates. The flourishing

municipalities were losing all power of initiative, compelling the imperial government to take more and more decisions and develop an increasingly large, and potentially rigid and inefficient, bureaucracy. The use of local troops to defend the frontiers risked the development of provincial loyalties and the possibility of secessions as soon as the grip of the central authority slackened; and the employment of barbarian auxiliaries settled within the frontier (begun by Marcus Aurelius, who brought groups of his German ex-enemies to live in plague-depleted areas) was potentially even more dangerous.

The potential weaknesses rapidly became actual with the madness and death of Commodus. The Age of the Antonines ended, and the Roman Empire plunged into a series of crises more serious than any it had known since the foundation of the principate.

Commodus, one of the more bizarre figures in Roman history. He fought as a gladiator in the arena and his self-identification with Hercules is apparent in this marble bust, where he sports the mythical hero's lionskin and club.

THIRD-CENTURY CRISIS

Roman emperors generally tried to give their autocratic power some appearance of legitimacy. Augustus did it by respecting traditional forms and pretending to be no more than *princeps* – first man in the state; the less stable emperors among his successors spoiled the illusion by capricious acts of tyranny that finally destroyed the dynasty. The Antonines gave imperial rule a firm moral basis: the emperor was 'best man' as well as first, visibly working hard and co-opting a successor of proven ability. The system broke down when Marcus Aurelius co-opted his irresponsible son Commodus. After Commodus' assassination the Senate chose one of their number, Pertinax, as emperor; but he was less fortunate than Nerva had been in a similar position a hundred years before. Pertinax's economies angered the Praetorians, who murdered him and blatantly put the Empire up for sale. The highest bidder was one Didius Julianus; but he had hardly assumed the purple when the armies in the provinces took a hand, acclaiming their favourite generals and marching

against one another. In the ensuing civil wars Didius Julianus perished, Lyons was sacked, and the leader of the legions in Pannonia, Septimius Severus, finally emerged as the master of Rome.

Severus was a tough military man, and ruled as such. He had little time for the Senate, which had backed one of his rivals, and he kept the favour of the army by increasing its pay. He also recognized military marriages, which had not been allowed in the whole period of professional soldiering since Marius' time, although this had not prevented unofficial unions from flourishing. After campaigning over much of the Empire Severus arrived in Britain, fought an indecisive war against the Caledonians in the north, strengthened Hadrian's Wall, and died at York in 211. He is said to have advised his sons to 'stick together, pay the army well and let the rest of the world go hang' – the clearest possible indication of the new status of the emperors as the chosen of the armies.

Severus was succeeded by his son Caracalla, who ensured his own supremacy by having his brother murdered, but in other respects followed his father's advice. The army's pay was substantially increased, and to help meet the cost Roman citizenship was extended to all free men in the Empire (making them liable to pay an inheritance tax). This completed the slow evolution of the Empire into a single, effectively uniform society where a man's status, rank and class mattered more than his geographical origin.

Despite some respectable military achievements Caracalla was killed by his officers – a fate that was to become increasingly common for Roman emperors. The prestige of the Antonines was such that even in these violent times emperors changed their names to join the earlier 'dynasty', and some sort of legality was observed; but this broke down in the 230s, when utter chaos reigned. Of the long, long list of emperors and pretenders over the next 50 years, Decius (249–251) is remembered as the first emperor to launch a general persecution of the Christians, while Claudius II and Aurelian distinguished themselves by driving back the barbarians who were menacing the Empire; Claudius was spared

Doctored dynastic record: this painted panel shows Septimius Severus, his wife Julia Domna, and their son Caracalla. The scraped-away head of the fourth figure represented Septimius' other son, Geta, murdered by Caracalla.

Remains of the Aurelian wall, built in the early 270s to protect Rome, which had previously seemed safe from attack. By this period hostile barbarians were penetrating deep into the empire and threatening Italy itself.

human ingratitude when he died of the plague, but Aurelian, hailed as *restitutor orbis*, 'restorer of the world', became yet another victim of discontented or ambitious officers.

During this period it must have seemed that the Empire was on the verge of disintegration. Economic decline, most marked in the West, accompanied civil wars and devastating bouts of plague. The Franks and Alemanni broke through the frontiers and ravaged Gaul and Northern Italy; Gothic barbarians took to the sea and looted the Aegean; and in the East, Persia again became a great power, inspired by a new dynasty, the Sassanids. The general insecurity showed itself in a new development, the building of defensive walls by municipalities (including the Aurelian Wall at Rome) that had never before felt the need. At one of the low points of Roman history, in 260, the Emperor Valerian was captured by the Persians – a shattering blow to Roman prestige – while Gaul, Britain and Palmyra became virtually independent and usurpers sprang up everywhere.

However, between 268 and 275 Claudius II and Aurelian restored the military situation; and in 284, when their fellow-Illyrian, Diocletian, was proclaimed as emperor by the troops in the East, he set himself the task of reorganizing the Empire from top to bottom.

The captured Roman emperor Valerian humbles himself before the Sassanian king Shapur; relief on a rock in Iran. The defeat and capture of Valerian in AD 260 was a blow to an empire apparently on the point of disintegration.

Ex-imperial grandeur. After a 20-year reign, Diocletian voluntarily relinquished power. He lived on in imperial style at Split (Croatia), in a palace that combined ceremonial opulence with fortress-like walls. 18th-century view.

THE EMPIRE TRANSFORMED

The Emperor Diocletian (284–305) saved the state, but at a cost: he turned it into an 'Oriental' despotism, served by a rigid bureaucracy, in a society increasingly organized on caste lines. For the most part these measures had been foreshadowed by existing tendencies in the Roman state. The emperor, for example, was already an object of religious veneration, and no longer *princeps*, 'first', but *dominus*, 'lord'; Diocletian took matters to their logical conclusion by secluding himself from the populace, identifying himself with Jupiter, and emphasizing his semi-divine nature through elaborate ceremonial. Similarly, the fiction that emperor-making needed senatorial approval was finally abandoned and all civil service posts were thrown open to senators and equestrians alike, ending the remaining distinctions within the ruling class.

For administrative purposes the Empire was organized into a dozen dioceses run by vicars –

terms that were to survive as ecclesiastical divisions within the Christian Church. Military and civil functions were separated to make defence more efficient and slow down any separatist tendencies in the provinces; 'dukes' and 'counts' were created with responsibility for repelling barbarian attacks. More than ever, the army was localized. Peasant militias, and barbarian auxiliaries who had settled down within the frontiers, bore the brunt of attacks from outside, assisted by smaller units of mobile regulars; heavy cavalry rapidly became more important than the once-invincible legions in which the infantry had been the supreme arm. The badly depreciated currency was reformed and (with rather less success) prices were fixed by government decree. Bureaucracy and taxation bore heavily on the peoples of the Empire, making municipal responsibilities even less attractive; but evasion became harder as an increasing number of offices and crafts were declared hereditary, compelling sons to follow the same occupations as their fathers. It all sounds worse, perhaps, than it really was. In an insecure world any order may be better than none, and caste societies, however unattractive, have often proved to be extremely durable. In the event, much of Diocletian's work was to outlive him and to last as long as the Empire itself.

There can be no doubt that Diocletian's system was the creation of realism rather than megalomania, for he showed a remarkable willingness to share power and eventually to renounce it. Previous emperors had co-opted colleagues, but Diocletian tried to institutionalize the practice and give it a geographical basis. He promoted an old comrade-in-arms, Maximian, to Augustus (that is, co-emperor) and gave him the western empire to rule; the west-east boundary ran from the Danube to the Adriatic. Diocletian's creation, the Tetrarchy (rule of four), was completed by appointing a Caesar, or junior emperor, as the assistant and heir of each Augustus. Significantly, Diocletian reserved for himself the East, where wealthy cities continued to flourish; he set up his court at Nicomedia, strategically placed on the Bosporus. With Italy in economic decline, Rome had lost much of her old importance, and Maximian made his headquarters at Milan, closer to the frontier areas where trouble might arise. Some of these arrangements proved temporary, but the realities that prompted them did not. The strength of the Empire was becoming concentrated in the East; the West was declining, and only the prestige attached to the name of Rome disguised the fact.

While Diocletian ruled, his system worked. In 305, after 21 years on the throne, he abdicated – a voluntary act, unique in imperial Roman history. The last 11 years of his life were spent at his enormous palace in Dalmatia, later the nucleus of the town of Spalato (modern Split), where he planted gardens and studied philosophy. He reappeared briefly in 308 to preside over an attempt to sort out the tangled affairs of the Empire, where Maximian, the Caesars and their relations were already battling furiously; but his system was already beyond repair. The marching and countermarching went on long after Diocletian's death, until Constantine, the son of Maximian's first Caesar, emerged as sole victor.

Imperial harmony. Diocletian created the tetrarchy, the system by which four men ruled the Roman world. This group, carved in porphyry, represents the tetrarchs; each Augustus embraces his Caesar, his junior partner.

CONSTANTINE AND CHRISTIANITY

In 306 Constantius I Chlorus, formerly a Caesar, was co-emperor, ruling the West. He and his son Constantine crossed to Britain and drove back an invasion by the untamed tribes north of Hadrian's Wall. When Constantius died suddenly at York, Constantine was hailed as emperor by his troops and became a Caesar, controlling Gaul and Britain, in a reconstituted Tetrarchy. Six years of military and political intrigues followed, until in 312 Constantine was strong enough to invade Italy, defeat his rival Maxentius at the Milvian Bridge, and become emperor of the West. Before the battle he is said to have looked at the sky and seen a cross and the legend *in hoc signo vinces*: 'In this sign, conquer.' Whether or not this actually happened, Constantine favoured Christianity from at least this time, by contrast with earlier emperors who had looked to the old Roman religion to restore the old Roman virtues. (Diocletian, for example, had persecuted Christianity during his last years.) By the Edict of Milan (313), Constantine and the emperor in the East, Licinius, proclaimed general toleration and the restoration of confiscated Christian property. Later, Licinius began to persecute Christians, perhaps because the new faith had become politically identified with Constantine. War broke out, Licinius was defeated, and by 324 Constantine was master of a re-united Roman world.

Christians were far more numerous in the East, and Constantine could now safely lavish patronage on the Church. Having long made way against imperial indifference or active hostility, Christianity flourished throughout Constantine's reign, no doubt gaining strength as doubters realized that it did not involve un-Roman weaknesses such as pacifism. One of Constantine's earliest actions as ruler of the Roman world was to convene an ecumenical council at Nicaea in Bithynia (325), which attempted to resolve the conflict between those who believed Jesus and God were of one substance and those who believed they were separate – the Arian heresy, as the victors later called it; despite the orthodox victory at Nicaea, Arianism was to play an important part in the later history of the Empire. By the end of Constantine's reign Christianity was effectively the state religion, although it was not as yet persecuting its rivals.

Constantine's greatest material legacy was a new capital, begun in 326 and dedicated in 330 on the site of the old Greek city of Byzantium. New Rome, which was soon to become known as Constantinople, 'the city of Constantine', was planned as a Christian capital; although pagan as

Colossal head of Constantine; the head, along with a single hand and other fragments, survives from a huge marble statue. Its solemn, abstracted air reflects the new concept of the emperor as a remote, god-like being.

well as Christian ceremonies were discreetly allowed at its foundation, no pagan temples were built within its walls. The site was superbly chosen – the end of a small peninsula on the European coast of the Bosporus where it joins the Sea of Marmara. Surrounded on three sides by the sea, it became near-impregnable when immensely strong walls were built across the peninsula; indentations in the coastline provided good harbours; and a long inlet, the Golden Horn, was large enough to shelter a navy but narrow enough for defenders to keep out enemy ships by stringing chains across the entrance. The city controlled the natural land route from Europe to Asia and the sea route from the Mediterranean into the Black Sea; and it served as a well-placed headquarters for an Empire apparently most strongly menaced from across the Danube and the Tigris. Constantine's choice, not so very far from Nicomedia, confirmed Diocletian's wisdom in making the East the new heart of the Empire; and

Constantinople would be a Christian imperial city for the next eleven hundred years.

In many other respects Constantine furthered Diocletian's work. The imperial bureaucracy grew still larger and was equipped with ever-wider powers and duties; the separation between civil and military powers became complete; the admission of barbarians as army recruits continued; taxation remained onerous, and measures were taken to prevent peasants from leaving the land and the wealthy from evading municipal office. The attempt to create a rigid but stable society had some success; for although the value of the old silver denarius continued to depreciate there was at least a partial economic recovery, mainly thanks to the introduction of a new coin, the gold solidus. And by favouring the new Christian faith Constantine promoted an ideology that was to prove effective in increasing social cohesion and would long outlive the Empire and the world of late antiquity.

The walls of Constantinople, built in the early 5th century by Theodosius II. Founded by Constantine and named after him, Constantinople remained the greatest city in the western world until the 15th century.

DECLINE AND FALL

After Constantine's death in 337, his sons and nephews allowed neither their blood ties nor their Christian faith to hinder them from murdering one another. Ironically, the last survivor of the family was Constantine's half-nephew Julian, a passionate classicist who attempted during his brief reign (361–363) to revive the worship of the old gods, maintaining a policy of toleration but shifting state patronage and funding from churches to temples. In 363 Julian died while campaigning against a revived Persian empire before his religious policy could have much of an effect; having been raised as a Christian and freely rejected the faith, Julian was long reviled as 'the Apostate'. With the extinction of Constantine's line the army raised to the purple one of Julian's senior officers, Jovian, who made a hasty peace with Persia and restored Christianity as the religion of the Empire before dying in 364.

The next army-made emperor, Valentinian (364–375), appointed his brother Valens co-emperor and ruler of the East. From this time onwards West and East were effectively, though not officially, separate realms. Valentinian, an able general, was constantly on the move from the Danube to Britain, in an unending and just-successful effort to repel invaders and mend breaches in the frontier defences. The first decisive breakdown occurred in the East, three years after Valentinian's death, when a Germanic people, the Visigoths, crossed the Danube into the Empire. Ironically, they arrived not as invaders but as

The Emperor Julian and his wife, on a sardonyx cameo. Julian's attempt to restore the old gods has been seen as inevitably doomed; but the emperor's early death may well have been a turning point in religious history.

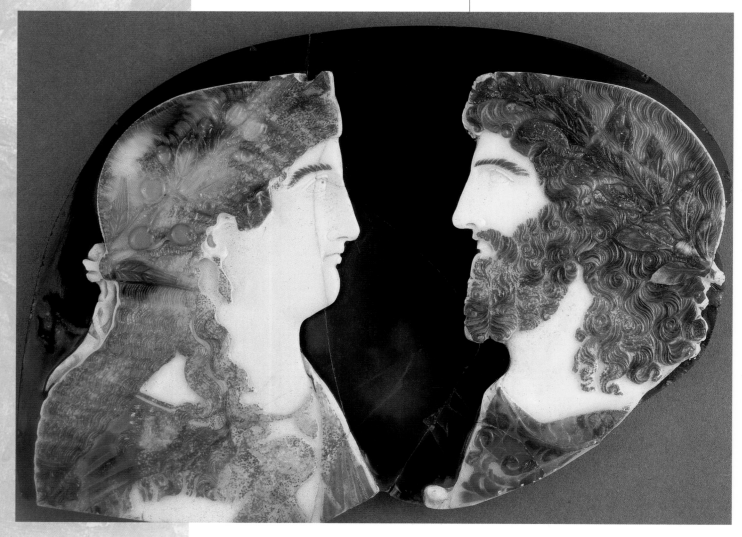

refugees from ferocious Central Asian nomads, the Huns, whose crushing victories and savage behaviour set the entire barbarian world on the move. After an initially friendly reception, the Visigoths were so carelessly handled by the Romans that they took to arms, ravaged the Balkans, and then, in 378, defeated and killed the emperor Valens at the battle of Adrianople. A new Eastern emperor, Theodosius, failed to defeat the intruders but managed to pacify them and settle them in Thrace as military allies. The precarious situation of the Empire was now clear. More frightened but formidable peoples were fleeing the terrible Huns and approaching the frontiers at a time when the Romans could no longer rely on their military superiority over barbarians; indeed, Roman armies were increasingly manned by other imported barbarians, creating a situation in which the distinction between defenders and invaders easily became obscured.

Theodosius restored order in the East and intervened in the West to put the youthful Valentinian II back on his throne. Under the fervently devout and orthodox Theodosius, the future of Christianity as an exclusive state religion began to take shape: Arians and other heretics were persecuted and the pagan temples were closed or taken over. In the final months of his life, having invaded Italy and overthrown a usurping warlord, Arbogast, Theodosius became the sole ruler of the Empire. He was the last: in 395 his dominions were divided between his sons Arcadius and Honorius, and although the division had no special significance at the time, it proved to be permanent.

In the West, things soon began to fall apart. The Visigoths became restless again, while Vandals, Alans and other peoples poured into Gaul. Only the ability of a barbarian general in Roman pay, the Vandal Stilicho, gave much hope that Rome could hold on; but Stilicho's behaviour was ambiguous and in 408 his son-in-law, the Emperor Honorius, became fearful of his general's intentions and had him murdered. Britain was effectively abandoned at this time; it was the second fully Romanized province to be lost (trans-Danubian Dacia had been evacuated as early as 270). Then, in 410, the Visigoths under Alaric

sacked Rome itself. The city had been replaced by Milan as the imperial capital in the late 3rd century, and had been eclipsed by Constantinople; but the name of Rome was still redolent of past glories, and for Roman citizens everywhere its sack was a symbolic and psychological catastrophe of the first order. The Visigoths moved through France into Spain, driving the Vandals in front of them: the Vandals crossed into North Africa, from where they were later to sack Rome with a gleeful thoroughness that has made their name a byword for mindless destruction.

Imperial recognition of the barbarian Spanish and African kingdoms amounted to an admission that they were no longer part of the Empire. But

The Mausoleum at Ravenna of Theodoric, Ostrogothic king of Italy from 493. Like other rulers after the fall of the empire, Theodoric imitated Roman ways where he could, and had himself buried in Roman fashion.

Byzantine masterpiece. The tall minarets of Muslim Istanbul have modified the impression that would once have been made by St Sophia (centre), the vast domed church built in Constantinople for the Emperor Justinian.

there were still times at which it seemed that something might be salvaged. The Huns plundered the eastern empire but were driven out of Gaul, bought off or bluffed out of Italy, and then, after the death of Attila, broke up – to the relief of the Romans and other barbarian peoples alike. But the Vandal sack of Rome followed three years later (455) and the history of the West became a shambles in which the emperors were often no more than the puppets of 'Roman' barbarian generals. The last western emperor, Romulus Augustus, was the most grandiosely named; in spite of which he was deposed on

4 September 476 after reigning for a year, and the Roman Empire in the West came to an end. For a time Romulus Augustus' barbarian successors kept up the fiction that they were the representatives of the eastern emperor, but by the 490s Italy had become ruled by another Germanic people, the Ostrogoths, who set up their own entirely independent kingdom.

The great folk wanderings were far from over, but the likely outcome was already apparent: the Empire was dead, but the barbarians would eagerly accept the religion of Rome (at first in its heterodox Arian form) and as much as they could assimilate of its culture, which they admired even as their activities helped it to crumble all around them.

The East was terribly battered by the events of the 5th century, but it managed to survive thanks to its greater resources, the strong walls of Constantinople, and the subtlety displayed by its emperors in playing off barbarian armies against one another. The reign of Justinian (527–565) witnessed a recovery so brilliant that for a few years it even seemed that the Mediterranean might again become a Roman lake: North Africa (533–534) and, much more arduously, Italy (535–554) were recovered by Justinian's generals Belisarius and Narses, and the south-east of Spain was conquered from the Visigoths. Justinian had a genius for being well served – and even well partnered, for his wife Theodora, a former actress whose past may have been more than a little shady, proved to be a strong-willed and politically capable empress; it was her firm stand that dissuaded Justinian from fleeing when the Nika riots of 532 threatened to turn into a revolution. Justinian himself was an able administrator who reformed and purged the civil service, though his ambitious policies still put a great strain on the Empire's resources. Like Constantine he had a powerful voice in the affairs of the Church, although he too failed to reconcile the hostile factions, now quarrelling over whether Jesus had a single or dual (human and divine) nature.

One of Justinian's greatest achievements was to preside over a codification of the law that ultimately influenced western Europe even more than the East. Above all he initiated a great building programme throughout the Empire; at Constantinople it was crowned by the completion of the church of St Sophia, whose domed splendour caused Justinian to cry out 'Solomon, I have surpassed thee!' There was even a literary revival, although not all its manifestations can have pleased the emperor: Procopius, the court historian, took his revenge for the constraints of official record-making by compiling a *Secret History*, which he filled with very rude stories about the imperial family.

Justinian's reconquest of Italy was completed in 554; but only 14 years later a new people, the Lombards, overran much of the peninsula. Rome remained technically under imperial control, but the city's real rulers were its bishops, the popes. With new doctrines and structures developing in the old imperial capital and the eastern empire becoming increasingly Greek in character, during the 6th century the history of ancient Rome can reasonably be said to have come to an end.

Loot from the East: four superb gilded Greco-Roman bronze horses, carried off from Constantinople by the Venetians after the scandalous Second Crusade. For centuries the group stood over the entrance of St Mark's Church in Venice.

2

LIFE IN THE ROMAN EMPIRE

MORE THAN A SINGLE CHAPTER, EVEN A SINGLE BOOK, WOULD BE NEEDED TO DESCRIBE THE
VARIETIES OF LIFE EXPERIENCE IN AN EMPIRE SUCH AS ROME'S, FAR-FLUNG OVER SPACE AND
TIME. WHAT FOLLOWS IS IN EFFECT A SERIES OF SNAPSHOTS OF SOCIAL CLASSES, OCCUPA-
TIONS, DWELLINGS, DRESS, CUSTOMS AND HABITS, PASTIMES AND OTHER ASPECTS OF ROMAN
LIFE. THE DESCRIPTIONS ARE MAINLY DRAWN FROM THE IMPERIAL PERIOD, FOR WHICH THE
FULLEST EVIDENCE HAS SURVIVED, BUT SOME OF THE MOST IMPORTANT CHANGES BETWEEN
REPUBLICAN AND IMPERIAL TIMES ARE GLANCED AT; AND SINCE ANY BRIEF SURVEY
INEVITABLY FOCUSES ON ROME ITSELF AND, AFTER ROME, ON ITALY, SEVERAL SECTIONS ARE
DEVOTED TO A HANDFUL OF PROVINCES – FROM SUN-BAKED AFRICA TO CHILLY BRITANNIA –
WHERE THE ROMAN WAY OF LIFE WAS MODIFIED BY LOCAL CUSTOM OR CLIMATE.

Preparations for marriage as
recorded in a 1st-century BC
painting, the *Aldobrandini
Wedding*. The occasion combines
religious ritual with music and
merrymaking; but the bride is
evidently apprehensive.

FAMILY AND ROMAN VALUES

For Romans in early Republican times, the family, religion and the state were parts of a complex of feelings and attitudes of peculiar intensity. The values they enshrined can be summarized as *pietas* and *fides*, terms that translate rather feebly into words such as 'piety' (or 'duty') and 'faith', which no longer have their former force in English. The household was at the centre of life in a way that it never was for the Greeks, who were in so many other respects models for the Romans; and for a farmer-hero such as Cincinnatus it was the small kingdom from which he briefly emerged to rule Rome itself. In this kingdom the oldest male, the *paterfamilias*, had *patria potestas* – supreme authority over the lives and property of his family. His wife, like all women, was regarded as immutably child-like, and therefore to be kept in lifelong subjection: she passed straight from her father's authority to her husband's, and when he died she could be commanded by her son; once she had left the paternal home her only possible protector was a male relative from her own family who could be appointed as her legal guardian, empowered to reclaim her dowry if her husband put her away. (In very early times a husband could divorce his wife without any shadow of excuse; but this was such an unsatisfactory arrangement that even in the 3rd century BC he was obliged to prove that she had committed some serious offence.) By contrast, a son could hope one day to become a *paterfamilias* himself, although in the meantime he remained in leading-strings even when he had become the grey-bearded father of a family. In law a *paterfamilias* could kill his son, sell him into slavery, or formally expel him from the family. Such actions must always have been rare, and probably unthinkable in most families, but the fact that they were countenanced by the law does serve to emphasize the limitless nature of paternal authority.

A young woman in bridal yellow rearranges her hair, while a cupid holds up a mirror; wall painting from Pompeii. The scene represents the nuptials of the Greek god Dionysus (Roman Bacchus) and the mortal Ariadne.

Memorialized by a funeral feast. This mosaic from a tomb reunites a married couple in death; each is shown reclining on a couch in characteristic Roman fashion. The flat pictorial style is typical of the period, the 4th century AD.

The stern rectitude to which Romans aspired during their early history is exemplified by the legend of Lucius Junius Brutus – not the assassin of Julius Caesar, but the aristocrat who is said to have led the revolt that drove the last king from Rome: according to a legend that the Romans evidently regarded as admirable, Brutus discovered that his sons were plotting with the Etruscans and unhesitatingly condemned them to death. In historical times stern rectitude was exemplified by Cato the Elder, whom we have already met demanding the destruction of near-helpless Carthage. His puritanism was almost a mania. Discipline was rigid in the home, and shows of affection were forbidden. Even when holding high office Cato dressed simply, went about on foot and dispensed with retinue and display. He argued for the perpetuation of wartime austerity measures that had forbidden women to wear embroidered clothes or drive in carriages within the city (but the women of Rome demonstrated so vigorously in favour of a repeal that they got their way); and when, holding the office of censor, Cato was empowered to purge the Senate of wrong-doers, he expelled one member for kissing his wife in public. When he held the office of censor he also taxed luxury goods and works of art; for above all else he detested the Greek culture and Greco-

Eastern refinements of life that were beginning to captivate Roman society. Cato was fighting a losing battle, and his contemporaries' admiration for his unyielding virtue was strongly tinged with hypocrisy – 'the tribute vice pays to virtue'. Both his puritanism and his more positive qualities – his sense of justice and his incorruptible behaviour in public office – were increasingly praised rather than copied.

The nature of Roman marriage changed greatly over the centuries. At any time the husband had advantages in law and also in practice: any manifestation of female independence must have been restricted by the fact that girls married at an early age, between about 12 and 15 years old; except in the most sophisticated circles the majority must have been trained into docility and circumscribed by motherhood before they became adults. On the other hand even a very young girl among the better-off became the mistress of a household on marriage, and rapidly learned responsibility or autocratic caprice. Despite the non-existence of women as separate legal personalities, a good deal was expected of them in practice. The ideal Roman matron was chaste, frugal and fertile; she capably managed her own household domain and, when occasion arose, displayed a heroic loyalty to her husband. Roman legend had its female equivalents to Junius Brutus in heroines such as Veturia and Volumnia, mother and wife of the disaffected general Coriolanus, whom they persuaded to give up his assault on Rome at the cost of his life. Although such episodes can be dismissed as simply reflecting male values, they do suggest that more active female roles were possible. And in fact Roman women always enjoyed a greater physical freedom than women in most other ancient cultures. By contrast with the segregation of the Greek wife, who had to retreat to the women's quarters when there were visitors, the Roman matron dined with her husband even when there was company and, provided she behaved decorously, also moved about in public without censure.

By the 2nd century BC women were playing even more prominent roles, partly as a result of Roman losses in the Carthaginian and other wars, which left the fate of many families in the hands of widows. As the Republic approached its end a general softening of attitudes – perhaps the result of victory and affluence – seems to have influenced family relationships, bringing greater freedom for women and, as far as it is possible to judge, a greater warmth of affection between husband and wife and parents and children. The form of marriage in which the wife had a relative-guardian became universal, while at the same time the guardianship became increasingly perfunctory; so that by the 2nd century AD the wife was a free partner in the marriage, able to keep an eye on her own property and to will it to whomsoever she pleased. Partners were also more or less freely chosen by this period, or at least consented to; inevitably, among the upper classes 'suitability' in terms of rank and property continued to influence choices, as they have in periods

Intense encounter: an erotic scene from a wall painting at Pompeii, the city overwhelmed by a volcanic eruption. Among the many items preserved under its ash were paintings, including a wealth of erotic subjects.

committed to far more romantic conceptions of married love. Convincing evidence of how women were valued is provided by inscriptions and literary references, which indicate that a loving spouse was increasingly counted as one of life's treasures. Pliny the Younger, a highly successful advocate and imperial administrator of the early Antonine period, appears in his letters as a devoted husband, delighted by his wife Calpurnia's interest in his literary productions and missing her – haunting her bedroom – during her absence. Since Pliny published his own letters, arranged in self-consciously artistic selections, his sincerity can be questioned; but it is evident that he expected his readers to warm to a picture of a marriage based on affection and shared interests. Even allowing for the difference between written and lived relationships, it seems certain that attitudes changed radically between the age of Cato and the age of Pliny.

Another aspect of the new freedom was easy divorce. In imperial times this again became possible for men without the excuse of a serious offence on the wife's part; but in the 'modern' form of marriage women too could put away their husbands and come away none the worse, although the practical difficulties must have been greater for them unless they were heiresses. Among the outrageous examples (but with a distinctly modern resonance) was that of Cicero, who divorced his wife of 30 years to wed a rich young girl. Augustus too, though he later set himself up as a moral reformer, divorced his own wife *and* arranged the divorce of 19-year-old Livia (pregnant with her second child by her husband, Tiberius Nero) so that he could marry her. This must have been a love match (at least on Augustus' side), but generally speaking the many marriages and divorces of men like Sulla, Caesar and Pompey were politically motivated; and later on, according to Martial and other satirists, high-society people changed partners so often that marriage was no more than legalized adultery. It seems unlikely that divorce was so common among other classes; no doubt it offered much the same pros and cons as it does today.

The sexual availability of slaves must have put a considerable strain on many marriages, although we hear little of the subject. There is some evidence that female sexuality was regarded as not quite respectable, although occasional suggestions that wives should be grateful if their husbands turned their carnal attentions elsewhere smack of wishful thinking on the husbands' part. As in most societies, sexual attitudes were so contradictory and fluctuating that it is hard to make any meaningful statements about them. This applies equally to homosexuality, which was formally less acceptable than in Greece, yet was often casually referred to in a way that implies tolerance in practice. The law prohibited it between citizens, yet moralists of the 2nd century BC vociferously blamed Greek influence for its prevalence at Rome. Augustus tried to revive the prohibition, yet his poets sang happily of the pleasures offered by boys and girls without insisting on distinctions; whether this was a mere poetic convention – a graceful tribute to the Greek lyric – is unclear. The most famous homosexual relationship in antiquity was the one between Hadrian and the exceptionally beautiful Antinous, whose death by drowning caused the grief-stricken emperor to make him a cult figure all over the Empire.

Children at play. This lively scene is all the more touching in that it appears on the side of a sarcophagus made for the body of a dead child. The rate of infant mortality was appallingly high and troubled Romans of all classes.

One of the more mysterious aspects of Roman life is the decline in the birth rate, at least of the upper classes, which occurred from the late republican era. Neither Caesar nor Augustus managed to produce a male heir, although they married five times between them; and the infertility of the Antonines, though beneficial to the state, is not likely to

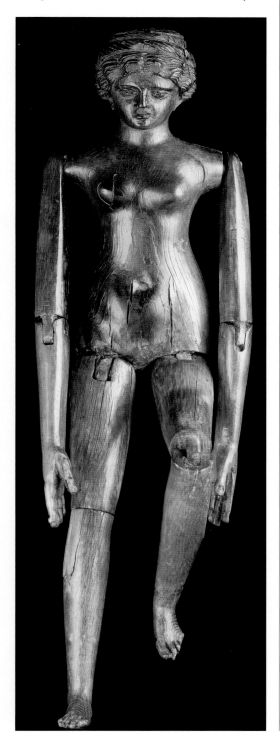

have been deliberate. The old patrician families, having survived for centuries, died out in an astonishingly short time during this period; and the surprisingly large number of freedmen (that is, ex-slaves) who are known to have inherited their former masters' property indicates that the phenomenon was socially and statistically significant. Augustus certainly thought so, since he introduced legislation to combat it, penalizing bachelorhood, requiring widows to remarry, and conferring privileges on families with more than three children; but his measures seem to have had little effect. The privileges became just one more mark of imperial favour, conferred for faithful service on an individual such as the younger Pliny, despite the fact that he had no children. As so often in demographic matters, most of the explanations are implausible or (like 'widespread irresponsibility') explain nothing.

The children who did come into the world were better – or more affectionately – looked after. Infanticide by exposure had been practised by the early Romans (as it had been, earlier still, by the Greeks) to dispatch weak, deformed or unwanted children. This extreme example of the *patria potestas* came to be regarded as immoral and was finally made illegal under the Empire, although the very poor no doubt continued to abandon offspring they could not support; occasional gestures were even made by the emperors towards the upkeep of poor children in Rome. Infant mortality was appallingly high, and in the more humane atmosphere that prevailed from late republican times, monumental and literary laments for dead children multiplied; even Martial, most savage and foul-mouthed of satirists, mourned the little six-year-old slave girl Erotion in verses touchingly reproachful of a personified, and criminal, Destiny. One result of the declining birth rate may have been to encourage parents to feel that their offspring were precious; at any rate they became far more affectionate and indulgent. Stories about spoiled children began to circulate, although here, as in the case of women, conservative grumblings are not indisputable evidence of widespread depravity.

Left: A wooden doll with jointed limbs. This well-made and finely carved object probably belonged to the child of a wealthy family. Most children would have had home-made dolls or toys such as balls, marbles and hoops.

EDUCATION AND CULTURE

Roman family affection may have varied in intensity over the centuries, but children were of prime importance to all classes. Without them a noble family would become extinct and its name would in time be utterly forgotten; while poor people looked to their children as the only source of support in old age. Every birth was a hazardous event, threatening the lives of mother and child. Roman women were delivered at home, usually by a midwife, sitting more or less upright in a birthing chair. If the child was in some way disabled, or there were too many mouths to feed, it might be abandoned or simply done away with; discoveries of bones beneath the floors of houses suggest that infanticide may always have been fairly common among the poor. When the child was eight or nine days old the father performed the ceremony of *sublatus*, taking it into his arms to signify its acceptance into the family, after which it was named and presented with a good-luck charm. This was of limited efficacy, since something like one in three children died within the first year of life, a fact that helps to explain why the Romans of the early Republic regarded fertility as a cardinal wifely virtue.

In early times the education of Roman children was supplied by the parents themselves, even in the upper classes. As in so many things, Cato the Elder followed the old customs when others were abandoning or modifying them: he supervised his son's bath night, taught him to read and write, and personally took the boy through a

gruelling course of physical training that seems to have enfeebled him for life. By this time (the 2nd century BC) other upper-class parents were employing tutors for their children and/or sending them to school; and ideas about what needed to be learned had been profoundly affected by the impact of Greek culture on the Romans. The tutor, or *paedagogus*, was likely to be a Greek and might well also be a slave. Some children were educated entirely at home, but many went to an elementary school at about the age of seven, accompanied by the *paedagogus*. Girls as well as boys of good family attended and were taught reading, writing and arithmetic by a master (*litterator*), whose school was known as the *ludus litterarius*. (Even in antiquity the use of the word *ludus* ['game'] in this context was regarded as puzzling; one commentator suggested that it was adopted with a deliberate intention to deceive

children by making them believe that school would be fun!) All schools were fee-paying, but quite a large number of children seem to have gone through the primary stage and acquired basic literacy; one indicator is the abundance of Roman graffiti, much of it clearly done by ordinary people.

Elementary schoolteachers were low in status and often found it hard to make ends meet; classes were large in order to maximize fees, but even so, many teachers took second jobs. School began at dawn and carried on till noon or the early afternoon. Evidently not everybody got up so early: in one of his verses Martial complained that a local teacher woke the poet and his neighbours, making it impossible to sleep through the din created by his bellowings and beatings. An advocate of 'progressive' education appeared in Martial's contemporary and fellow-Spaniard Quintilian, a

Stages in a boy's life, from babe in arms and play-charioteer in a toga to schoolboy reporting to his master; relief from a sarcophagus of the mid-2nd-century AD. The little cart drawn by a goat is a particularly delightful touch.

Funerary relief of a child in a toga; the goat beside him must have been his pet. Around his neck the child wears a *bulla*, an amulet that was only discarded at puberty. Beneath his feet is a dedication to the spirits of the dead.

successful advocate whose book on the training of orators roundly condemned corporal punishment and argued that better results were obtained by making lessons enjoyable and providing incentives for the pupil such as prizes and praises. However, the teacher described by Martial was probably closer to the reality of Roman teaching.

The education of girls ended when they were about 12, and only a small minority of boys went on to secondary education with the *grammaticus*, whose lessons concentrated exclusively on works of literature. In the later centuries of the Republic the literature was mainly Greek, but under the Empire the works of the Roman writers Virgil and Cicero were recognized as Latin classics, fit to be studied beside Homer and Menander. The teaching method was uninspiring: the pupil read or recited a prepared passage, then the teacher explained it word by word, concentrating on grammatical and metrical points but also elucidating the mythological, geographical, historical and other allusions as they occurred. In this way a boy could pick up a good deal of incidental information; but that was not the main object. The bilingual literary education created a unified ruling-class culture that was inaccessible to outsiders. Criticisms of it on utilitarian grounds may seem justified but in fact miss the point: a ruling class has no pressing need for 'useful' knowledge in a relatively stable, low-technology culture, whereas it always does feel impelled to put obstacles in the path of would-be members; the English public school operated in the same way (and with the very same languages and literatures) in the 19th and early 20th centuries.

Although physical training with a military flavour was encouraged, the Romans had nothing like the Greek passion for athletics; in fact this was one pursuit where the associations with Greek practices (nudity and pederasty) were a negative influence; even as spectators the Romans were not enthusiastic about the Greek games, which Julius Caesar, Augustus, Nero and other philhellene emperors attempted to popularize; however, it is arguable that Roman taste in this respect was corrupted by addiction to the carnage of the Colosseum, which made bloodless sports seem tame. Music too was not part of the regular

curriculum, although specialist teachers were available; neither the character nor the fate of the outstanding amateur practitioner, the Emperor Nero, can have provided much inspiration.

At 16 the well-born youth left off his purple-striped *toga praetexta*, assumed the *toga virilis* that marked him out as an adult, and was formally registered as a citizen. He was then attached to some prominent person and served a sort of political apprenticeship, accompanying his mentor on civic and ceremonial occasions. He also underwent a period of army service, at first in the ranks and later as an officer on the staff of a general. Finally he spent up to three years studying rhetoric, the art of speechmaking, argument and persuasion. This gave him the confidence and verbal skills he needed for public life. However, over time the discipline became increasingly artificial

and the cases to be argued came to have less and less contact with reality, although 'technique' was constantly refined and terminology elaborated. This development was probably connected with loss of political freedom under the Empire, which deprived oratory of its prime subject matter, contentious political issues; even 'practice' political speeches might be dangerous (liable to misinterpretation by suspicious imperial authorities) as well as futile. Declamation remained an admired talent, but decoration and ingenuity began to loom large when content became stereotyped and non-controversial. Stylistic flights, not relentless arguments, were called for, and the object was to win applause (and perhaps advancement) rather than to influence decisions. That being so, there was something to be said for ingenuity-provoking exercises in historical or legal fantasy: should the

School scene from a pillar found at Neumagen (Roman Noviomagus) on the Mosel River in the Rhineland; 2nd or 3rd century AD. Nothing changes: one boy is hard at work, while a late comer is being told off by the master.

Nicknamed 'The Orator', this life-size bronze statue of one Aulus Metallus shows his eloquence in full flow. In a society where a small ruling class met regularly in assemblies and courts, the arts of persuasion became a vital part of a young man's education. Etruscan, early 1st century BC.

Greek king Agamemnon sacrifice his daughter for a favourable wind that would carry his fleet to Troy? Is the gold ingot swallowed by a fish part of the pre-sold catch? So rhetorical teaching was not useless to those who underwent it, although its usefulness was not of a kind we see fit to admire.

Given the power of fashion, rhetorical embroidery was probably useful in the law courts, which provided ambitious men with an alternative career to political and administrative work. In practice the two were often combined. Pliny the Younger, for example, made his name as an advocate in property suits while following a conventional senatorial career; after that he worked in the treasury; and finally he undertook an extended troubleshooting mission as the Emperor Trajan's representative in Bithynia and Pontus, dying in office. Special schools existed at Rome for those who wished to study law, offering the detailed knowledge that classes in rhetoric largely ignored. This was the most distinctive Roman contribution to education, in line with their devotion to the law, and was one subject in which they outshone the Greeks. Contracts and wills were of palpable importance quite early in Roman history, and the sanctity attached to legal agreements was in marked contrast to the more casuistical and often downright unreliable practice of the Greeks. The first coherent body of Roman law, the Twelve Tables promulgated by the magistrates of the Republic, dates from 450 BC. This brief code was expanded over the centuries by 'case law', consisting of rulings and opinions that formed precedents covering more and more permutations of events. Later on, the continuing Roman interest in law must have been further sharpened by the conditions of imperial times, when the courtroom provided the only outlet for qualities that had once been developed in political battles – and when, thanks to the size and wealth of the Empire, litigation flourished as never before. The result was the development of a specialized legal profession (not just advocates but authorities and compilers of textbooks) and of a body of law that increasingly aimed to secure justice rather than merely uphold custom. A code of law as well-made and rational as a Roman road was to be one of the Empire's most durable bequests to mankind.

In most other areas of Roman culture, Greek influence was a powerful force from the 2nd century BC. Religion, drama, literature, philosophy and the arts (the subjects of later chapters) were all modified by Greek examples where they did not directly copy them, although in most instances the Romans made contributions that reflected their own down-to-earth and practical attitudes. The Roman genius for conquest and reconciliation spread the Latin tongue all over the western Mediterranean and north-west Europe, and with it a common Greco-Roman culture. Some Romans were out-and-out philhellenes, but most were ambivalent in their attitudes, scorning contemporary 'Greeklings' as degenerate while they imported Greek statuary, studied Greek philosophy and literature, and even employed the living Greekling jewellers and metalworkers who had emigrated to Italy. For their part, many Greeks affected to despise the Romans as uncultured while they rushed to supply them – at a price. Educated Romans were bilingual, and equally familiar with Virgil and Homer, Livy and Thucydides; educated Greeks all too often knew no Latin – to their own loss, since (with one or two exceptions) the Greek literary achievement belonged to the distant past, whereas the Latin tradition lived on into the age of the Antonines.

Professional couple: wall painting from Pompeii, believed to show the lawyer Terentius Neo and his wife; their double portrait has a startling immediacy reminiscent of a photograph. They appear anxious to establish their status: he grips a papyrus scroll, while she insists on her literacy by holding up a stylus and a note-tablet.

Unfriendly welcome in the style of the 1st century AD: floor mosaic at the threshold of a Pompeian house, carrying the warning *Cave canem*: 'Beware of the dog!' The Romans kept dogs for many reasons, not least as pets.

HOUSE AND HOUSEHOLD

The peoples of the Roman Empire inhabited a great variety of dwellings, from huts and cottages to city tenements and palatial villas. But the traditional Roman house was the *domus*, where one or more generations of a single family lived under the guardianship of the *paterfamilias*. The *domus* was a type of building long common in Mediterranean lands, with a blank, undistinguished exterior broken at best by small, high windows. This arrangement, reminiscent of a castle, provided a degree of security against criminal entry and ensured the privacy of those inside. Lack of pride or interest in the outside was such that, in towns, the facade facing a street of any size usually had a row of shops added to it.

The front door opened more or less directly on to the most hallowed room, a lofty hall known as the *atrium*. Here stood the *lararium*, the shrine to the household gods (*lares* and *penates*), whose goodwill was retained by regular sacrifices.

Niches held masks or busts of the family's ancestors, and its material treasures, stored in the family strongbox, were also kept in the *atrium*. An opening in the roof let in daylight and also rain, which was collected in a basin set in the floor; although aqueducts brought water to Roman cities, only a few private dwellings benefited directly, and collecting rainwater saved unnecessary trips to the nearest well or municipal tank. Bedrooms and other small chambers led off from the *atrium*, and behind it lay the *tablinum*, the master's office, where he received dependants and conducted private business; to one side of that was the *triclinium* (dining room). Beyond these rooms there was a walled garden in early republican times, but once Greek influence began to permeate life the garden area was transformed into an elegant courtyard with a colonnade or peristyle, filled with lush plants, topiary work, statues and eye-catching items such as fountain niches; these were intended to be seen as the crowning features of a view straight through the house from the front door. In summer the courtyard was the pleasure-centre of the house, and the letters of the younger Pliny describe dining alfresco, with small delicacies floating in the basin of the fountain, ready to be picked out at leisure.

Among the other amenities valued by the well-off was a bath-suite. This was the part of the house most likely to be heated by the ingenious hypocaust system, which has often been compared with modern central heating. However, it was usually restricted to one or two rooms in private houses and was only applicable to the ground floor. Basically, air warmed by a furnace circulated in a space below (and co-extensive with) the floor, which was supported by stacks of tiles. Vents carried the soot and fumes outside the house, avoiding the disadvantages of other forms of heating such as charcoal braziers; nevertheless these were used in most rooms, thickening the atmosphere and also creating a fire hazard. Fires could also be started by the main form of artificial lighting, oil-burning lamps made of terracotta or bronze, which were often fashioned in ingenious animal or grotesque shapes. The winter trade-off between retaining the heat and blotting out the light with shutters became a little less acute as

time went on and the romans made increasing use of window glass.

Roman houses had little furniture, and the general effect in a substantial *domus* must have been one of spaciousness and simplicity. Tables, even when made of bronze or marble, were relatively small; the legs on many of these and other items were in animal form or terminated in paw-feet, setting a fashion that has reappeared intermittently ever since. Chairs, benches and stools appear to have been plain and uncomfortable-looking. The most important item was probably the couch or bed: the definition depends on location rather than any variation in appearance, since the same item was used for sleeping and dining. Bedrooms were very small and seem to have been solely functional – left immediately on rising – rather than pleasant environments. What little is known of Roman furnishing suggests that it was, by modern standards, rather austere, but quantities of fabrics and cushions were probably used in the house to brighten and soften its appearance.

From the 2nd century BC, Greek influence and growing affluence brightened the bare mortar

Middle-class luxury: the outdoor dining room of the House of Neptune and Ampheitrite at Herculaneum. The mosaic-lined walls are witnesses to the prosperity of the shop-proprietor to whom the house belonged.

Underfloor heating for Roman baths. The piles visible here supported the floor, but also allowed warm air to circulate beneath it. In the northern provinces the system was used to warm several rooms in the house.

floors and plastered walls of the *domus*. An attractive and durable form of decoration was the mosaic, a pattern or picture made with many tiny pieces of coloured glass or stone (*tesserae*); it had the advantage of maintaining the cool, hard surface of the floor, highly agreeable during the summer, although there were also purely ornamental wall mosaics. Walls could be painted to imitate the veining of marble and to create fantasy architectural or theatrical frameworks for scenes of landscape or mythical events; quite often perspective devices were used to create a 'window' effect that deceived the eye into believing that the painting extended into the outside world and so made the room seem more spacious. (The same effect is achieved in modern interiors by the use of wall mirrors.) Mosaics and paintings were luxury items, and in all but the grandest houses they were confined to public areas such as the *atrium*, where they showed off the family's wealth and good taste. Decorative objects also

beautified the house, the most important being statuettes of bronze or stone and, especially in the courtyard among the shrubs and trees, stone figures and reliefs.

Romans ate two or three times a day, but very frugally except for the main meal, taken in the cool of the evening while reclining on a couch and preferably in the company of friends. Although snack bars and taverns existed to serve the lower orders, there were no restaurants, and well-off Romans dined in their own homes or as guests of people of their own class; where the standard of domestic fare was inadequate for an ambitious entertainment, an expert cook could be hired for the night. Cooking was done with charcoal on a raised brick hearth; in poorer households only frying and boiling were possible, but brick ovens existed in which food could be baked or roasted. Cookery books were published, and one survives from the late imperial period, attributed to a well-known gourmet named Apicius. A wide variety of foodstuffs were consumed, including soups, meat, fish, poultry, vegetables, fruit, nuts, bread and pastries (but not, of course, potatoes, tomatoes, chocolate and other items unknown to Europeans until they began to trade with the Americas). Nevertheless the Romans were liberal in their use of herbs and sauces and had a positive mania for *garum*, a kind of fermented and pickled fish sauce. One possible reason for disguising natural flavours was that by the time produce reached households in large towns it was no longer fresh; but taste and custom seem to have played a part too. One of the Romans' more unusual preferences was for foods that confounded the diners' expectations, causing them to anticipate eating a chicken and find that the dish was in fact a knuckle of pork.

Such artifices were not devised for everyday meals but for banquets, and inevitably the most costly and decadent of these have attracted attention; as a result accounts of peacocks' and larks' tongues and stuffed dormice rather distort our ideas of Roman habits. The most famous description of such a banquet is given in a novel, the *Satyricon*, by Petronius Arbiter, who may well be the 'arbiter of taste' known to have been employed by Nero to supervise imperial diversions until he fell under suspicion and was compelled to take his own life. The banquet in the story is given by the wealthy ex-slave Trimalchio, and is a wild exhibition of tasteless nouveau-riche extravagance culminating in a maudlin display by Trimalchio himself, who shows off his wealth, vulgarity and ignorance in about equal parts. Perhaps the Neronian period (one of excess and danger) really was more gluttonous than some others; at any rate Nero's sometime mentor, the philosopher Seneca, hits off the most repulsively bulimia-like of Roman gourmandizing habits when describing people who 'ate to vomit and vomited to eat'. However, there is no reason to suppose most Romans were like this, and some of the more high-minded, like Pliny the Younger, took the opposite tack and consciously made their banquets feasts of intellect and reason.

Humble but indispensable: pottery stacked in the corner of a room at Pompeii. With glass and metal in relatively restricted supply, huge numbers of earthenware vessels were used for storage, transport, or eating and drinking.

COSTUME AND ADORNMENT

High fashion in Flavian times. The lady's locks were a product of the hairdresser's art; her bust displays the dexterity of the Roman sculptor, who on occasion created even more extravagant examples of high-piled marble curls.

For the Romans, ordinary dress consisted of tunics, mantles and poncho-like cloaks: in distinguishing rich from poor and fashionable from frumpish, cut was less important than quality of material, colour and ornamentation. The most distinctive item of Roman clothing was the toga, a voluminous garment of fine wool worn by male citizens on formal occasions. Draped over one arm, it was evidently tiring and difficult to keep under control, hot, and perhaps scratchy; at any rate one emperor after another felt compelled to insist that it must be worn at public ceremonies, which implies that there was considerable public reluctance to do so. There were various types of toga including a grey one for mourning; boys wore the purple-hemmed *toga praetexta* until they could assume the adult's plain *toga virilis*; while various stripes and colours on togas (and, for that matter, shoes) distinguished senators, equestrians and magistrates. Everyday dress was more likely to be a sleeved and belted tunic, worn at knee-length, supplemented when necessary by a cloak and cape. Footwear became more specialized over time, and cobblers turned out sandals, slippers, fancy town shoes, and boots for heavy work and soldiering. A girl wore an under-tunic, tunic and shawl (the *palla*); when she married she replaced the tunic with the longer and fuller *stola*, decorated only with coloured hems. Although the tradition of sobriety was kept up in public, both men and women dressed more brightly at banquets.

Beauty aids, scents and jewellery were abundant by imperial times, and they were used to a greater or lesser extent by both men and women. Greek craftsmen probably made the finest jewellery, repaid with a characteristically Roman mixture of contempt and envy for their cunning art. One important way in which a Roman woman could appear beautiful and distinctive, while at the same time advertising her wealth, was by adopting an elaborate coiffure: the range of hair styles was such that it left little scope for future invention, and some of the more elaborate must have been triumphs of leisured immobility and the art of the slave-girl expert wielding curling tongs.

Men too had increasing recourse to the barber in imperial times, although a sterner age had contented itself with a pudding-basin cut and straight combing. Julius Caesar was an early dandy, though forced in middle age to conceal his baldness beneath the victor's laurel wreath. Hair-consciousness was still more intense by the time of Hadrian, who made a mop of curly hair *de rigeur* for the would-be-fashionables of all ages. During the same period beards began to be worn again after three clean-shaven centuries. Shaving was another custom adopted from the Greeks, who had largely abandoned beards in imitation of Alexander the Great; appropriately enough, the Roman most often compared with Alexander – Scipio Africanus, the conqueror of Hannibal – introduced the new fashion to Rome, and by the 1st century BC it was becoming the norm: Sulla, Cicero, Caesar, Augustus and other men of the late Republic – men whose images are perhaps the best-known of antiquity – were all clean-shaven. Since soap did not yet exist and iron blades were not very sharp, shaving must have been an uncomfortable business even in the hands of experts: no man shaved himself, and a barber who acquired the reputation of being a smooth worker could make his fortune. The long vogue of the clean-shaven face

suggests that it fulfilled some psychological function, perhaps expressing the sharp-edged nature of ambitious men in a dangerous age. It is said to have been the Emperor Hadrian who finally set a new fashion by growing his beard to cover a scar; but it is tempting to believe that the double change he initiated (curly hair and full beard) also corresponded to a change in sensibility, possibly one favouring a more 'romantic' appearance in an otherwise rather staid age.

Bearded romantic. The facial hair grown by Emperor Hadrian ended the 400-year-old fashion for clean-shaven chins on mature men; combined with the 'soft' style of 2nd-century sculpture, this gives portraits a new, mild look.

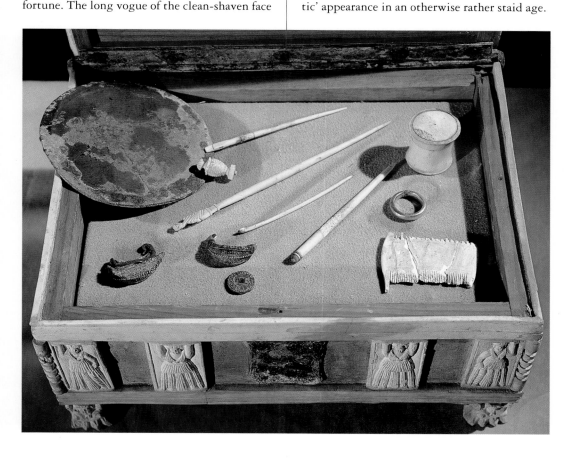

A case with mirror and cosmetic equipment. By the 1st century AD, when these were made, upper-class Roman women took great pains over their make-up, using foundation, lipstick, mascara, and face powder made from white lead or chalk.

CITY LIFE

Mass entertainment for city-dwellers: the superbly preserved amphitheatre at Arles in southern France, where beast-hunts and gladiatorial combats were staged for an audience which might number more than 20,000 people.

At the beginning of its career of conquest Rome was a city-state, and the Empire it created was filled with cities to an extent never equalled in ancient times. As in so many other respects, the Greeks had gone before, establishing the basic city-state layout, with its hill-citadel (*acropolis*) and meeting- and market place (*agora*). In Rome the Capitol and the Forum served the same purpose, and temples, baths, gymnasia and theatres were derived from Greek models, initially absorbed through contact with the Etruscans and the Greek cities of Southern Italy. The Romans

made contributions of their own, turning the outdoor Greek theatre on the edge of the city into an indoor urban institution, and adding new features such as the circus for chariot racing, the amphitheatre for gladiatorial contests, triumphal arches, commemorative columns, and new and more efficient hygienic arrangements.

This model prevailed throughout the Roman world. The eastern half of the Empire already had

many cities, and few new foundations were needed there; but Roman cities grew up all over the West from North Africa to Britain, at key points for trade, communications or military strategy. Municipal pride was strong, and the competitive spirit made both new and old towns eager to acquire symbols of the Roman way of life such as baths and amphitheatres; where the imperial authorities were unwilling to supply any deficiencies, wealthy and ambitious individuals stepped into the breach in order to further their political careers. As a result Roman cities presented a remarkably uniform appearance, with relatively small variations caused by differences of climate and custom.

Ironically Rome itself became something of an exception, largely thanks to its huge size. The Romans themselves often referred to it simply as *Urbs*, 'the City'. It was the undisputed capital of the Empire until the late 3rd century AD, by which time it had well over a million inhabitants. The original Forum, the Forum Romanum, remained a great civic centre but was supplemented by new *fora* built by Julius Caesar and others. These were increasingly administrative, banking and legal centres, surrounded by colonnades and large-aisled halls (basilicas). The largest of all was the Forum of Trajan, which was part of a larger complex including Trajan's Market and overlooking the great column commemorating the emperor's campaigns against the

The Porta Nigra (Black Gate) in the German city of Trier. Two huge rounded towers flank and control access to the two arched gateways. It was begun by Septimius Severus at a time when Roman cities were no longer safe from attack.

Dacians. The palaces on the Palatine Hill, the Capitoline temple, the Colosseum, the Baths of Caracalla, the Circus Maximus, the Theatre of Marcellus and many other monumental structures made public Rome an awe-inspiring sight.

Much of the residential city was very different, with narrow, winding streets that were permanently in shadow because of the height of the buildings. The affluent, well-born Roman dwelt with his family in a private house on the courtyard plan, but by the imperial period the overwhelming majority of the inhabitants lived in large apartment blocks known as *insulae* ('islands'). Most other towns and cities had only a few *insulae*, but in Rome 'high-rise' building was the only solution to the housing problem caused by the disproportionate increase in the size of the population. A survey made in the 4th century AD found that there were 1,797 family houses in Rome and no less than 46,602 *insulae*; the best-preserved examples now are at Ostia, the harbour

town of Rome, which also needed to build *insulae* to take the population overspill from the capital. Most *insulae* seem to have been warren-like tenement blocks, crammed with dole-fed poor tenants, although some are said to have been designed for 'middle-class' residents or at least to have been relatively spacious and pleasant on the ground floor; conditions generally became worse towards the top (anticipating the later garret), where the rooms were smaller and the fabric was less soundly constructed.

Building on the cheap and building too high made the *insulae* unsafe, and collapses were frequent. The scandal became acute enough for Augustus to issue regulations limiting the height of a building to 20 m (65 ft; about half a dozen storeys), but it is questionable whether he managed to enforce it. He also instituted a night-watch system to give early warning of fires in the city. Both tenants of *insulae* and families in private houses cooked on open stoves and used charcoal-burning braziers to keep warm and oil lamps for lighting, making outbreaks of fire a common occurrence. Tenants of *insulae* were supposed to keep water in their rooms at all times in readiness to fight a blaze, but the difficulty of bringing any large amount up from the street makes it doubtful whether the regulations were widely observed. The ill-success of Roman firefighting is shown by one of the strategies used by Crassus, the millionaire associate of Caesar and Pompey, to increase his fortune. When a building caught fire, Crassus made the despairing owner an offer for it. Although it was derisory the owner was glad to salvage something, after which Crassus moved in his team of slave architects and builders, who cleared the site and threw up a profitable new apartment block. By this method Crassus was said to have acquired very large areas of Rome – testimony to the frequency with which fires broke out.

The absence of a direct water supply increased the fire hazard and must have added to the discomforts of life on the upper floors of an *insula*. Some blocks were equipped with a cistern in the courtyard, but more often the tenant or paid carrier had to bring water from one of the tanks in the street that were supplied by the municipal system; pipes carrying water directly from this

The Palatine, one of the celebrated seven hills of Rome. During the imperial period the emperors built their palaces there, competing with one another in size and luxury until the entire hill was covered.

system were connected to only a few of the wealthiest families in private houses and ground-floor 'luxury flats' in the *insulae*. Nevertheless the existence of an assured water supply, brought by aqueducts that were marvels of engineering, remains one of the Romans' most impressive achievements. The city's first aqueduct was built as early as the 4th century BC; the oldest of its sewers, the Cloaca Maxima, was (and is, for it still exists) even older, since it is said to have been installed during the reign of Tarquinius Superbus in the 6th century. The sewers kept the lower-lying areas free from flooding and carried away waste from the public latrines and some ground-floor residences; but the lack of any physical link between the upper floors of the *insulae* and the drains and sewers was another of the drawbacks of flat-dwelling – and also one of the hazards of walking by night, since residents were apt to save themselves effort by flinging their slops out of the window. In the circumstances the existence of hundreds of public baths and a system of cheap and efficient public latrines did much for the health and happiness of the Romans; a difference between ancient and modern sensibilities is revealed by the fact that in the often pleasantly decorated latrines up to 20 customers at a time sat side by side on an open row of seats, chatting without embarrassment.

Roman writers complained at length about the discomforts of the city, and even allowing for the exaggerations of satirists it was noisy, cramped and overcrowded. During the day the streets were thronged – despite which barbers and even teachers were known to save paying rent by pursuing their professions out of doors. Shop-goods spilled over on to the pavement, and stalls further obstructed traffic. The cries of shopmen and stall-holders advertising their wares was only a small part of the noise problem: since many objects for sale were made as well as sold in the shops, which were open to the street, there was, depending on the nature of the trade, a constant sound of banging, hammering or sawing, accompanied by shouted instructions. Heavy traffic was not permitted except for builders' wagons, but these, piled high with masonry and lurching along, were given a wide berth by the wary.

The night brought other problems. The unlighted streets were dangerous, and most people stayed at home. The wealthy diner could venture forth with a bodyguard of slaves carrying flaming torches, but the less affluent individual who left a friend's or patron's house, perhaps rather the worse for drink, might be robbed or, at best, wander around all night in the dark, trying to find his way back to his own home. Not that the streets were empty. Julius Caesar found a partial solution for traffic congestion by decreeing that all supplies from outside the city must be brought in during the hours of darkness. This worked so well that it was adopted for cities all over the Empire; but, the satirist Juvenal complained, the noise of men, animals and creaking cart-wheels made it impossible to sleep . . .

So, despite its amenities and entertainments, the city was a place that those who could afford it were glad to leave when their affairs permitted. Not surprisingly, urban Romans found much to admire in country living.

Communal latrines at Lepcis Magna in Libya. Roman sanitary arrangements favoured sociability rather than privacy, but were otherwise admirable from the point of view of public provision and waste disposal.

THE COUNTRYSIDE

During their early history the Romans were citizens of the city but also farmers. They lived near-self-sufficient lives, ploughing while their wives ran the house and spun and wove their clothing; at the call of duty, like Cincinnatus, they forsook the plough and took up the sword, returning to work when peace was made. Their holdings were small and they worked hard, with relatively primitive tools, to wrest a living from the soil.

The realities of life on the land changed as Rome became powerful and wealthy, but in Roman minds the countryside remained identified with simplicity and virtue. Significantly, in a culture that had no great respect for money-making, the ownership of land was seen as the only completely acceptable way in which could be combined prestige with profit.

The character of farming in Roman Italy began to change as the wars with Carthage and other enemies inflicted heavy casualties, and holdings suffered from damage or neglect. Wealthy absentees built up large estates (*latifundia*) that were run by bailiffs and worked by slave labour. Large-scale production and cheap labour gave them a competitive advantage over small producers, many of whom were driven out of business, allowing the large estates to expand still further; however, some independent and tenant farmers did survive, along with the colonies of veterans settled on the land by victorious commanders. With the swollen population of Rome (including former smallholders) reaching an unprecedented size, the *latifundiae* had an assured market for grain, olives, wine, vegetables and other produce; even so, more was needed, and agricultural practice in the provinces was also revolutionized, and in some cases became for the first time market-oriented, to fill the million mouths of the capital.

At the heart of the *latifundia* was the *villa rustica*, a working farmhouse equipped with a threshing floor, barns, oil and wine presses, wine cellars, stables, cattle sheds and quarters for the bailiff and slaves. Thanks to the power of literature, the most famous Roman farm is a smaller *villa rustica* at Sabinum, just outside Rome, which was immortalized by its owner, the Augustan poet Horace. He received it as a gift from his patron, Maecenas, and it was big enough to relieve him from financial anxieties – reason enough for him to have sung its praises so often in his verses. However, for the most part the poet was less interested in market produce than in the joys of a refuge from the noise and summer heat of Rome: red wild cherries and sloes grew there, oaks and ilex trees offered pleasant shade, and flocks of sheep formed an appropriately pastoral backdrop for his musings.

On some estates the house was separated from the farm buildings, allowing the owner to enjoy

Treading the grapes in September to make wine; the workers are hanging from straps to prevent themselves from slipping. The picture is part of a floor mosaic from the city of Thysdrus (El Djem) in Tunisia; 2nd century AD.

his country retreat while leaving business affairs to the bailiff. Since discipline on the *latifundia* was harsh, this meant that toiling gangs of slaves and wealthy leisured families were near neighbours; but if the Romans were insensitive to such contrasts, they were not much different in that respect from 19th-century plantation owners in the American South, Victorian factory proprietors, and a good many others over the centuries.

A much grander feature of the rural scene was the *villa urbana*, a large country house. Like the country houses of 18th- and 19th-century Britain, it was at once a place of civilized leisure and a monumental assertion of status. Though found in Pompeii and other places, many *villae urbanae* were built in the countryside around the capital, like Pliny's villa at Laurentum, 27 km (17 miles) from Rome, so that, as he told a friend, 'it's possible to stay here and still do a full day's work in the city'. The *villa urbana* was laid out on the same lines as a town house, but colonnades dignified the exterior and the ceremonial *atrium* was much smaller or might even be dispensed with altogether; picture galleries and libraries advertised the cultivated tastes of the owners, and outdoor pleasures were emphasized by the provision of extensive garden courts, arbours, fish ponds, walks and fine views.

Harvesting olives; a scene from a 3rd-century AD Tunisian mosaic. Olives were one of the great staples of Roman civilization; as well as food, they provided oil for cooking, burning in lamps, and massaging and cleaning the body.

SOCIAL CLASS AND SLAVERY

Slave combing a girl's hair while the mistress of the house looks on; wall painting from Herculaneum, 1st century AD. The fine quality of the fabrics is apparent, and the mother's sandals have been neatly shaped to her feet.

The chief social distinctions at Rome, in both republican and imperial times, were between three groups: the senatorial or noble order, the *equites* (equestrians or knights), and the over-whelming majority of plebeians, their ranks swollen by the ever-increasing numbers of freed-men (ex-slaves) who took only a generation or so to achieve full citizenship rights. At the bottom of the social hierarchy, vast numbers of slaves laboured in widely varied conditions and with a variety of prospects, from ultimate emancipation to death by exhaustion in the mines.

Under the Republic, the Senate was indirectly elective: a man joined it after holding a number of

minor magistracies such as *aedile* and *quaestor*, for which he was chosen by the citizenry. However, in practice almost all magistracies were occupied by members of the hereditary class of great landowners, so that the Senate and the nobility were largely the same people. During the imperial period the hereditary principle was openly accepted, and the nobles of Rome and Italy were joined in the senatorial order by representatives of the provincial upper classes.

The equestrians, as their name suggests, originated as a category of citizens enrolled to serve on horseback in wartime; but their membership soon became identical with that of the wealthy business class. In republican times most equestrians remained outside politics, their ambitions discouraged by the ruling that no senator could have dealings in shipping or in the lucrative state contracts that multiplied with Rome's victories; but a handful of 'new men' (the term habitually used by the Romans themselves) did reach the Senate from an equestrian background, the outstanding examples being the general Marius and the great orator Cicero. Under the Empire the equestrians

flourished, carrying out a range of civil and military functions created by the expansion of imperial bureaucracy. More and more offices were opened to them, until only a relatively small number of key posts remained the exclusive

Above: A Roman lady and her servant. The relief captures the languid condescension of the mistress as she chooses an item from the box held by her servant. However, slaves in domestic service were relatively well off.

Left: A procession of the joiners' guild. The members are carrying a litter on which stand a cult figure and models who perform craft tasks such as using a two-man saw; wall painting from Pompeii, 1st century AD.

Asserting her status to the end: the tomb of Caecilia Metella is a famous landmark on the Appian Way outside Rome. Ironically, little is known of the lady – except that she was the daughter-in-law of the millionaire Crassus.

preserve of the senatorial order. By the end of the Antonine period it was apparent that Roman nobles, provincial notables and equestrians – the propertied classes – were blending into a single ruling class.

The *plebeians* can hardly be called a class at all, ranging as they did from well-to-do tradesmen to the 150,000–200,000 men on the corn dole. Although they had shown that they were capable of collective action in early times, when faced with open discrimination on the part of their patrician superiors, they made only sporadic use of the rights they had won; their lack of any visible community of interests no doubt accounted for this, and for the failure of the Gracchi and other revolutionaries to form an effective opposition to the Senate.

More important bonds linked Romans as members of societies such as religious fraternities, mutual-aid clubs and trade guilds. But the most important relationship, cutting across classes, was that of patron and client. In republican times this

was a matter of life-or-death political strategy: Caesar, Pompey and other men of power needed political friends who would return favour for favour, as well as veteran soldiers, settled on the land, who would rally to them at a call, and wealthy provincial cities that would accept their leadership.

In the imperial period, patrons and clients abounded. At the lowest level, poor men got up before dawn every morning and went to salute their patron at his house. Each man wore a toga and carefully addressed the patron as 'my lord' (*dominus*); failure to do so might forfeit the little gift – probably a few coins – which the client expected on his departure. The most disreputable clients probably hoped for little more from their patron than this daily hand-out and a more substantial gift of money or food on special occasions; poets and other halfway respectable, down-at-heel persons angled for invitations to dinner; and tradesmen hoped for special orders. The patron also extended to his followers a degree of protection against legal oppression; all he derived from the relationship in return was a visible retinue, flattery, verses in his honour, and a train of mourners at his funeral – quite a lot, in fact, on the non-material level.

As soon as his clients disappeared, the patron rushed round to *his* patron and went through much the same performance, no doubt with more substantial benefits in view than a few coins. Political support, help in making a career, climbing the social ladder or winning a contract – on this level the process looks familiar. However, the importance of the quasi-ceremonial side of the relationship should not be underestimated: the Roman found it very gratifying to cut a great public figure surrounded by dependants. The actual extent of patronage is not very clear, but there are some authorities who believe that only

the emperor, at the apex of the hierarchy, was not simultaneously somebody's patron and somebody else's client. The whole phenomenon appears less strange when we realize that it has existed at many other times and places under different names. The Democratic political machine in Tammany Hall, New York, 'protected' immigrants and found them jobs in return for votes. The 18th-century English nobleman held a levee that was crowded with suppliants who hoped his 'influence' would be employed to find them army commissions, pensions, or jobs in the customs and excise; the situation of English author-clients was so much like those of ancient Rome that the famous Dr Johnson was able to adapt the verses of the satirist Juvenal to lament the tribulations of the Grub Street writer: 'Toil, envy, want, the *patron* and the gaol'.

A palatial villa by the sea; wall painting from Stabiae, a resort on the Bay of Naples. Wealthy Romans enjoyed seaside holidays, and those who had time headed south, using their villas as staging-posts on the journey.

The complexities of social relationships sometimes cut across economic realities, but the law was quite unambiguously on the side of the rich and respectable. Ignoring other distinctions, it treated men as *honestiores* or *humiliores* – 'honourables' and 'dishonourables'. The categories were not precisely defined, and in each case the courts decided where a man belonged; but it seems clear that property and position were the decisive considerations, grouping the better-off plebeians and professional men alongside senators and equestrians as *honestiores*. The main difference between the two categories lay in the punishments that were meted out to them. If convicted of a serious crime *honestiores* were most commonly condemned to banishment and confiscation rather than death; whereas *humiliores* were liable to crucifixion, a bloody end in the arena, or death by exhaustion and ill-treatment in the mines, working alongside slaves.

The *humiliores'* crimes were regarded as the more serious because they did not own property; but those unlucky enough to be slaves *were* property. Roman slavery existed on such a vast scale

In the market: a customer sits while the merchandise is weighed. Rome itself had a series of markets erected by popularity-seeking emperors; the most ambitious was Trajan's Market, built into the Quirinal Hill.

that it had profound effects on society and the economy. From the 2nd century BC, when Roman arms triumphed in both east and west, enslaved prisoners-of-war were brought back to Italy in such numbers that they could be allocated to specialized functions, often though not always on a geographical basis: Africans were employed as body slaves; Greeks as nurses, tutors, physicians and craftsmen; Spaniards as herdsmen; and so on. In the following century their ranks were swollen by Gauls who had resisted Caesar, and later by Germans and other barbarians from beyond the Rhine and the Danube, while wars in the Near East brought a renewed flow of more or less Hellenized prisoners.

As a result, the Roman economy became adapted to the use of a slave workforce, and this had the effect of depressing the wages of free labour and helping to increase the numbers of the Roman unemployed. It also made it difficult for smallholders to compete against capitalist farmers, who could undercut them by large-scale production based on slave-labour. In Rome, about a third of the inhabitants are estimated to have been slaves, and in Italy the numbers were so large that masters could never feel entirely secure. There were in fact slave revolts in 2nd-century Sicily, followed by the spectacularly near-successful rising led by Spartacus, which must have shaken any belief Romans may have had in their innate superiority. Understandably, then, Roman masters lived under a certain strain: 'so many enemies, so many slaves' was a widely quoted maxim, and in one of his books of advice Cato the Elder warned his readers to watch out for conspiracies when slaves lived together in harmony. In his household slaves were flogged if the meals they served were not up to standard; they were not allowed to enter any house but their master's; and stable relationships between slaves were discouraged by compelling the females to prostitute themselves within the house according to a tariff fixed by Cato himself. As this implies, even Cato found it prudent to give slaves some incentives to acquiescence by allowing them to earn money; but his general attitude can be summed up in his celebrated advice to farmers that they should sell their worn-out oxen and old or sick slaves.

On the treadmill. Slaves employed for labour-intensive tasks led hard lives. This relief comes from the tomb of the Haterii; the presence of the windlass suggests that they were building contractors. 1st century AD.

Naturally, everybody was not as determinedly unfeeling as Cato, who loved rigour even better than virtue; but many of his attitudes were no harsher than the state of the law. A master could sell, prostitute, castrate or murder his slave; if a slave murdered his master, the whole household was to be executed; and in criminal cases the evidence of a slave was only regarded as worth having if it was extracted under torture.

In practice slavery could mean many things, depending on the nature of the slave's employment and the temper of the master. The worst fate was to work in the mines or provide brief entertainment as animal-fodder in the arena; it seems quite likely that this was the reward of carelessly displayed spirit or intelligence as well as crime, although some legal safeguards were introduced against sheer vindictiveness on the part of masters. The herdsman was almost certainly better off than field-workers, who could be organized in gangs and locked up together at night; but the household slave had most advantages of all – a relationship with the owning family that became humanized through close contact, plus opportunities to pilfer and benefit from left-overs and discarded items. Household slaves could also make the most of the Saturnalia on 17 December, a Christmas-like holiday when people exchanged presents and topsy-turvydom prevailed; masters waited on slaves, and slaves were able to indulge

in some plain-speaking forbidden all year long – within severe limits, no doubt, since there might otherwise be a reckoning to pay on the morrow.

The confusions of town life must have been even more favourable to the household slave, and they also gave him more opportunities for advancement. If he was a skilled worker he would probably be allowed to take a job on the side, or even to set up on his own and pay his master a percentage of the takings. And eventually, if his master was too mean or too poor to grant him his freedom, he could hope to buy it and join the growing numbers of active, prosperous freedmen. Under the Empire, the condition of slaves

The reality of slavery: a master strikes his servant. In this theatre scene, art imitated life: however kindly the relations between owner and owned, the relationship was ultimately based on force backed by the law.

improved remarkably both in law and practice. Claudius laid it down that any master who killed a sick or 'useless' slave was guilty of homicide; castration was forbidden; rights of appeal against injustice were established and could even lead to the enforced sale of a badly treated slave to a new master; and emperors intervened in a number of legally ill-defined situations to rebuke or punish a cruel owner. Cicero's relationship with his secretary, Tiro, was one of touching friendship, culminating in Tiro's manumission (release from slavery) when he was only 30; Cicero was such a good master that his slaves refused to desert or betray him even when Antony put a price on his head. In the 1st century AD Seneca, admittedly the most sympathetically high-minded man in antiquity, argued that a master should have only so many slaves as he could get to know well, and that slaves should look up to a master rather than fear him. Later still, Pliny the Younger boasted that his slaves' and freedmen's quarters were comfortable enough to be used as guest-rooms; and he affected to be astonished when he heard of some slaves who had attacked their master.

This change in attitudes runs parallel with the milder family situation noted earlier, and probably affected household slaves more than others. The slowing-down of military expansion has been suggested as a contributory reason; with slaves no longer pouring into Italy, slave-holdings stabilized; new generations of slaves were born into households; and a more genial patriarchal relationship inevitably developed. In effect, many slaves were simply domestic servants, perhaps a little less independent than labourers and craftsmen but with greater security; the Roman equivalent to the butler or maid was arguably a little better off in real terms than his or her Victorian counterpart.

An improvement in the treatment of slaves is easier to account for than the tremendous increase in the numbers who were actually set at liberty. By Augustus' time manumissions had reached such an alarming rate that he imposed age limits (the owner must be 18 and the slave 30) and a sliding scale establishing ratios of slaves owned to the number of slaves it was permissible to manumit; Pliny, for example, liberated the maximum number (one hundred) in his will, which indicates that he owned at least five hundred. Even with these limitations, such huge numbers had been freed by the Antonine period that a majority of the inhabitants of Rome are believed to have been of servile origin.

This is difficult to explain, and some puzzled historians have been driven back on unconvincing hypotheses such as a fashion (a remarkably long-term fashion) for generosity. True, a kindlier atmosphere prevailed among the slave-owning classes; but there is little trace of a conviction that slavery as such was wrong, and the only people who might have thought so were of a philosophical or religious turn that emphasized inner rather than real, worldly liberation. Economics may well have played a large part. An unproductive slave actually consumed his master's resources; and in the unregimented circumstances of town life, slavery was probably even less efficient than elsewhere: no slave in his right mind would do much work except for a reward or under supervision. Better, perhaps, for the master to free skilled men to earn their own livings, keeping down the number of servants to be fed and building up a following of grateful freedmen.

For the liberation of the Roman freedman was not unconditional: he owed his ex-master certain services and, perhaps more important, the *obsequium* with which a client treated his patron. In many instances the patron-client relationship survived for very long periods, despite the fact that within three generations all the freedman's legal disabilities were removed and he could aspire to any office in the state. (The Romans' eventual identification of a free man with a full citizen is, incidentally, unique in antiquity.) The position attained by freedmen under Claudius was exceptional and temporary, but in later times they continued to provide the Empire with many of its best civil servants and businessmen. Inevitably they were mocked, like all newly arrived men: Trimalchio, the ex-slave and dinner-party host in the *Satyricon*, is the classic new-rich vulgarian. But for all that, freedmen often inherited from their infertile ex-masters, and their role in the later Empire was an important one.

Bust of a Syrian slave. This curious item, made of bronze and lead, was part of a container. The suggestion of degeneracy in his close-set eyes and bat-like ears perhaps reflects a conviction that slaves were congenitally inferior.

FAMOUS WOMEN

Roman women exercised very limited authority in their own right. But they could still become famous, or notorious, for their virtues or vices, and the shrewdest of them could on occasion exploit accidents of birth or marriage to wield real power. The earliest Roman heroines were models of chastity such as Lucretia, who stabbed herself after being raped by the son of Tarquin the Proud, or patriotic icons like Veturia and Volumnia, mother and wife of Coriolanus, who persuaded the disaffected Roman warrior to abandon his attack on the city. Later, Cornelia, daughter of Scipio Africanus and mother of the Gracchi, was such a model figure that the Romans put up a statue of her; while Paulina, the youthful wife of Seneca, insisted on her duty to die with her husband when Nero ordered the aged philosopher to kill himself.

But the Empire also gave women the opportunity to acquire power or influence. The most clear-sighted female politician was probably Livia, the wife of the Emperor Augustus. She is known to have taken an active part in decision-making, and to have retained Augustus' love and respect to the last. They had no children, and Livia seems to have diligently but discreetly promoted the career of Tiberius, her son by her first marriage. Rumour said that she disposed of any popular young man who threatened Tiberius' chances of succeeding Augustus, and after the sudden death of Tiberius' nephew Germanicus, his widow Agrippina – herself a formidable personality – was certainly convinced that Livia was responsible; the feud that followed was, inevitably, fatal for Agrippina.

Tiberius succeeded, but resented his mother's political influence so strongly that he avoided erecting the memorials to her decreed by the Senate; and it was left to her grandson Claudius to declare her officially divine. Claudius' own marital experiences were so bizarre that it is difficult to believe that the accounts we have are not wildly exaggerated or lacking some political key that would allow us to make sense of them. The emperor's first wife, Messalina, carried sexual

indiscretion to incredible extremes, of which Claudius seems to have been the only man in Rome who knew nothing; some Roman historians rather implausibly suggest that, since the emperor had told his courtiers to follow his wife's instructions whatever they might be, they inferred that he didn't mind how she behaved. Eventually Messalina went through a public 'marriage' with a young lover, perhaps as a preliminary to a political coup, and when the emperor was told he had her put to death. In his resentment Claudius decreed that every monumental or written reference to Messalina should be expunged.

Untaught by experience, Claudius took a second wife, Agrippina, who proved to be more interested in power than sex. Having put her son Nero in a position to succeed Claudius, she is said to have poisoned her husband; at any rate, in AD 54 the 16-year-old Nero became emperor. For a time he was content to enjoy himself and leave political matters to his mother, whose power was such that her image appeared along with Nero's on Roman coins. But Agrippina's influence was rapidly undermined by Nero's tutor, the philosopher Seneca, and Burrus, prefect of the Praetorian Guard; though apparently high-minded in their political aims, they were not above finding Nero a mistress, a freedwoman named Claudia Acte, in order to weaken the emperor's dependence on his

Opposite: Livia, consort of the first Roman emperor, Augustus; the bust owes its unusual appearance to the material from which it was carved, basalt. Despite rumours about political murders, Livia was eventually declared a goddess.

Agrippina, wife of the Emperor Claudius, whom she was said to have poisoned, and mother of Nero. Her image, on this coin minted at Antioch, emphasizes her near-imperial status during the early years of her son's reign.

mother. The plan worked and Agrippina moved out of the imperial palace. Within a few years Seneca and Burrus were finding Nero increasingly difficult to control, and his homicidal tendencies began to reveal themselves. Agrippina's schemes to regain influence irritated him, but he was evidently still unable to stand up to her directly; so he decided to have her killed. There followed a black comedy of failed assassination attempts that reached its climax in 59, when Nero provided his mother with a collapsible boat to take her on a trip in the Bay of Naples; the craft duly sank but the indomitable matron swam to safety. Having apparently failed to realize that Nero was capable of matricide, she wrote to announce the good news of her survival. His response was to send a party of soldiers to her villa, where their swords provided the comedy with its bloody anticlimax; finding herself surrounded, Agrippina is said to have pointed towards her womb and invited the soldiers to strike her in the place where she had borne Nero.

Most of the women in Nero's life were victims, but the beautiful Poppaea used her hold over him to have his first wife murdered and become empress. During her three-year tenure (62–65) Poppaea exercised considerable political power. Nero was besotted with her – in spite of which he flew into a rage and kicked her while she was pregnant; she died, and the remorseful emperor deified her. Surprisingly, Nero himself was capable of inspiring devotion: after his suicide in 68, the long-discarded Acte claimed his body and ensured that it was placed in the family tomb.

Rome's only female 'dynasty' was provided by the women of a Syrian family who ruled and ultimately ruined their menfolk. Julia Domna was the wife of Septimius Severus, the African general who made himself emperor in AD 193, ending the chaos that followed the assassination of the last Antonine, Commodus. As Augusta, Julia Domna vied for influence with other members of Septimius' inner circle. But after the emperor's death in 211 she became the principal adviser of her son Caracalla (though she failed to prevent him from having his younger brother Geta killed), and as the imperial secretary in charge of correspondence in both Latin and Greek she knew everything that went on and could control the quantity and nature of the information that reached the emperor.

When Caracalla was murdered in 217, Julia Domna died or, more probably, killed herself. Caracalla's successor, Macrinus, made the mistake of allowing Julia Domna's sister, Julia Maesa, to live. From her retirement in Syria she organized Macrinus' overthrow and the elevation to the

Julia Domna, the first in a family line of strong-minded Syrian women who dominated imperial politics in AD 211–35. As Septimius Severus' wife, she acquired the political skills that she exploited during the reign of her son Caracalla.

The Empress Theodora and her entourage; mosaic in the church of San Vitale, Ravenna, 6th century AD. With a scandalous past behind her, Theodora became a formidable figure, strongly influencing her husband, the Emperor Justinian.

purple of her grandson, Elagabalus. When Elagabalus' exotic religious and sexual practices made him a bad risk, Julia Maesa secured promotion to the rank of Caesar for another grandson, Severus Alexander. The consequent intrigues and confrontations ended in 222 with a Praetorian mutiny in which Elagabalus and his mother (Julia Maesa's daughter) were murdered. Julia Maesa remained in control until her death in 226, when her daughter Julia Mamaea (Severus Alexander's mother) took over the reins. The last of these extraordinary Julias was so greedy and arrogant that she and the emperor were killed in another military mutiny, ending the Severan line.

Other women figured in Roman history as victims of imperialism, but victims whose activities profoundly influenced the course of the Empire. By the time that Cleopatra VII became its queen, Egypt was in effect a client-state of Rome, and her notorious relationships with Julius Caesar and Mark Antony represent, if nothing else, attempts to retain some kind of autonomy for her dynasty. By contrast, Boudicca, queen of a British tribe,

the Iceni, led a revolt by a people who had been conquered but not yet thoroughly tamed.

The turbulent, barbarian-dominated later years of the western empire were unfavourable to female influence, but at least one remarkable career is on record. In 414 Galla Placidia, the half-sister of the Emperor Honorius, was married off to a barbarian, the powerful Visigothic king Athaulf. She survived the ordeal, and Athaulf, only to be married off again by Honorius in 417 – this time to an ambitious military man, Constantius, whom Honorius was forced to appoint co-emperor. Constantius died suddenly in 421, leaving Galla Placidia with two children. In 425, after further vicissitudes, including some incestuous designs on the part of Honorius, her son became emperor as Valentinian III (425–455) and Galla Placidia ruled in his name for a number of years until she was forced into private life. Having experienced to the full the instability of fortune, she died in 450, when the tottering western empire had only a quarter-century more of its history to run.

Catching fish with nets; detail from a mosaic in the catacombs of Hermes at Hadrumetum (Sousse in Tunisia), late 2nd century AD. The mosaic expresses the variety and abundance of fish, a staple food and also a Roman gourmet taste.

THE WORLD OF WORK

Cicero, the great Roman orator, lawyer and politician, was in no doubt about social and economic priorities. Writing to his son, he dismissed any form of hired manual work as degrading, declared that retailers could only make profits by swindling, and scorned fishmongers, butchers, cooks, poulterers, actors and dancers on the rather odd grounds that their work appealed purely to the senses. Nor was becoming a merchant an option, although a businessman who operated on a large enough scale – one that required significant organizing ability – might be just about acceptable; even so, such a man should retire as soon as possible and become a landowner. By implication, then, only public life, the army or being a gentleman farmer were suitable careers for 'a free man'. As so often, these ancient Roman attitudes find echoes in the very recent past, when well-brought-up people would have nothing to do with 'trade' and there was some question as to whether gentility was even compatible with having made a fortune, rather less vulgarly, in 'wholesale'.

Just as genteel disdain for most forms of work flourished during the western Industrial Revolution, Cicero's elite values were held in the heart of a bustling urban culture where building and rebuilding went on constantly and economic activity gave rise to hundreds of specialized trades, crafts and professions. Rome above all, with its huge population of workers and parasites, was filled with activity and stimulated activity on the part of other peoples; their goods poured into the imperial capital, enriching the port of Ostia, where tenements and vast warehouses sprang up on a scale almost rivalling those of Rome itself. The city absorbed huge quantities of imports from the provinces, most of them representing taxes and tribute for which no return had to be made, but on-the-spot manufactures and services also existed there on an unprecedented scale: over 150 Roman trade guilds have been identified, and this number does not of course take in a variety of professions and occupations ranging from lawyers and civil servants to gladiators and prostitutes.

Evidence about working lives and conditions is patchy, since the main literary sources are the satirists Juvenal and Martial; their verses are full of brilliant thumbnail sketches, but these invariably highlight the grotesque or the ridiculous sides of their subjects. Other evidence can be gathered from mosaics and wall paintings, tombstones, and archaeological remains such as the shops and workshops of Rome and buried Pompeii. But apart from occasional graffiti, the workers' own thoughts, feelings and experiences have gone unrecorded and can only be guessed.

The routines of existence are another matter. In the city, the working day began at dawn. Those who were clients but also had some gainful employment hurried round to salute their patrons and collect a few coins as early as possible before getting down to business. The day was divided into twelve 'hours', each representing one-twelfth of the time when it was light; consequently the length of the hour varied with the season and the latitude. Most Roman citizens worked a six-hour day for seven days of an eight-day week. Shops opened during the morning and possibly reopened in the late afternoon (a pattern still found in some parts of the Mediterranean), allowing the ordinary Roman to combine his siesta with a visit to the public baths.

Generally speaking it was men who went out to work. Although a few women professionals (doctors, teachers) and clerical staff are heard of, most women stayed at home. Many must have helped their husbands in shops, which were extensions of the home. The normal shop was a large hole in the wall of a tenement or house, opening directly on to the street. At night substantial folding shutters were drawn across the threshold and locked; the shopkeeper, his family, and probably any assistants he employed, retired to a room above or behind the workplace. There the inhabitants cooked, ate and slept, possibly in conditions worse than those of their fellow-tenants in an *insula*. During the day the staff may have served customers from behind a counter, but

At the sign of Tiberius Julius Vitali, the butcher. Tiberius is shown as a highly respectable man who could be taken for a senator; his employee is a more workaday figure, his cleaver poised to cut up a porcine head.

any workshop activity – preparing food, repairing shoes, making objects of wood or metal – was done in full view of passers-by. A variety of scales and other weighing devices were employed for foodstuffs and other goods; the simplest were bowl-shapes let into the counter which held a known quantity of a particular commodity. Despite Cicero's aspersions there is no evidence of widespread dishonesty, although regular checks of weights and measures by officials doubtless encouraged fair trading.

Much of the city's work was done by slaves, but they were not necessarily unpaid or under supervision. Some acted as agents for their masters, but others set up in business for themselves; in law their earnings belonged to their owners, but since insistence on the point would have destroyed the slaves' motivation, masters were content to take a percentage and allow the entrepreneurs to accumulate profits with which they could ultimately purchase their freedom. The prominence of the freedman in many walks of Roman life has already been remarked on.

Traders in Rome lived in cramped quarters and were often behind with their rent. But they worked a relatively short day and had access to the public baths and the splendid entertainments staged by the imperial regime to keep the un- and under-employed masses docile. They also enjoyed some collective advantages as members of a trade guild. Each guild specialized in a single commodity or activity, and among the 150 or so organized occupations there were not only bakers and shoemakers but also florists and goldsmiths, porters and mule-drivers. Members' subscriptions were used to give communal dinners or even to purchase a permanent banqueting hall which could also serve as a club. There were some communal religious activities, including funerals and setting up memorials, but the guilds seem never to have been used to formulate trade regulations or pursue common commercial interests; if they had done so they would probably have fallen foul of the imperial authorities, always sensitive about anything smacking of political activity.

Though melon-sellers, pastrycooks and sausage-makers flourished, milling and baking were essential and closely linked occupations.

A bronze weight made for use with a set of scales. Here, as so often a small utilitarian object has become the medium for artistry of a high order: the weight takes the form of a little bust of Minerva, goddess of wisdom.

At Pompeii hardly anyone seems to have bothered to make bread at home; over 30 bakers' shops are on record, and a line of flour mills has survived next door to a large oven. Essentially such a mill consisted of a large, distinctively waisted upper stone that was rotated by ass- or slave-power so that it moved round an only slightly smaller stone beneath it; grain poured in from above was ground between the two stones. In his novel *The Golden Ass*, Apuleius gives a heart-rending description of the flogged and scarred workers and sore-infested animals employed at a mill-house, but it is hard to know whether this was a common or an exceptional situation.

Another essential was wine, sold by the cup-measure at wine-merchants and available at taverns. The quality varied greatly, and wealthy connoisseurs made subtle distinctions between wines and vintages. Among other things, the Romans were effectively the founders of the French wine industry, planting vineyards in areas that are still renowned for their products. A particularly important trade in Pompeii was fulling, the preparation of woollen cloth by treading, beating, bleaching, brushing and scraping it; fullers also served as laundrymen, using the same methods to renovate already worn garments. A number of chemicals, including potash and alkaline-rich fuller's earth, were involved, and urine was used as a grease-solvent; supplies were obtained by leaving jars on the street which passers-by were invited to fill.

One of the most striking features of the Roman world of work is its extremely labour-intensive nature. A kind of crane was employed in building work; on the land there were reaping-machines with multiple knives; and some water-mills came into use during the imperial period. But cheap labour, and Ciceronian contempt for those who undertook it, inhibited technological advance and ensured that human- and animal-power would always underpin the impressive and complex Roman economic system.

The baker's shop; relief from a tombstone at Metz in north-eastern France. Despite clumsy carving, there is a real sense of a transaction taking place, and the aerial view of the baker's wares can be regarded as effective posthumous advertising.

Girl with a stylus and writing block; wall painting from Pompeii, 1st century AD. This lovely image of a reflective young woman is often called 'Sappho', after the famous Greek woman poet, although she is equally likely to have been a bright young Pompeian with literary leanings.

BOOKS AND WRITING

Latin, the language of the Romans, was originally spoken only in the small region of Central Italy known as Latium. It might well have been displaced by geographically more widespread Italian tongues such as Oscan and Umbrian, but Roman conquests made it the received speech of the peninsula, and ultimately of most wealthy or educated people all over a vast empire.

Writing began in the 7th century BC, when the Latin alphabet was devised as an adaptation of the Greek letters used by the Romans' Etruscan neighbours. The earliest known written Latin is on the Lapis Niger, an inscribed block of stone, found in the Forum Romanum, that probably dates from the early 6th century BC. There is no way of establishing how many Romans became literate, but written records, orders and transactions were vital to the efficient running of the Empire, while poems, plays, political and philosophical reflections, letters, prayers and graffiti provided outlets for vivid self-expression that often bring the Romans very close to us.

Commemorative inscriptions and some official decrees appeared on stone or bronze, but a variety of materials were available for other purposes. A wooden tablet with a coating of wax was particularly useful for temporary personal memoranda and school work; the metal or wooden stylus that scratched letters into the wax had a flat top that could be employed for corrections or to erase all the written content so that the tablet could be used again. However, on occasion this unstable medium also seems to have served for quite important documents.

Letters and other short personal statements could be written with pen and ink on thin sheets of wood. Pens were made of metal, or sharpened reeds or feathers; Roman ink, variously mixing soot, resin and cuttlefish ink, was surprisingly black and durable, as surviving documents have shown. Those who could afford it bought a much less cumbersome, paper-like material made from the papyrus reed (an Egyptian invention from which the word 'paper' is actually derived). This was also used for Roman books, which took the form of long papyrus scrolls. A book, or part-book, was called a *volumen*, or roll (the origin of the English word 'volume'); the reader held it in both hands, simultaneously rolling and unrolling it so that the text was progressively revealed. Under the Empire, parchment and vellum (made from hides) were also used as writing surfaces, and the book with pages, or *codex*, began to be made; but, surprisingly, it never replaced the much clumsier roll.

Roman interest in books only became intense under the influence of Greek culture in the 2nd century BC, when libraries were part of the booty brought back from the East by Sulla and other successful generals. An influx of well-educated

Greek slaves facilitated the development of the book trade in Rome, where something resembling mass production was achieved by booksellers whose slaves wrote out copies of texts dictated by one of their number. The influence of ardent collectors such as Cicero helped to create a fashion for possessing a private library, and booksellers flourished in the capital and ultimately in most parts of the Empire, advertising the latest authors on the pillars outside their shops. The first public library in Rome was founded during the reign of Augustus by the retired politician-poet Gaius Asinius Pollio, and within a century there were over 20, some of which allowed members to take out books for private reading. Authors were paid an outright fee for their works, and even the most famous were unable to live on their literary income; Martial, for example, complained that, in spite of being read even on the Danube and in Britain, his work brought him little profit. The bookseller-publisher could not afford to be generous, since there was no copyright law and consequently he could never acquire exclusive rights to any publication: as soon as he put a work on sale, a rival bookseller could acquire a copy, put his own scribes to work on it, and publish his own edition. Impecunious authors were therefore dependent on the generosity of one or more patrons – and, as Martial lamented, there was not a Maecenas in every generation.

Writing materials used by Romans at various times. The hinged 'book' was filled with wax (shown here as a separate item in ready-to-melt block form), which when hard could be written on with the elegant stylus; pen and inkpot are to hand for more durable writing, along with a lighted lamp, a spare wick and a seal.

LEISURE AND PLEASURE

The Romans enjoyed their pleasures most intensely in company; as well as gambling, gaming and banqueting together, they preferred communal to private bathing, and congregated in huge numbers to watch spectacles and shows. In time they became readers, although many people probably chose to listen to their slaves reading out loud rather than pore over a manuscript. However, the Romans' capacity for solitary reflection is shown by the number of literary compositions (only a fraction of which have survived) produced by individuals who would not have considered themselves primarily writers: both Caesar and Augustus, for example, are known to have written copiously in poetry and prose.

But writing led on to social events, which took the form of public readings. Patrons who thought their poet-clients would do them credit arranged readings in their houses; for the poet this was a chance to win fame and – just as important – to

Banqueting couple; wall painting from Herculaneum, 1st century BC or AD. The robust banqueters are in striking contrast to the small, frail servant girl in attendance. Note the idiosyncratic tripod table and the fine glassware.

attract new patrons from the audience. Readings had become tremendously popular by the Antonine period, and not merely for the impecunious and ambitious. The Emperor Claudius, who had written several historical works before his accession, gave readings in his palace. Pliny the Younger often performed for an invited audience and, to judge from his letters, felt more nervous on these occasions than when appearing in court. As the vogue spread, a successful public reading became a social triumph. Many people reserved a special room in the house, the auditorium, for these events, and the Emperor Hadrian built the Athenaeum in Rome to hold them. The extent of Roman reading-mania can be judged from the fact that Pliny went to one every night for weeks at a time, apparently without feeling fatigued – although not everyone felt the same, for on occasion he complains bitterly of audiences' bad manners and inattention.

The Roman passion for the baths was less high-minded but still very civilized. Bathing was a social rather than a merely hygienic activity, which is why people favoured public establishments; in the cities, many quite well-off people never bothered to put baths into their houses at all. Republican Rome boasted a multitude of public baths, available on payment of a small entrance fee; then Marcus Agrippa, Augustus' best general, built the first imperial baths, which were open to all free of charge. Later emperors strove to outdo one another in building enormous complexes with medium, hot, cold and 'Turkish' baths, gymnasia, massage rooms, lounges, playing grounds for games, walks and enclosures with fountains, and even museums and libraries. The most impressive in their ruined grandeur are the Baths of Caracalla in Rome, dating from the 3rd century AD; but remains on every sort of scale have been found all over the Empire from Hadrian's Wall to the Lebanon.

Some kind of bathing establishment was one of the earliest buildings put up in any colony or military settlement, and in cities the baths became as much a part of the civic scheme as the forum. At Rome, mixed bathing became common under the early Empire, although not for really respectable women; but the practice was banned altogether by

Hadrian, who decreed that women should use the baths in the morning and men in the afternoon. The most popular time for men seems to have been just before dinner, although the unemployed poor probably lingered for most of the afternoon, glad to be in a hotel atmosphere after the rigours of tenement nights; those who could not afford the services of bath attendants to scrape them down (steaming and scraping took the place of soap) accomplished it by mutual aid or by rubbing themselves against the marble walls. The central place of the baths in the lives of both rich and poor is summed up in elegiac vein by an anonymous artist in graffiti: 'baths, wine and sex corrupt our bodies, but they make life worth living'.

Eating and drinking were also sociable occasions. Workers frequented their guild halls or stopped off at snackbars and taverns; the rich entertained one another and their more presentable clients at banquets, where readings and conversation might be supplemented by performances of mimes, music and dancing. The most common musical instruments were flute-like pipes with reeds, and the lyre and the cithara

Lady giving a concert on the cithara, a form of lyre; wall painting from Boscoreale, c.40 BC. It is believed to be a copy of a lost Hellenistic Greek work in which the player was probably a royal personage.

(both stringed, with soundboxes); percussion instruments such as cymbals and drums were used in processions, and military musicians flourished a large horn, the *cornu*. Most music was intended to accompany singing, but there were evidently other kinds of popular hit, since the poet Martial describes with distaste a man about the town whose accomplishments included an ability to 'hum the tunes of Alexandrian and Spanish dances'. Little is known about Roman music or musicians, but the general impression is that neither was of great creative interest; this is perhaps not surprising in a society where musicianship was left to slaves and the base-born. Nero was an outstanding exception, performing in public and funding competitions; but since he always won first prize and was dangerous to know, it is not likely that his activities promoted talent or enhanced the popularity of music. The social standing of dancing was more ambiguous: like music, it was supposed to be performed only by the lower orders (Cicero declared that you would have to be drunk or insane to be seen dancing), but some households are known to have employed dancing masters, and the poet Ovid even implies that during a dance the would-be seducer could achieve some sort of preliminary physical contact with his prey.

Romans enjoyed gambling on dice and board games such as *duodecim scripta*, which closely resembled backgammon. At the baths they played ball games and worked out in the gymnasium; but despite their enormous cultural debt to the Greeks they never shared the Greeks' passion for athletics, whether as participants or spectators. Philhellene rulers from Sulla onwards attempted to establish regular competitions, but it was only in AD 86 that a permanent cyclical event, the *Agon Capitolinus*, was inaugurated by the last of the Flavian emperors, Domitian. Held every four years, the *Agon* mixed competitions in a fashion that now seems incongruous, combining athletics, field events, boxing, poetry and music; it had a brief vogue under its founder but was always a minority taste. When they wanted public entertainment, the great majority of Romans headed for the circus or the arena (in Rome itself to the Circus Maximus or the Colosseum), where the contests were fast and dangerous or blood was certain to be spilled: to the chariot races or the gladiatorial and other 'games'.

Chariot-racing was a genuine sport, to some extent comparable with present-day motor racing. But homicidally dangerous driving was both permitted and indulged in: a driver might try to 'bump' a rival to break his axle, or ram him from behind to smash up the light car in which he stood; but if he cornered too tightly he would be overturned by grazing a track marker. Since drivers raced with the reins wound round them, they needed to react fast in an accident, slashing through the cords before they were dragged along the track behind their horses. The sport was at least as popular as the games, and evoked more permanent loyalties. Although there were star drivers and horses, what mattered was the colour

Opposite: A bird among the shrubs and flowers of a garden; detail from a Pompeian wall painting, 1st century AD. This exquisite, tapestry-like painting exemplifies the Roman passion for gardens and the countryside.

Mosaic fountain niche, an indispensable item in the Roman garden; it was often the visual focus of the house. This example provided a natural-looking setting for the fountain that played in front of it. 1st century AD.

Women playing knucklebones, a dice-like game still played by children. The scene is painted in red lead on marble, and may be only a preliminary sketch. It was found at Herculaneum and is signed by the otherwise unknown artist, Alexander the Athenian.

they raced under. The circus 'factions' – red, white, blue and green – were the closest the Romans came to supported team games, and their successes and failures were followed with the same breathless interest as modern football matches: when his faction won an event, the manager let the city know by releasing a flock of swallows painted with the appropriate colour. Only the big cities could afford a permanent circus or hippodrome, but Rome had no less than five including the famous Circus Maximus, roughly 600 m (1,950 ft) long. As an entertainment the races were more respectable than the games: drivers, though mainly slaves, were envied, and Roman intellectuals were not ashamed of being partisans, traditionally of the Blues.

A diet of blood and equestrian thrills must have made the drama seem dull fare to a mass audience, and may account for the increasing sensationalism of Roman theatrical performances. Still, the Romans did build theatres all over their empire, each capable of seating thousands, as well as three in the capital itself. These were not outdoor structures set into slopes in Greek fashion, but were free-standing. The stage was raised and roofed, with a wall behind it; the actors performed in front of a set designed to look like a row of houses with three doors and 'town' and 'country' street exits at either side. The auditorium was semi-circular, and in fact the first amphitheatre for the games is said to have been made from two wooden theatres, placed back to back, so ingeniously constructed that they could be swivelled round after the morning performances and interlocked to accommodate gladiatorial shows in the afternoon. The drama was an integral part of festivals and celebrations, just as the games were; and it is possible that there were rather more theatrical performances and fewer games during any particular period than has generally been supposed.

Despite the magnificence of public provision for the theatre, its creative record was poor. The outstanding comic dramatists, Plautus and Terence, flourished in the late 3rd and early 2nd centuries BC as translators or adapters of Greek playwrights such as Menander, even retaining Greek settings for their works. Plautus is lively and loquacious, whereas Terence writes in a quieter, more self-consciously finished and apho-ristic style; but both dealt in stock characters such as the crafty slave and the professional diner-out, and the plots have a typical fairy-tale love-story quality in which, for example, the slave-heroine proves not to be a slave after all and can marry the well-born hero. Roman tragedy is said to have reached its peak in the 2nd century BC, but the works themselves have not survived. After this, drama consisted almost entirely of revivals; 'seri-ous' plays became library productions like the gory tragedies of Seneca, written to be read aloud to a select audience. Pompeii had theatres that catered to both tastes: a large open-air theatre that seated five thousand people, and a smaller covered theatre (by Roman standards a 'little' or intimate one) for an audience of a thousand or so.

Roman theatre soon witnessed the development of a 'star system' that turned every play into a vehi-cle for the idol of the day. Ruthless editing of clas-sics, or specially prepared 'scripts' or libretti, focused attention on the star in spectacularly mounted performances that increasingly resembled opera or ballet, with a chorus singing on stage and instrumental backing. The supreme star was the *pantomimus* who acted entirely in dumb-show, by all accounts with superb command of gesture, posture and dance-movement. Though such professional performers, like gladiators, were technically *infames* (degraded), like gladiators they attracted a devoted following and female attentions; one *pantomimus*, Paris, received the favours of the Empress herself. Comedy seems to have remained closer to conven-tional drama, although in the debased form of 'mimes', quasi-realistic improvised productions in which women were allowed to appear and masks were not worn. They seem to have mixed sentimen-tality, sex and violence in soap-opera style, but with the occasional distinctively grim Roman note, as when a real criminal was substituted for the fictional villain and tortured and executed on stage. Many of these developments represented attempts to com-pete in sensationalism with the most popular and infamous of all Roman entertainments: the games.

Actors wearing comedy masks; terracotta statuettes, 1st century BC. The drama was a Greek invention, adopted by the Romans – who, however, preferred the broader effects of comedy and melodrama to the high seriousness of Greek tragedy.

SPECTACLE AND SLAUGHTER

The Roman who thought that 'sex, wine and the baths' corrupted the body was strangely silent about the spiritually corrupting 'games' where untold thousands of men and beasts were slaughtered. As a spectacle 'with a cast of thousands' there has never been anything quite like it – especially since a high percentage of the 'cast' made only a single appearance. The games were the most unmitigated evil in antiquity, all the more difficult to comprehend because society was tending to become more humane in other directions. At Rome, the games were the opium of the people: it was state policy to entertain the two hundred thousand men on the dole who might otherwise have become dangerously restless, and 'bread and circuses' went naturally together. But the games were not just the pastime of the Roman mob: they spread all over the Empire, and in time even the Greeks – in their own estimation much more civilized than their Roman masters – succumbed to their ghoulish allure.

The most notorious feature of the games – gladiatorial combats – began as a variation on human sacrifice, derived from Etruscan funeral games: in 264 BC the sons of Brutus Pera staged three simultaneous gladiatorial combats between pairs of slaves, with the intention of making a pious blood offering to the shade of their father. Decade by decade such displays became more elaborate, and their connection with religion more perfunctory, until by the late Republic every ambitious politician borrowed or beggared himself to put on a show that would win the favours of the electors. By this time there were already hundreds of participants; and from the reign of Augustus, when the whole business came under imperial control, both the numbers involved and the calendar days devoted to games began to soar. By the 4th century no less than 175 days were earmarked for games, and these did not include gratuitous shows such as the four-month-long event put on by Trajan to celebrate his victories in Dacia, during which ten thousand animals died and one hundred thousand gladiators took part. Gruesome entertainment of this sort prompted the invention of an impressive and capacious stadium, the amphitheatre, of which well-preserved examples survive at Verona, Nîmes, Arles, Thysdrus (El Djem) in North Africa and other sites. The largest and most famous of all was the Colosseum at Rome, built under Vespasian and Titus, which seated at least fifty thousand spectators and must still rank (in spite of its purpose) as one of humanity's most awe-inspiring achievements.

In their developed form the games consisted of two distinct elements: massacres and professional fights. The first involved both animals and humans. Hunts were staged in which wild animals, imported by the thousand, were slaughtered: lions and panthers, elephants, bulls, bears, rhinoceroses and hippopotamuses, crocodiles, snakes, ostriches, seals and similar exotica. At other times men were the victims: criminals and prisoners-of-war were tied to stakes for ravenous beasts to consume; set to fight one another; alternately armed and forced to kill, and then disarmed and delivered to the next killer-victim (both parties urged on by whips and hot irons), and even primed and lit to create human torches. The dramatic performances staged in the arena and elsewhere were even more extraordinary, with actors whose tragedies were real: in one, a doomed Icarus might be borne aloft on wires until he was plunged into an enclosure of wild beasts; in another, two parties of prisoners-of-war might be set to re-enact the battle of Salamis on a lake, fighting each other for survival with all the desperate ferocity of the original combatants.

Gladiators proper were a group apart: men trained to fight with skill and style, and more or less evenly matched. Most gladiators were criminals, or prisoners-of-war, or slaves (though owners were forbidden to despatch unoffending and unwilling slaves to the arena); but there were always some free men prepared to risk their lives in the hope of recouping shattered fortunes or becoming a star. The gladiator's position was equivocal. In law he was a degraded being and the lowest of slaves, having sworn a terrible oath to

Opposite: Combat between gladiators. These lethal games were popular all over the Empire, where amphitheatres and scenes like these were widely found; this floor mosaic is from Nennig in the Saarland, Germany.

endure fire, chains, whips and cold steel at the behest of his master (in imperial Rome a specially appointed official, one of the praetors). He was a virtual prisoner, unarmed, in the barracks-like training schools at Rome, Capua and Ravenna. (The military feats of Spartacus were never forgotten by Rome's rulers.) Yet there were rewards too: freedom for the criminal (and probably, although less certainly, for the slave) at the end of a three-year stint in the arena and a period of work around the schools; the palm and prize money for every victory; and, for the star performer, fortune, adulation and women galore. In the training schools gladiators developed a strong esprit de corps, and a pride in their profession so pronounced that some expressed their impatience at long spells away from the arena.

The games were surrounded with a ritual and pageantry reminiscent of Spanish bullfighting. The night before their appearance, the gladiators were feasted in their quarters under the eyes of privileged members of the public. Clad in gold-embroidered purple cloaks, they went in procession to the arena, marched round it and greeted the emperor with the famous words 'Hail, Caesar: we who are about to die, salute you!' In combat too the ritual went on: the defeated man flung away his weapons and held up one finger to appeal for mercy; the emperor, prompted by the crowds,

gave the thumbs-up or down for life or death; and if it was death, the loser was supposed to prop himself up and offer his throat to the sword without flinching. Then an attendant dressed as Charon, ferryman of the dead, removed the corpse while others raked the sand and sweetened the air with perfume.

The combatants were always unalike in equipment and tactics. 'Thracians', 'Samnites' and 'Gauls' were accoutred in some versions of the national arms and armour, whereas *secutor* (follower), *retiarius* (net man) and others were named after their equipment or fighting style. Labelled pictures and descriptions of the various types are confused and contradictory, but the principle on which they were paired was clearly that of balancing offensive against defensive strengths, and better protective equipment against superior mobility. *Retiarius*, for example, fought almost naked with net and trident against *secutor, myrmillo* or some other armed man with sword and shield; one was mobile and hoped to enmesh and pin his opponent, whereas the other was almost invulnerable, but deadly only if he could come to grips with his opponent.

Though indefensible, gladiatorial displays were at least a little better than massacres staged to satisfy the audience's blood-lust. They were fair(ish) fights, with something of

Horse and chariot races in a Roman hippodrome; the mosaic, from Lyons in France, is typical of the 3rd century AD in its simplified, schematic style. In the centre, two officials hold up a wreath and palm for the winning horseman.

A beast fight in the arena; detail from a 3rd-century AD Tunisian mosaic showing men fighting four leopards. Huge numbers of animals were imported from Africa to take part in such spectacles, with significant environmental effects.

Wrestlers limbering up and practising holds; 3rd-century AD mosaic from Thaenae, North Africa. Compared with the modern versions of the sports, wrestling and boxing were brutal free-for-alls, and serious injuries were common.

the atmosphere of a boxing match: excited audiences shouted *'Habet! Hoc habet!'* ('Yes! He's had it!') and, perhaps more to the point, both combatants had some chance of victory or mercy. The skill involved in such displays has probably been underestimated: gladiators, like top-class boxers, fought only about three times a year. And as their training must have made them valuable investments, it seems possible that bouts were often arranged to put the audience in a good mood by giving them value for money, so that the eventual loser had an excellent chance of being spared. The epitaph of the 30-year-old gladiator Flamma suggests that the mortality rate for gladiators may have been lower than has commonly been supposed: he won twenty-one victories, fought nine no-decision bouts, and was beaten but spared on four occasions.

Despite such possibly mitigating factors, the games can only be pictured as a horror; the public brutalities of the more recent western past, such as would-be deterrent public hangings and impalings of traitors' heads, scarcely make this centuries-long mass sadism more comprehensible. Even in the context of ancient warfare and punishment (massacres, burning cities, chopped-off hands, crucifixions) the Roman games were unique, since their motive was not revenge, hatred, rage or punishment, but entertainment. Yet even Romans who disliked the games seem to have regarded them as an unavoidable evil. Tiberius, Hadrian and Marcus Aurelius gave as few as possible; Julius Caesar used them to win popularity, although he found them so tedious or repellent that he could be seen working during his mandatory attendances. Cicero and Pliny, otherwise humane men, feebly recommended the games as a school of valour; and other intellectuals seem to have despised them as the boring pastime of the boring populace, but to have felt no great impulse to stop them. During the centuries of Rome's greatness, only Seneca, Stoic philosopher and minister of Nero, accepted the logic of the Stoics' belief in universal brotherhood and unequivocally condemned the games.

A street in Pompeii, familiar in its raised pavements but not in the regularly positioned sets of stepping stones, with gaps between them for vehicle wheels. The high windows of the buildings preserved the inhabitants' privacy.

TRADE AND COMMUNICATIONS

The Roman Empire was knitted together by a network of roads, bridges and seaways that was without equal in the ancient world. Its existence made it easier for the army to defend the frontiers, encouraged trade, promoted the spread of ideas, customs and fashions, and brought the provinces into frequent and useful contact with the heart of the Empire. Without its advanced system of communications Rome might still have made conquests, but it could never have evolved into a cosmopolitan civilization.

Roman roads have always been famous for their durability, and for their long, straight stretches, which made no concessions to natural obstacles. This was a function of their initial purpose — to allow troops to deploy as rapidly as possible; the first major Roman road was the Via Appia, built as early as 312 BC from Rome to Capua in order to control Campania, and later extended to Brundisium on the heel of Italy, from which there was a short sea crossing to Greece. Skilfully layered, pounded down and bonded with the Roman engineer's 'secret weapon' – concrete – Roman roads were driven along every line of march; once a new province had been pacified, their upkeep was transferred to the cities on the route, which generally extended the local network to suit their own requirements.

Those who travelled the roads could monitor their progress by reading the regular milestones set up by imperial decree, and they were served by wayside inns or taverns; however, these were generally rough-and-ready places, and upper-class Romans were more likely to buy villas for their own use on routes that they regularly followed, or to arrange for hospitality from people of their own class. Well-maintained roads also facilitated the postal service set up under Augustus, with relay stations at regular intervals holding fresh horses for the couriers, who were enabled to travel some 240 km (150 miles) a day. Non-official letters had to be carried by private couriers, who often executed a number of commissions at a time; Cicero's extensive surviving correspondence with friends all over the Empire suggests that this was a satisfactory, although expensive, way of keeping in touch. The road system was complemented by imperial and municipal bridges, some of them considerable feats of engineering that have outlived the Empire by 1,500 years.

Romans were less eager to venture on board ship, and the number of wrecks discovered on the Mediterranean seaboard suggests that their fears were well-founded. Pirates were a menace in disturbed periods, and at all times vessels were at the mercy of storms and rough seas. There were no passenger ships, so a traveller had to negotiate a passage on a merchantman. Nevertheless the sea lanes were busy, since cross-Mediterranean travel – for example from North Africa to Italy – was obviously much faster than circuitous land journeys; and in fact most voyages were quicker than land travel, especially where heavy consignments were concerned. The Romans built very substantial artificial harbours, notably at Lepcis Magna in North Africa and Ostia, the port of Rome. During the early imperial period the priority given to supplying Rome with grain led to the construction of huge new installations at Ostia and a canal linking them with the Tiber and the city. The work was only a partial success, as has been demonstrated by recent archaeological finds of sunken boats in the harbour (now inland).

The communications network was widely used for military and administrative purposes, but travel for pleasure was rare except for excursions to seaside villas on the Bay of Naples or cultural tourism in Greece. The importance of long-distance trade has been much debated. Most Romans certainly lived by agriculture and traded locally. But it is easy to underestimate the importance of the international market for grain, wine and olive oil, and of exports such as British metals, Gaulish pottery, glassware and cheap textiles, Sardinian salt and Cappadocian horses and livestock. Though the silks of China and spices of India passed through many hands to reach the Empire, it is true that these were mere luxury items; but it is hard not to be impressed by the fact that trade carried Roman artefacts across the frontiers to distant lands such as Scotland, Scandinavia, Russia and South-East Asia.

A wagon of a type used by travellers; relief found in the wall of a church in Carinthia, Austria. The lack of springs made journeys uncomfortable; wealthy people preferred to travel on horseback or in a litter.

PROVINCIAL LIFE

The vast scale of the Romans' conquests meant that the provinces of the Empire were filled with an extraordinary mixture of peoples. Gallic tribesmen, Berber nomads and Syrian city-dwellers lived in very different climes and differed from one another in language, customs and religion. Yet this was only a problem with an exceptional group like the Jews, whose exclusive religion made most of them unresponsive to the potential benefits of Romanization. In dealing with subject peoples Rome promoted its own city-based way of life. Finding that the Romans respected their local beliefs and customs, the affluent classes in conquered lands succumbed in short order to the twin incentives of citizenship and urban pleasures; and they also followed the Roman example in developing a passion for rural leisure based on luxurious villas that doubled as the centres of large farm estates.

The East was urbanized even before the arrival of the Romans, but large areas of the West were transformed by Roman foundations, initially in the form of military colonies, or of army camps around which native settlements grew up. Every tribal area was allocated a capital where the chief men were encouraged to meet on a regular basis, and the provision of amenities for them soon turned even the most artificial centre into a true city. Conquered Gaul became thoroughly Romanized, and even chilly Britain supported a widely distributed villa

Shops in one of the main streets of Pompeii, a prosperous provincial city in Southern Italy. Its chance preservation under volcanic ash has made it world famous, providing important information about everyday life.

Hands across the counter, buying and selling; a lively market scene on a relief from Ostia, the port of Rome, 2nd century AD. It repays scrutiny, being filled with fascinating details that may escape the attention at first.

culture; the historian Tacitus, torn between imperial pride and a tendency to romanticize a political freedom he had never known, described the Romanization of Britain in terms that might have been used of many other peoples: 'Those who once refused to learn the Roman tongue now aspired to become eloquent in it. Our national dress was honoured, and togas became a common sight. Gradually the Britons succumbed to the lure of Roman vices: lounging under arches, at the baths, and at elegant entertainments. The naive referred to all this as "gracious living" when it was simply an aspect of their servitude.'

Aware of the classes to whom this way of life would appeal, the Romans not only promoted cities but also favoured oligarchies – control by wealthy elites – within them; otherwise they hardly interfered in municipal affairs. Each city had its own senate and magistrates, who expressed their local pride through public works duly recorded by a marble inscription. Later, such endowments turned into a competitive frenzy, became expected of each and every magistrate, and ended by making men reluctant to assume the expensive burden of office. By the late Antonine period the imperial government was being compelled to take over responsibility in many places – a development that encouraged the growth of an over-extended bureaucracy and actually weakened the real cohesion of the Empire. But by that time both those who accepted responsibility and those who shirked it undoubtedly regarded themselves as Romans.

Until the end of the 2nd century AD urban culture grew steadily stronger in all the provinces of the Empire, and Latin could be heard on the street from York in Britain to Timgad in North Africa; though not in all cases the first language of provincials, it was indispensable for official business and as a lingua franca for all who had trade or other dealings with people from other parts of the Empire. Those who worked on the land (in most places a majority of the population) were less directly affected, and being 'Romans' may have made little or no difference to them. In less advanced societies Roman rule brought the burden of taxation, which may or may not have been counterbalanced by the benefits of peace, better communications and new markets; in a number of areas Roman demand for taxes and commodities seems to have caused a switch from subsistence farming to more intensive methods that produced a surplus intended for the market.

Whatever reservations may be made about some aspects of Roman life, the overwhelming impression given by the Empire at its height in the 2nd century is of cosmopolitan splendour. The provinces were flourishing and accepted as full members of the Roman commonwealth. Rome tolerated most religions and was remarkably free from national or racial prejudice. A Spaniard like Trajan could become emperor; an African like Terence, who was also a slave, could become the favoured playwright of a sophisticated elite. In a world of local loyalties and narrow sympathies, it was a significant achievement.

Riot in the arena. This wall painting from Pompeii records the city's main claim to fame until excavation began in the 18th century: the violence that flared up in AD 59, only 20 years before it was destroyed by Vesuvius.

POMPEII

Descriptions of everyday Roman life are heavily dependent on the evidence of one archaeological site: the city of Pompeii, destroyed in AD 79 by the eruption of Vesuvius, the only active volcano on the European mainland. Buried metres deep in pumice and ash, Pompeii and the area for kilometres around were trapped in time, concealing for 1,700 years a wealth of evidence about what should have been an ordinary day in a Roman town and the lives of its citizens.

Pompeii was a city of about 20,000 inhabitants, not far from the Bay of Naples. In August, AD 79, plumes of smoke and rumblings from Vesuvius alerted the population to the danger, and only about 2,000 are thought to have stayed too long in the city and perished. The younger Pliny was staying at Misenum, the northernmost cape of the Bay of Naples, when the actual eruption took place on 24 August; and years later he wrote an account of what he had seen. His uncle Pliny the Elder, an indefatigably encyclopaedic writer, was in command of the fleet at Misenum and set out to investigate the mys-terious cloud that had appeared to the south-east. He landed at Stabiae, making notes on everything he saw, but seems to have overdone the business of restoring calm by example: having bathed, dined and slept, he was only persuaded to leave when there was a danger that falling volcanic debris would trap him in the house where he was staying. Pliny and his companions reached the shore, where a churning sea made escape impossible. Though supported by two slaves, the corpulent Pliny, then in his mid-fifties, collapsed, either asphyxiated by the fumes or struck down by a heart attack brought on by their effects. Meanwhile Pliny the Younger, still only 17 years old, had remained behind at Misenum with his mother. That evening there were violent earth tremors, and by next morning 'the buildings around us were tottering'. Pliny and his mother decided to leave, and crowds of townspeople followed them. A convulsed sea rolled away from the shore and the volcanic cloud descended. It became black as night and ash rained down; but despite Pliny's 'conviction that the entire world was dying with me, and I with it', the worst was over, the sun reappeared and they were able to return.

Entombed and forgotten, Pompeii and the smaller town of Herculaneum remained intact through late antiquity and the Middle Ages. Indications of their existence received little attention during the Renaissance, and it was only in the 18th century that they were rediscovered. Excavations began in 1748 and are still not completed. They revealed the everyday life of the 1st century but also recovered evidence of the catastrophe in the form of human and canine 'corpses', obtained by injecting plaster into the voids left by bodies that had long before perished; these casts of figures contorted by the struggle to breathe are hauntingly memorable.

Pompeii itself was revealed as a city with thoroughly up-to-date buildings and amenities, which had not long before replaced older fabric damaged in the major earthquake of AD 62 or 63. Laid out with paved streets on a typically Roman grid-plan, Pompeii had all the requisite public facilities: a forum surrounded by temples and a market hall; three public baths; two theatres; an exercise ground (*palaestra*); and the oldest known amphitheatre, dating from 80 BC. Only 20 years before the eruption, in AD 59, the amphitheatre had been the scene of a riot, as Pompeian fans and spectators from neighbouring Nuceria fought and killed one another; the Emperor Nero punished the city by forbidding it to hold games for ten years.

There were few apartment blocks on the Roman model in Pompeii, but buildings were frequently extended or adapted to new uses. Rows of shops concealed often spacious colonnaded private houses, creating interesting social mixtures, and there were many taverns (often doubling as brothels) and snack bars. Unlike smaller, mainly residential Herculaneum, Pompeii was a thriving commercial and industrial centre, producing textiles, wine and a particularly popular line of *garum* (fermented fish sauce). However, the most poignant spots for most visitors are the interiors of the finest houses. In this affluent but provincial place the paintings and mosaics of the interiors, with their variations of style and treatment and their images of myth and religious ritual, can hardly have been unusual; their survival in near-isolation brings home to us just how much of the ancient world has vanished for ever.

The sumptuous colours in this corner of a Pompeian house suggest the effects achieved simply by painting walls. The corner is in a garden court, and the left-hand painting shows Mars against an appropriately natural background.

THE EAST

In many of the lands they subdued, the Romans regarded themselves as standard-bearers of civilization. But the Hellenistic kingdoms of the eastern Mediterranean were different – richer and more sophisticated than their Roman conquerors, with a shared Greek culture and splendid cities unequalled in the West. It was the Romans who dutifully learned Greek and imported Greek teachers and artefacts. During the long *Pax Romana* they embellished existing cities but founded few new ones; and Greek remained the principal language of the entire region.

Alexandria, on the coast of Egypt, was the second city of the Empire, with a population of about half a million. Although the Egypt of the pharaohs lived on in the hinterland, Alexandria was a Greek city with a strong cosmopolitan admixture provided by Jews and other outsiders. It had been the capital of the Ptolemies, the Greek dynasty that ended with the death of Cleopatra, and under their rule it acquired most of the features for which it was renowned, including the great Library, reputed to hold the entire knowledge of the ancient world, and the lighthouse on

the island of Pharos, one of the Seven Wonders of the World. A causeway from the mainland to Pharos created a twin-basined harbour from which the huge grain surpluses of Egypt were carried to Rome. During the Hellenistic period Alexandria's main rival was Antioch, the great Syrian city that became the capital of the Seleucid dynasty, sometime masters of western Asia. Like Rome, Antioch was not on the coast but channelled wine, olive oil and other local products through its downriver port, Seleucia.

A similar rivalry existed in Asia Minor between Pergamum and Ephesus. Pergamum had been the capital of a small but successful Hellenistic kingdom, made wealthy by its silver mines and manufacture of parchment. It made a smooth transition from the Hellenistic to the Roman age, since its Attalid rulers were shrewd enough to become faithful allies of Rome. In 133 BC the last of the Attalids bequeathed the kingdom to Rome, and it continued to be favoured; in 19 BC the Pergamenes were permitted to build a temple to Rome and Augustus, becoming the first citizens in the East to establish an imperial

THE ROMAN EMPIRE AD 106
— Imperial frontier AD 106
  Roman expansion to 201 BC
  Roman expansion 201–100 BC
  Roman expansion 100–44 BC
  Roman expansion 44 BC–AD 14
  Roman expansion AD 14–96
  Roman expansion AD 96–106
GAL Roman province
Agri Roman region
● Roman provincial capital

cult. Nevertheless Ephesus was a worthy rival, with a large harbour, fine colonnaded streets, a famous theatre, the two-storey, marble-columned Library of Celsus, and above all the Temple of Artemis (another of the Seven Wonders) to which thousands of pilgrims flocked each year.

The culture and way of life of the eastern elites and city folk were Greco-Roman, but in many places older languages, customs and beliefs persisted; except for tax obligations, the life of the Egyptian peasant probably changed little when native pharaohs gave way to Ptolemies and then to Roman emperors. As elsewhere, the Romans displayed a genius for conciliation by patronizing the native gods and temples and allowing the emperors to be portrayed and worshipped as pharaohs. No such compromise was possible with the Empire's most troublesome eastern subjects, the Jews, with their belief in a single, exclusive god and their fierce national pride. The revolt of AD 66–70 culminated in the destruction of the Temple and the sack of Jerusalem by Titus; and a second full-scale revolt in 132–135, ruthlessly suppressed, hastened the dispersal of Jews throughout the Empire.

From the 3rd century AD life in the eastern provinces was less secure, as emperors were made and unmade and a new Persian empire gathered strength. The most remarkable phenomenon of the period was the rise and fall of Palmyra, a wealthy city in the Syrian desert, lying on the great cross-continental trade routes. Led by Odaenath and then by his queen, Zenobia, Palmyra inflicted heavy defeats on the Persians and ruled most of the East for a few years (260–272), until Zenobia's armies were totally defeated, and her empire was reclaimed for Rome, by Aurelian.

Christianity was born in the East and spread rapidly there. In 330 Constantinople was founded as the Empire's new eastern capital, but Alexandria proved more theologically fertile, nurturing both Athanasius, the great champion of orthodoxy, and Arius, author of the rival and heterodox Arian doctrines. The four patriarchates (most important sees) were Rome and three eastern cities, Constantinople, Alexandria and Antioch; and the eastern empire retained much of its vitality until the 7th century, when most of it fell to the forces of Islam.

The Roman Empire as it was at its height in AD 106, after Trajan's conquest of Dacia; subsequent advances were made in the East, but proved short-lived. The prowess of the legions and an international trade network bound the Empire together.

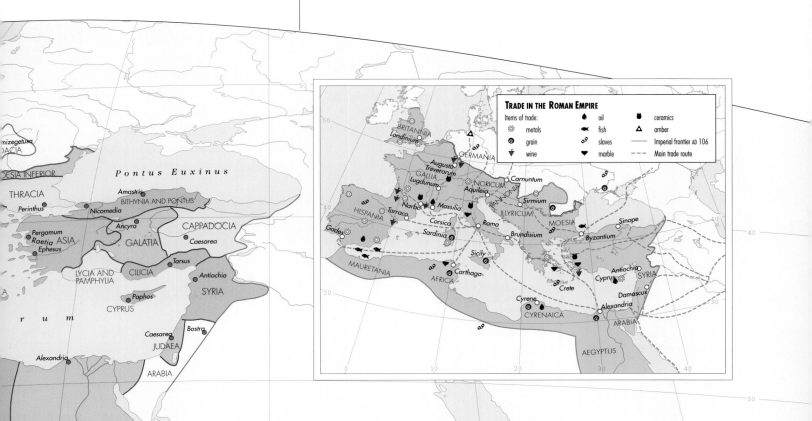

ROMAN AFRICA

The Roman way of life became well established, and had particularly successful results, in North Africa. From the Egyptian border to the Atlantic, the native population and Roman colonists prospered, and hundreds of exemplary Roman settlements and cities grew up. Peace and security were general, especially during the 1st and 2nd centuries AD, partly thanks to the accident of geography that placed the Sahara Desert along most of the southern frontier; it afforded protection from large-scale attack, and only a single legion was stationed in the entire region.

The North African provinces were reorganized several times over the centuries, but four main divisions can be identified: Africa, Numidia, Cyrenaica and Mauretania. Roman involvement in North Africa began with her wars against Carthage, which ended with the destruction of the city in 146 BC. The Carthaginian heartland – roughly modern Tunisia – and most of the Libyan coastline formed the Roman province of Africa. Immediately to the west, Numidia was an independent kingdom until the defeat of its king, Jugurtha, in 106, after which it was ruled by client kings until its complete incorporation into the Empire in 25 BC. To the east of the Roman province of Africa lay Cyrenaica, which was taken out of Egyptian hands in 96 BC and formally annexed in 74. Finally, in 25 BC, Augustus transferred the last Numidian king, Juba II, to the larger but wilder territory of Mauretania, 'the land of the Moors', which stretched beyond the Pillars of Hercules (Gibraltar) to the Atlantic seaboard. Raised as a Roman, Juba laboured to civilize his new kingdom, but remained dependant on Roman help in dealing with the restless tribes, and Mauretania was always to be the most troublesome of the North African provinces.

Grain, olive oil and wine were the most important products of a region whose fertility was greatly increased by Roman irrigation schemes. Tunisia was only a two-day sail from Rome, and North Africa became second only to Egypt as a supplier of grain to the city. In 146 BC Carthage had been destroyed, in intention for ever, but its site on the Gulf of Tunis was too good to ignore; colonists began to move in, encouraged by Julius Caesar, and in 29 BC Augustus refounded it as a Roman city. It became the capital of the province and the centre of a network of roads that ensured its dominance as an entrepôt serving the African hinterland. In time, beautified by imperial gifts such as the vast Antonine Baths, Carthage became the rival of Alexandria and Antioch, if not of Rome itself.

Another magnificent city, Lepcis Magna, fulfilled a similar function further east, on the Libyan coast. Cereals and olives left its harbour in huge quantities, it acquired all the public buildings required to rank as a fully Roman city, and then it was further aggrandized by its most famous son, the Emperor Septimius Severus. It is

Rome in Africa. This villa at Utica, Tunisia, is the only one to have survived in any of the North African provinces, once thoroughly Romanized and offering avenues for their citizens to rise in the empire's cosmopolitan society.

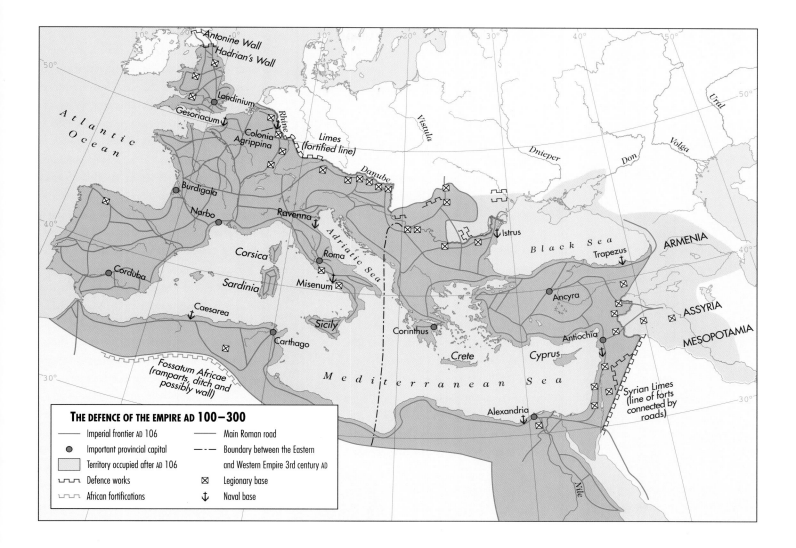

THE DEFENCE OF THE EMPIRE AD 100–300

—— Imperial frontier AD 106
● Important provincial capital
▨ Territory occupied after AD 106
⊓⊔ Defence works
⊓⊔ African fortifications
—— Main Roman road
–·–· Boundary between the Eastern and Western Empire 3rd century AD
⊠ Legionary base
↓ Naval base

now the most spectacular Roman site in North Africa, but many other impressive monuments survive – at, for example, Cuicul, Thugga, Timgad, Sabratha, Thysdrus, Volubilis and Theveste – as testimony to the thriving urban culture of the region.

Christianity took hold rapidly in North Africa, producing such influential figures as Tertullian, one of the Fathers of the Church, St Augustine of Hippo, and the heresiarch Donatus. However, the peace of North Africa was broken by the civil wars of the late Empire, notably when the governors of Carthage attempted to assert their independence;

in AD 308 Domitius Alexander's revolt was crushed by the forces of the imperial prefect, which went on to sack the city. Rebuilt by Constantine, Carthage was captured in 439 by a Germanic people, the Vandals, notorious for their depredations ('vandalism'). During the 5th-century collapse of the western empire, neglect of the irrigation systems weakened the North African agricultural base and the decline of international trade caused a general decay of Roman cities and prosperity; finally, the 7th-century Arab invasions destroyed any but the monumental remnants of the Roman way of life.

Once the Empire ceased to expand, its immensely long frontiers created potentially serious problems. As the map shows, the Romans dug in along natural barriers such as the rivers Rhine and Danube and the margins of the Sahara and Syrian deserts.

FAR-AWAY BRITANNIA

Opposite: triumph over the barbarous northern British; Roman relief set up on the turf Antonine Wall, built in AD 146 across southern Scotland, and held by the Romans – briefly, before they fell back to Hadrian's Wall again.

In Roman eyes Britain was an exotic place. The people were not very different from their neighbours in Gaul, but they lived still further away and were, as the poet Virgil wrote, 'completely separated from the whole world'. Their remoteness was emphasized by the fact that their homeland lay in the waters that the Romans simply called 'Ocean', believed to surround the European-Asian-African landmass that constituted the known world; and although the cross-Channel voyage to Britain was short, the stormy ocean waters were unpredictable and intimidating to peoples who were cautious even when sailing the tideless, relatively placid Mediterranean.

As if to reinforce the point, wild weather disrupted both of the expeditions undertaken to Britain by Julius Caesar in 55 and 54 BC. Caesar later presented them as essentially punitive and fact-finding ventures, but they were conducted on a scale leaving little doubt that he hoped to achieve a permanent conquest. This was particularly obvious during the second expedition, involving some 27,000 troops and offering good prospects of exploiting the rivalries between the

The well-preserved Roman baths in the city of Bath in south-west England. They were built to take advantage of the hot spring on the site, which was already known to the British and possibly credited by them with curative powers.

British tribes. The legions inflicted several defeats on the British leader Cassivelaunus and penetrated deep inland, but another storm had delayed the campaign and Caesar, aware of unrest in the recently conquered province of Gaul, accepted Cassivelaunus' offer of peace and tribute rather than risk spending the winter in Britain.

The Gauls did break out in a major revolt, and Caesar never returned to Britain. But his exploits at the end of the world deeply impressed the Romans, and the conquest of Britain remained a desirably prestigious project, proposed but never carried out by both Augustus and Caligula. It was taken up by an emperor who badly needed a popular success: Claudius, a civilian in his 50s who had come to the throne unexpectedly and rather ingloriously. In AD 43 Claudius despatched four legions, commanded by an able general, Aulus Plautius, which landed at Richborough in Kent and rapidly struck across the Medway and the Thames. Claudius hastily joined the expeditionary force from Gaul, bringing war-elephants with him, in time to lead the assault on Colchester, the capital of the most important southern British king, Caratacus. The stronghold was stormed, Caratacus fled, and tribes began to surrender or, if not directly involved in the conflict, to align themselves with the Romans.

Under Aulus Plautius and subsequent governors Roman control was extended over most of what is now southern and central England. Caratacus remained at large, moving from place to place and inspiring resistance, until AD 51, when he was defeated, captured and displayed to the Roman populace by Claudius, who then pardoned him and pensioned him off. But a few years later there was a serious setback. The Romans' policy was to conciliate the ruling groups in conquered lands, granting them privileges and showing them the advantages of living within the Empire; it tended to work, unless the rapacity of local officials or military men spoiled things. This happened to the client kingdom of the Iceni in East Anglia, where the widowed Queen Boudicca (Boadicea) and her daughters were plundered and

brutally treated. In 60 or 61 Boudicca led a revolt of the Iceni that was joined by other tribes and caught the Romans off guard at a time when the governor, Suetonius Paulinus, was away campaigning in Anglesey. Roman settlers were massacred and the new towns of Colchester and London were burned to the ground before the rising was crushed and Boudicca poisoned herself rather than be captured.

The Romans' forward momentum resumed a few years later. Cornwall and Wales were subdued, and the defeat of Rome's sometime allies, the Brigantes, brought the legions to the modern border between England and Scotland. Led by Gnaius Julius Agricola, the Romans pushed on deep into Scotland, and in 83/84 won a great victory in the far north at Mons Graupius, an unidentified spot near the Moray Firth. But after Agricola was recalled the Roman hold on Scotland progressively weakened. Eventually the legions retreated to the Solway-Tyne line, which the next visiting emperor, Hadrian, chose as the location for his famous defensive wall. This was one of the Romans' most spectacular achievements, a stone and turf barrier some 3 m (9 ft) thick and standing up to 6.5 m (21 ft) high, with huge ditches to front and rear, and forts, milecastles (small forts) and signalling turrets at regular intervals over its 117-km (73-mile) length. Hopes of further conquests in Scotland were revived under Antoninus Pius in the 140s, and for a few years the turf Antonine Wall between the Forth and the Clyde served to demarcate a new frontier. The last serious attempt to conquer Scotland was made by the Emperor Septimius Severus in 208–211, before his death at York. For most of its remaining history Roman Britain ended at Hadrian's Wall. However, Roman influences and artefacts spread north of the Wall and also across to Ireland; a Roman-style fort has been unearthed north of Dublin, but its discovery has not yet convinced historians that the Romans themselves were even briefly present on the spot.

Roman Britain was furnished with towns and a network of roads linking the Channel ports with London, and London with Exeter, Cirencester, Wroxeter, Chester, Carlisle, York, Lincoln, St Albans (Verulamium), Colchester and other urban centres. Villa culture spread slowly and, by Roman standards, was on a modest scale, although an unusually opulent palace has been unearthed at Fishbourne, near Chichester; it was probably the residence of Cogidubnus, a client ruler whose support for the Romans was important during the early decades following the conquest. Agriculture remained the occupation of the majority, perhaps conducted a little more efficiently thanks to Roman improvements. The same was probably true of mining (gold, silver, lead), and both the use of coinage for regular commercial purposes and the presence of the army and administrators acted as economic stimuli. These may have counterbalanced the burdens imposed by Roman government and the cost of an urban lifestyle with such familiar features as the baths and the amphitheatre; but of course the British beneficiaries mainly came from the upper class. As Tacitus noted, Britons of this class acquired most of the Roman 'vices', and they or their children became fluent in Latin and aimed to play prominent roles in provincial or even imperial affairs.

Over the centuries Germans, Syrians and traders and soldiers from many other lands settled in Britain. They brought their religions with them, and Celtic and Roman gods, Eastern deities such as Astarte and Isis, the Persian Mithras and Sol Invictus (the Unconquered Sun) all acquired devotees. Christianity made considerable progress in the 4th century, when it became the state religion, but just how well it fared by comparison with its rivals has proved impossible to establish.

Britain seems to have suffered relatively little during the disastrous 3rd century, when the Empire came close to collapse. A breakaway 'Gallic empire', including Britain, survived for 14 years (260–74), and soon afterwards (287–296) the province was ruled by the usurpers Carausius and Allectus, who were defeated by the Caesar Constantius I. When Constantius died at York in 306, his son Constantine was proclaimed by the troops and began his momentous career. During this period, British villas became more numerous and luxurious, and the first half of the 4th

century seems to have been a kind of Romano-British golden age.

However, the construction of forts along the southern 'Saxon Shore' suggests that the activities of Germanic pirates were already causing concern. From the mid-4th century the pressures intensified, and defence problems were aggravated by Britain's usefulness as a base for mutinous commanders with imperial ambitions. In 367 Scots from Ireland, Picts from north of Hadrian's Wall, and Saxon seafarers attacked Britain simultaneously in what has been called 'the Barbarian conspiracy', causing widespread havoc. Despite a partial recovery the pressure continued, while would-be emperors marched away to pursue their ambitions, all too often taking with them troops who would never be replaced. By the early 5th century the empire itself was at bay and incapable of defending Britain against predatory barbarians. By 410 the last legion had gone. Urban and commercial life rapidly broke down, but Romanized elements persisted in British life for very much longer.

Opposite: Hadrian's Wall, the longest surviving Roman structure, winds from coast to coast across northern England. Roman advances beyond the Wall, in what is now Scotland, proved ultimately impossible to sustain.

A cultural hybrid. This head from Bath once stood on the temple of Sulis Minerva (a composite Romano-British deity); it seems to fuse elements of some British god with the Greco-Roman (and female!) head of Medusa.

MEDICINE, DISEASE AND DEATH

The Romans suffered from very many illnesses, and life was always precarious – even for the rich, who could afford the best advice and extended treatment. Most present-day ailments already existed, from the common cold to tuberculosis and malaria. Diseases caused by malnutrition were widespread among the poor, and Romans of all classes suffered from bad skins, bad teeth and eye problems, along with disabilities caused by conditions in early life that were impossible either to diagnose or to treat. Furthermore the Roman world was smitten from time to time by death-dealing plagues that were mysterious to the Romans and remain so to us because of the lack of descriptive detail, which few uninfected observers would have lingered long enough in the vicinity to record.

Beset by ill-understood afflictions, many people believed that these ailments were sent by the gods, or at any rate were curable only through divine help. Romans worshipped a number of healer gods and goddesses, but the most important was Aesculapius, a Romanized version of the Greek Asclepius. Appeals to the gods might be

A physician examines his patient, using his hand to check for any abnormality in a way that is still familiar; relief, 2nd century AD. However, diagnostic skills were variable, and the line between magic and medicine was blurred.

answered by a sudden recovery, or by a dream in which the supplicant was told how a cure could be effected. Although the study and practice of medicine was important, it seems likely that the majority of patients preferred – or found it easier to afford – religious, magical or folkloric treatments. Temple sites have yielded inscriptions gratefully recording cures, along with very large numbers of votive objects, often in the form of the affected limb or organ.

The line between religion and medical treatment was by no means clear, since the curative power of drugs and herbs could be interpreted as magical rather than natural. Moreover there was no organized medical profession, and seers, 'wise women', charlatans and physicians were not always easy to tell apart. However, a tradition of serious medical investigation existed among the Greeks, going back at least as far as Hippocrates, who was said to have been a 6th-century BC physician; a mass of 'Hippocratic' writings survive that were actually from a number of different hands. By the Hellenistic period would-be physicians were enrolling as students at Alexandria and other centres, although it seems unlikely that there were medical schools such as; the main method of study must have been to work under, or at least to observe the procedures of, established physicians.

Greek doctors appeared in Rome, where they were initially regarded with suspicion; according to tradition the first was Archagathus, whom the Romans nicknamed 'the butcher'. By the imperial era an elite of physicians was well established, and Augustus and Claudius maintained long-serving personal physicians (Antonius Musa and Scribonius Largus respectively). Augustus seems to have been impressed by the profession, for he granted physicians generous tax privileges. Those who were in private practice visited their wealthier clients, but the poor had to come to them for treatment. Municipalities and trade guilds employed physicians on a permanent basis, but little is known of the duties involved and it is not clear whether this meant that free treatment was widely available.

There were also doctors and other medical personnel attached to the Roman armies. Although studied, surgery was drastic and potentially dangerous, and consequently in civilian life it was undertaken only as a last resort; but during military campaigns it was frequently unavoidable, and the reliefs on Trajan's Column show field hospitals at work. A range of specialized instruments has survived, including knives, probes, forceps, tweezers, scissors and clamps. Amputations and other operations were performed without anaesthetics, and although some

An impressively specialized collection of surgical instruments used by Roman practitioners. The fact that they would have had to be employed without anaesthetics, often on the field of battle, is not pleasant to contemplate.

A Roman citizen, dressed in his toga, carries busts of his ancestors. Such displays were customary at funerals and other public occasions, extolling the dead while also advertising the mourner's distinguished lineage.

enabled him to learn a great deal about anatomy without practising vivisection. During the early 160s AD he was in Rome and being consulted by Marcus Aurelius. After a brief residence in Pergamum Galen was summoned back to Italy to help combat an outbreak of plague, remaining imperial court physician until about 192; he then returned to Pergamum, where he died about eight years later.

Galen's voluminous writings remained the standard works on medicine for some 1,500 years. He made some outstanding advances in anatomical and physiological knowledge, accurately describing the human skeleton and pioneering the study of musculature; however, the virtual prohibition of human dissection led him to make a number of unwarranted inferences from the anatomy of oxen and monkeys. Many of his observations were of value despite a theoretical framework based on the four humours posited by an earlier Greek, Empedocles. According to this, four elements were present in the body – blood, yellow bile, black bile and phlegm – and were held in balance when a person was healthy; in most instances treatment of the sick was directed at restoring the balance. Like ancient medicine in general, Galen's diagnoses might be based on portents and omens as well as physical symptoms; and while aware of the value of rest and diet, he also recommended a wide range of herbs and drugs of varying effectiveness, and endorsed practices such as blood-letting, which remained an accepted, often lethal treatment right down to the 19th century.

Among other topics, Galen described the appropriate conduct for a physician, laying particular emphasis on creating confidence in the patient (or, put another way, belief in the physician's omniscience). Diagnoses could and should be made without questioning the patient, and the physician should not smell of garlic or burden the sufferer with over-lengthy explanations. The encyclopaedist Celsus counselled enlightened self-interest: it was better not to take a case if it was hopeless, since the physician was certain to get the blame when the patient died.

After death, fixed rituals were followed. Funerary practises varied from place to place

alleviation was offered by the use of mandrake root, many patients must have died of shock or infection. Surgery was also undertaken for non-military ailments such as hernias.

During the Roman period, encyclopaedic author-compilers such as Celsus and Pliny the Elder wrote extensively about medicine. But the most authoritative and prolific commentator was a Greek, Galen, who was also the most successful practising physician of his time. Born at Pergamum in Asia Minor, he studied at Smyrna, Corinth and Alexandria. On his return to Pergamum he became physician in attendance on gladiators, whose sometimes savage wounds within the Empire: the Egyptians, for example, despite their exposure to the Greco-Roman way of life, continued their ancient custom of mummifying the dead. Roman rituals were mainly designed to avert the misfortunes that might befall the living. Death was regarded as a curse or infection that had to be isolated and eliminated by following the proper procedures. Cypress branches laid in front of the house warned off priests, for whom it was particularly important to avoid contamination. The body was washed, laid out and loudly mourned, after which members of the family paid their respects and took their individual farewells. During the following eight days of ritual observance the corpse was taken out of the house (following the correct procedure, feet first), conveyed to the cemetery and buried. Bodies might be placed in coffins or sarcophagi, but until the 3rd century AD most Romans were cremated; however, some part of their remains still had to be covered with earth.

Because of the contaminated nature of corpses, cemeteries were always situated outside a settlement or town, usually next to the main road leading out of it. Whatever grave goods the family could afford were buried with the dead for their use in the underworld, although Roman ideas about the afterlife were at best vague and contradictory. They were far more definite about the consequences of failing to bury a corpse or to carry out the rituals properly: ghosts (*lemures*) would haunt the house or linger around crossroads until appeased or exorcised at the annual festival of the dead, the Lemuria, in May. Those who had been properly buried joined the shades (*manes*) and lived on as long as they received offerings of food and libations. In practice most poor Romans were consigned to graves that were reused many times, while the well-off were buried, or their urns placed in niches alongside those of other family members in mausoleums, accompanied by a stone with a carved commemorative inscription.

Humble memorial to a humble man. But according to this gravestone he thoroughly deserved to be remembered; he was 'Alexander, sausage-seller in the market, who lived thirty years, a good soul and a friend of all.'

A mosaic image of death. Around it are symbolic items including a carpenter's level and plumb line, a butterfly and a wheel. The *memento mori* was an apt picture subject in a society where death so often struck without warning.

LIFE IN THE LATE EMPIRE

In the mid-3rd century AD the Roman Empire seemed on the verge of collapse. Then it made a dramatic recovery, culminating in the reforms of Diocletian and Constantine and the adoption of Christianity as the state religion. In its new form the Empire survived for another two centuries in the West and very much longer than that in the East; but it was a rather different place from the Rome of Cato, Caesar or Augustus.

In the late imperial period any generalization is of limited validity, since circumstances changed rapidly and regional differences became more pronounced in the West, where there was a steady deterioration from the late 370s, with Germanic tribes breaching first the Danube and later the Rhine frontier and moving about restlessly within the Empire. There was most continuity in the East, where the challenges were less frequent and severe, and consequently a big-city culture survived; Constantinople, Alexandria and Antioch achieved a pre-eminence acknowledged by, among other things, their recognition as patriarchates of the Church – a distinction they shared only with Rome, which was living mainly on its past glory.

Most indicators suggest that the quality of life deteriorated in the late Empire; for example, the fact that underwater archaeologists have noted a steep fall in the number of Mediterranean shipwrecks dating from after AD 300 must mean that there was a very severe contraction in long-distance trade. The heavy taxes imposed to pay for increasingly large armies stifled economic life and, combined with oppressive bureaucracy and the failure of the authorities to provide good order or effective defence, made the benefits of Roman rule look increasingly dubious. City culture in the West began to run down. The wealthy retreated to their villas, which became centres of self-sufficient local economies, often organizing their own defences against raiding Germans or tax collectors; here the influence of local 'lords', who extended their protection to the neighbouring peasantry, foreshadowed the development of the feudal system. In areas where conditions became intolerable, peasants fled and joined roving groups of marauders, their ranks swelled by fugitives from conscription or deserters. Germanic tribesmen moved in to fill the vacancies as farmers and Roman soldiers, and even before they began to make war and found kingdoms on their own behalf, long-haired horsemen with boots and swords were a common sight on imperial territory. By the time that the last western emperor was thrust aside and Italy became a barbarian kingdom, the change would have made very little difference to the lives of most Romans.

Being alive in the 5th and 6th centuries was probably a less grim business than it can be made to sound when centuries of change are encapsulated in a few words. Moreover late Roman society

The Arch of Constantine, the last surviving triumphal arch in Rome. Its three bays and wealth of decoration make it an imposing sight, but the use of carvings from earlier monuments suggests some flagging in creativity.

was also influenced by imponderable factors, of which easily the most important was the changed spiritual climate created by Christianity. It is difficult to assess the impact of the new religion on the outlook and behaviour of people in general, but even the ordinary experience of worshipping together in a church must have seemed new and strange, since a pagan temple was not designed to hold congregations but served as the sanctuary of a god, closed to the laity. The reflective must also have been taken aback by the change from the polytheistic, essentially non-doctrinal worship of pagans to a religion in which doctrine was not only defined but fiercely debated. There had been nothing in the Greco-Roman world like the international church councils at which opinions

clashed violently, or like the subsequent acrimonious splits that occurred within the Church.

Christianity was to be the bridge from Rome to the Middle Ages, and its impact on late Roman life was considerable; but in many respects it was less dramatic than might have been expected. By the time Christians 'came out' – hesitantly in the 3rd century, then definitively, under the aegis of a military man, at the beginning of the 4th – any early communistic or pacifistic tendencies they may have harboured had been abandoned, and most of them regarded the Roman Empire as the divinely ordained vehicle for the propagation of the faith. Slavery was accepted as part of the social order, and even the games were allowed to continue until late in the 4th century, despite their

The Emperor Theodosius I and his entourage attending the circus at Constantinople, which replaced Rome as the imperial capital. The patterned and frontal treatment of the figures shows late Roman art moving away from naturalism.

Pagan survival: Hylus being taken by water-nymphs; from the Basilica of the Christian Prefect of Rome, Junius Bassus. The technique here is *opus sectile*, which resembles mosaic but is made with relatively large fragments of marble.

gruesome associations with Christian martyrdom. The passions aroused by chariot-racing raged on, and at Constantinople the Blues and Greens became identified with political factions; they sparked off the Nika riots that almost overthrew Justinian. In short, Christianity was no longer a subversive force but, on the contrary, provided a much needed emotional bonding for the struggling Empire.

Literature and intellectual life increasingly took their colour from the new state religion, but there were still a few representatives of the old classical tradition in the late 4th and early 5th centuries. Ammianus Marcellinus of Antioch, a pagan, wrote a remarkably candid history of Rome from the reign of Nerva to the disaster at Adrianople in 378; he discreetly ended his narrative before the reign of his contemporary,

Theodosius I, whose persecuting zeal on behalf of orthodox Christianity made him dangerous to offend. The last poet in the old style was Claudian of Alexandria, who turned from Greek to Latin and became the bard of Stilicho and the Emperor Honorius in Italy.

Nevertheless most intellectual endeavours were theological. Among a host of copiously eloquent figures, the outstanding Latin writers were St Jerome, whose translation of the Bible (the Vulgate) remained the definitive text for a thousand years, and St Augustine of Hippo in North Africa, author of two classics of Christian thought, *The City of God* and *The Confessions*. As an established institution the Church now sought to absorb as much Greco-Roman culture as seemed compatible with the faith, and Clement of Alexandria set himself to synthesize faith and reason by relating the philosophy of the great Greek thinkers, Plato and Plotinus, to Christianity. Significantly, St Jerome was the only one of these writers educated in Italy, and even he was not a native Italian, having been born in Dalmatia. However, it was the Roman-born son of a consul, Boethius, who wrote *The Consolations of Philosophy*, which was to become one of the most popular books of the Middle Ages.

One visible sign of the triumph of Christianity was the building of churches all over the Empire. As in other things, Roman usage was adapted to the needs of the new religion: the aisled nave and triforium lighting of the basilica, a large building used for public business or as a market hall, provided the space needed for the congregations not catered for in pagan temples; St Paul's-outside-the-Walls, Rome, is a classic example. Baptisteries on the other hand were successfully adapted from smaller circular Roman temples. Even in decline the Romans remained great builders, as Caracalla and Diocletian demonstrated; but from the 4th century, economic problems and political crises put an end to ambitious secular building in the western empire.

In the circumstances it is not surprising that official Roman art also showed a falling-off in competence and conviction: under Constantine there was such a shortage of skilled carvers that the reliefs used on his triumphal arch were mainly 1st-century work, purloined from Antonine monuments. However, this was only one aspect of a larger change in the arts, away from 'classical' realism and towards a style in sculpture, mosaics and painting that more directly expressed the concerns of Roman Christians.

By the reign of Justinian (527–565), Constantinople was indisputably the greatest city in the Christian world and, with its Greek language and culture, multi-domed churches and hieratic-figured mosaics, already belonged to a new age in which even its founder, Constantine, seemed remote and Roman. Elsewhere, men were turning away from the old world in a different sense by entering monasteries to escape the brutalities of life and find salvation outside the fray. In this age even Latin became a rarity, disappearing altogether in outlying parts such as Britain, and developing provincially into independent languages such as Italian, French, Spanish and Romanian; the Western Church alone maintained the universality of Latin, just as it maintained the Roman claim to universal dominion. A heaven-directed art, monasteries, church-Latin, disputes over doctrine, powerful but often no-longer-literate lords and peasants – here antiquity has been left behind and we are in the turbulent early Middle Ages.

The interior of St Paul's-outside-the-Walls, the largest early Christian church in Rome, built c.380. Though extensively restored, it retains the basilican layout of the period, with a large central area flanked by aisles.

3 PILLARS OF THE STATE

THE GOVERNMENT OF THE ROMAN STATE WAS ENTRUSTED TO ASSEMBLIES AND MAGIS-TRATES – THE SENATE, CONSULS, TRIBUNES – WHOSE NAMES HAVE RUNG DOWN THE AGES. THE ROMAN SYSTEM OF GOVERNMENT, THOUGH SOMETIMES CRUEL OR CORRUPT IN PRAC-TICE, SHOWED A REMARKABLE CAPACITY TO ADAPT TO CIRCUMSTANCES. IN TIME THE REPUBLIC FAILED TO COPE WITH THE CHALLENGE OF EMPIRE AND THE AMBITIONS OF MILITARY MEN, BUT, IN NAME AT LEAST, SOME OF ITS INSTITUTIONS SURVIVED FOR THE ENTIRE SPAN OF RECORDED ROMAN HISTORY AND EVEN BEYOND. THE OTHER MIGHTY PILLAR OF THE STATE WAS THE ARMY. AS LITTLE MORE THAN AN EXCEPTIONALLY TENACIOUS MILITIA IT DEFEATED CARTHAGE; THEN IT WAS CONVERTED INTO AN EFFICIENT PROFESSIONAL ARMY DURING THE 1ST CENTURY BC, WHEN THOROUGH TRAINING AND A HIGH LEVEL OF DISCIPLINE AND ESPRIT DE CORPS MADE THE LEGIONS THE MOST FORMIDABLE MILITARY MACHINE IN THE ANCIENT WORLD. THE DEFENCE OF ROME'S IMMENSELY LONG FRONTIERS EVENTUALLY REQUIRED DRASTIC CHANGES IN THE ARMY'S COMPOSITION AND TACTICS, BUT IT CONTINUED TO ACQUIT ITSELF VALIANTLY IN AN ULTIMATELY VAIN STRUGGLE AGAINST THE BARBARIANS AT, AND WITHIN, THE GATES.

Roman senators in a religious procession led by the Emperor Augustus; part of a relief from the Ara Pacis (Altar of Peace). The political elite is shown as personally dignified and endorsed by the state gods.

POLITICS
AND POWER

Rome began as a monarchy and ended as an empire. Not much is known about the way that early monarchical institutions functioned, but in all later periods the word 'king' (*rex*) was so odious to Romans that even the all-powerful Julius Caesar found it prudent to reject the offer of a revived royal title. Ironically, the system that then evolved under Augustus gave the emperor an autocratic power far greater than any enjoyed by the detested royal tyrant Tarquinius Superbus.

In about 510 BC Tarquinius was driven out and, despite some vicissitudes, Rome became a republic. The Senate had existed under the monarchy, and under the Republic it developed into a venerated institution whose advice carried immense authority. It was originally chosen on the basis of birth and rank, but by the 4th century BC senators were mainly men (admittedly from the same social class) who had held office under the Republic; over the following three centuries their numbers increased from about 100 to 300.

The place of the kings as chief executives of the state was taken by the consuls, of whom the first two were Lucius Junius Brutus, leader of the revolt that established the Republic, and Tarquinius Collatinus. The character of the consulate was defined in such a way as to avoid any further abuse of the executive power. The consuls held office for a single year and could not be elected two years running. They shared the *imperium* (supreme power) in complete equality, alternating in precedence month by month, and each had the right to command two legions. An overmighty consul could be restrained by his colleague, if necessary by a simple declaration that the omens for a given day were unfavourable and consequently no public business could be transacted. This tactic was used repeatedly in 59 BC by the consul Bibulus, one of the senatorial party, to frustrate the designs of his fellow-consul Julius Caesar; but by that time republican institutions commanded less respect, and Caesar, confident in the support of Pompey and Crassus, simply

ignored the omens, and Bibulus, so that it was wittily said that 59 was the year of 'the consulate of Caesar and Caesar'.

Like most constitutional arrangements, the twin-consulships worked satisfactorily while there was general goodwill. However, the disadvantages of dual command in an emergency were recognized by the arrangements made for nominating a dictator, who was entrusted with autocratic power for six months and might even be re-appointed for a further term. Between the 5th and 3rd centuries BC the dictatorship was held by men of integrity such as Cincinnatus and Fabius; but the rise of generals with strong personal followings changed the situation. Sulla's dictatorship was imposed rather than achieved by

Brutal despot: the Emperor Caracalla (AD 212–17) was always portrayed as fearsomely grim, presumably at his own wish; and he lived up to the image. Despite some military successes, he was murdered by an ambitious officer.

The sinews of government. This scene from the altar of Domitius Ahenobarbus, the conqueror of Greece, has been variously interpreted as a military census or tax-gathering; in either case, the Roman state is at work.

constitutional means, and after his death the Senate tried to avoid appointing another military man to this potentially dangerous office; the nomination of Pompey as sole consul during the crisis of 52 BC was a curious half-compliment, half-insult, granting him an executive authority that was exclusive but more circumscribed in law than that of a dictator. The subsequent ratification of Caesar's dictatorship, like Sulla's, was simply an act of acquiescence in rule by the sword; after which the establishment of an autocracy made the office of dictator redundant.

As republican Rome expanded, new offices were created to relieve the pressure on the consuls. *Quaestors* took over the administration of many financial matters; *aediles* supervised public works, tried to keep the city clean and presided over the games; praetors, ranking immediately below consuls, carried out a variety of juridical functions; censors, usually ex-consuls, maintained the registers of electors and senators, conducted censuses, and were also empowered to suspend senators who led flagrantly immoral lives or failed in their duties. Both praetors and consuls were likely to follow their year in office with the governorship of a Roman province, where they were known as proconsuls and propraetors. In time a recognized career-ladder (*cursus honorum*) developed, enabling those who held public office to make their way

into the Senate and achieve a consulship; Cicero, for example, was successively quaestor (75 BC), aedile (69), praetor (66), consul (63) and, after a period in the political wilderness, proconsul in Cilicia (Asia Minor).

These were the glittering prizes that republican Rome had to offer, and competition for office was intense. Yet the popular assemblies that elected officials never acquired very strong political identities, partly because the block-voting system was weighted in favour of the wealthier citizens and partly because voting had to take place without any preliminary debate, a rule that inevitably increased the influence of senatorial advice when serious issues arose. By contrast, the two tribunes of the people occupied an office created to protect the rights of the plebeian citizens and, in the persons of the Gracchi, were at the stormy heart of Roman politics in the late 2nd century BC. The tribunes had extraordinary powers within the city of Rome: their persons were sacrosanct, they could veto almost any decree, hold up any business, and summon the Senate or the popular assemblies at will. In alliance the tribunes and the popular assemblies should have been able to control the state, but the fate of the Gracchi demonstrated that this was an illusion. In practice tribunes and assemblies were part of the fragile balancing of constitutional parts that characterized the earlier Republic, and ultimately became caught up in the complicated political manoeuvring that preceded its fall.

Following this, Augustus became the first Roman emperor; but none of his titles suggested the autocratic grandeur now conjured up by the word. His achievement was to make everything seem the same while in fact altering everything. He 'restored the state' and contented himself with being its first citizen (*Princeps*) and victorious commander (*Imperator*). If anything, the powers of the Senate seemed to have been enhanced under Augustus, since the right to elect magistrates was transferred to it from the popular assemblies. The *cursus honorum* continued to be followed and the consulship remained a prize that the emperor himself thought it worth receiving from time to time. At five- or ten-year intervals the Senate granted Augustus an extension of the *imperium*, and an outsider reading official records might well have believed that ultimate authority remained with its members.

The reality was quite different. As well as packing the Senate with his own supporters, Augustus could use his position as First Senator and censor to appoint and eject anyone he pleased. He had been invested with the power of the tribunes (*tribunicia potestas*), leaving the posts themselves to others. As *pontifex maximus* he was the head of the state religion; his uncle was a god, and he himself was receiving divine honours in the East. On a less formal level, Egypt was his personal possession, enabling him to control the vital corn supply, Italy was garrisoned by his Praetorians, and the rest of the Empire was divided into long-settled provinces ruled by the Senate and front-line provinces that were placed under direct imperial command – where almost the entire Roman army was stationed.

By the end of Augustus' long life the situation had become irreversible. Subsequent emperors inherited the throne or, later, were raised to the purple by the troops with the acquiescence of the Senate. The old offices survived and new ones were created, widening career opportunities for equestrians in particular; and the creation of a substantial civil service offered further openings for equestrians and freedmen. But politics in the republican sense was dead, unlike intrigue and conspiracy. The *cursus honorum* carried on to the very end of the western empire, and the Senate and consulate actually outlived it, since the barbarian kings of Italy attempted for a time to imitate Roman ways by retaining institutions that had lost their reason for existing centuries before.

One half of 'bread and circuses': this painting is believed to represent a distribution of free bread by an ambitious politician. The Roman governing classes took pains to conciliate the urban masses and keep them docile.

Celebrating a military triumph with sacrifices; relief from one of Marcus Aurelius' monuments, incorporated in the Arch of Constantine. The military display casts the Roman army in a particularly glamorous light.

THE ARMED FORCES

Rome's empire was won by her army, and its survival depended on the efficiency and valour of its famous legions. The Romans' military genius lay in their ability to create and maintain a machine-like organization that could survive and overcome reverses, employing tactics that brought results without relying unduly on outstanding leadership. Ironically, some of the most brilliant generals (Sulla, Pompey, Caesar) slaughtered more fellow-Romans than enemies of the Empire.

The Roman army that conquered the Italian peninsula and defeated the Carthaginians was little more than a militia. Its legionaries were farmer-citizens, eligible to serve only if they satisfied a property qualification and could provide their own arms and armour. Many of their successes were attributable to sheer tenacity, but their style of fighting was also an important factor, revealing the Romans' tactical flair. At first they imitated the famous Greek formation, the phalanx, which was essentially a solid block of spearmen, many rows deep, that met its adversaries head-on. The Romans quickly discovered that such tactics were effective enough in set-piece engagements between similarly armed opponents on level ground, but had severe disadvantages when confronting other types of warrior in varied battle situations. Their response was to adopt a three-line formation, with each line of legionaries divided into groups of about 150 men (maniples); the maniples could be moved about, giving greater flexibility, while the gaps between maniples allowed the line in front to fall back if repelled or exhausted, or the line behind to join in the fray directly if the foe showed signs of yielding. The Romans also abandoned spears in favour of throwing javelins, used to damage and disarray the enemy front line before coming to grips with it, and the short, double-edged thrusting swords employed at close quarters.

Their flexible tactics served the Romans well in conflicts with Samnites, Gauls, Carthaginians and Greeks. But the further the empire spread, the greater the strain on the citizen army became. During Rome's early wars, her soldiers had fought in the summer and then returned to their farms, a cycle that was disrupted when conflict became continuous and campaigns were conducted far from Italy; moreover the requirements of empire included frontier and garrison duties that were incompatible with temporary service. In any case the system was breaking down by the late 2nd century BC, as capitalists used the loot of empire to set up large, slave-operated estates and independent smallholders began to disappear from the Italian countryside, eliminating the pool of manpower from which the army was recruited.

The transformation of the Roman army into a professional force was begun by Marius, who was spurred on by the need to finish the war in Numidia against Jugurtha (112–106 BC) and defeat the ferocious Cimbri and Teutones who invaded Italy (102–101 BC). Marius abolished the property qualification (although not the

requirement that legionaries must be citizens) and recruited from the urban poor; the manpower problem was eased still further as citizenship rights were extended, and Italian allies and other non-Romans became eligible to join the army. Soldiers were now paid, with deductions for their rations and equipment, and served for a fixed term (ultimately 25 years). Training became increasingly rigorous and weaponry was standardized, so that every legionary carried a javelin (*pilum*), a sword (*gladius*) and a curved rectangular shield (*scutum*). Rightly or wrongly all of these changes were attributed to Marius himself, and he was also said to have made the eagles the main legionary standards, and to have improved the *pilum* by having one of its rivets made of wood: this broke on impact so that the discharged *pilum* could not be picked up and flung back by the enemy. Such attention to detail became the hallmark of Roman military organization.

During this period the army took on the form it would keep throughout the high noon of the Empire. Under Augustus there were about 30 legions, each at full strength just over 5,000 men, giving a total of 150,000 men. Each legion consisted of 10 cohorts, the cohort of 480 men

Soldiers building a fortification; the relief, from Trajan's Column, stresses the energy with which the work is being done. It is one of many scenes on the column that exalt the professionalism, as well as the valour, of the legionaries.

officers were drawn from the senatorial or equestrian classes; with their characteristic clarity, the Romans had an unambiguous command structure, with a *legatus*, or general, ranking above the senior tribune, the camp prefect and five military tribunes.

As well as the famous legions, the army included auxiliary troops drawn from the provinces. Among these were light-armed skirmishers, infantry, cavalry and units of archers, slingers and other specialists, often fighting in the traditional style of their homelands. In total the number of auxiliaries was considerably greater than the number of legionaries; as precautions, positions of command were all held by Romans, and auxiliary forces normally served outside their native provinces. Among the rewards they could expect for faithful service on retirement was the granting of Roman citizenship for themselves and their descendants. Under Augustus neither the legions nor the auxiliary forces were stationed in Italy, where the main military presence was the emperor's personal guard, the Praetorians – a preventative against military risings that enjoyed only a temporary success.

More than in any previous army, the front-line soldiers were supported on a regular basis by specialists – clerks, medical orderlies, cooks, carpenters – and operated within a reliable infrastructure of roads, transport, mail and supplies. They obeyed regulations and performed duties that had been clearly laid down, and both punishments and promotions were awarded 'by the book' and not arbitrarily. The entire military system was designed to instil confidence in those who belonged to it.

There was also a standard pattern of service. Having been passed by the recruiting board, the newly enrolled legionary did his basic training. He was drilled until he could march in step with his comrades, use his weapons efficiently, and carry heavy gear including armour and weapons, rations and cooking utensils, a hammer and nails, a spade, an axe and a wooden stake. In this way Roman soldiers became virtually self-sufficient and able to survive without assistance from a baggage train or supply column. Even in peacetime, regular route-marches in full kit ensured that they remained in condition, and the heavy-loaded

Standard-bearer carrying an eagle; bronze statuette, part of a set of horse-armour. Each legion had its own eagle, which was guarded at all hazards. The 'eagle-bearer' (*aquilifer*) often played a decisive role in the outcome of a battle.

having replaced the maniple as the main unit for flexible deployment; however, the first cohort was almost double strength, bringing the notional legionary total over 5,000. A cohort was made up of six centuries (80 men), each commanded by a centurion, who was usually an experienced soldier who had worked his way up through the ranks. Senior

Roman bronze helmet with incised decoration. Like many surviving pieces of armour and weapons, it was probably made for display rather than use in battle: pieces damaged in combat have tended to be melted down and recycled.

legionaries called themselves 'Marius' mules'. On the march in friendly territory, the Romans pitched tents at the end of the day; eight men shared a tent, and a group of ten tents housed a century. During hostilities the troops constructed a camp before engaging in battle; this gave them a safe place to fall back on, surrounded by ditches and earth ramparts with a defensive line of stakes above them (this was why each legionary's kit included a stake). One of the best descriptions of Roman military habits was given by the Jewish general and historian Josephus, who wrote with something like astonishment about this methodical camp-making, the instant obedience of the soldiers, and the way that every activity was orchestrated by orders or trumpet-calls. Josephus also noted that the camp was constructed according to a standard plan and resembled a city with its forum and other facilities; and in fact many towns in the Empire were laid out in imitation of the permanent camps (that is, stone forts) that were also the work of the legions.

As well as fighting in open battle, the legionaries conducted siege warfare against cities and hill forts. Most of the techniques of siegecraft had been discovered in the Hellenistic East and

changed very little until the end of the European Middle Ages. The Romans were spectacularly successful in this area mainly by virtue of their methodical approach and persistence. Artillery, capable of use for attack or defence, consisted of catapults like huge crossbows that fired bolts, and slings that flung boulders. Assaults were conducted by soldiers who either carried their interlocked shields above their heads to form a kind of shell (the *testudo* or tortoise) or manned a wooden tower that could be wheeled close to the walls of the fortifications. Battering rams or hooks were used to break down the walls or weaken the foundations so that they collapsed.

At the end of a victorious campaign the general might be granted a triumph, during which he led his men through Rome itself. The individual soldier could win decorations, including the civic crown for saving a comrade's life; and on his retirement he received a lump-sum pension (ten years' pay), a bronze *diploma* attesting to his honourable service, and a grant of land in a *colonia* or veterans' settlement.

The Emperor Hadrian signalled the end of Roman expansion by building the famous Wall and other frontier fortifications. The civil wars

and invasions of the 3rd century AD brought further changes. Towns and other strongpoints were walled and fortified so that they could withstand a siege and protect forces that could sally out when appropriate and cut an invader's lines of communication. The army grew larger than ever, but its function and composition altered: the frontier legions were increasingly recruited locally, while a mobile field army was maintained to deal with emergencies. The legions were replaced by larger units and cavalry became more important than infantry, partly because its mobility enabled it to reach trouble spots more rapidly, and partly because more and more barbarian horsemen were being enrolled from 'federate' groups that had been allowed to settle within the frontiers. In the East the population remained large enough to provide army recruits; in the West the tribalization of the army, though perhaps inevitable, led to a disastrous situation in which both the 'Romans' and their enemies were Germanic. Towards the end, the appearance of magnates with personal military followings, soldiers settled on land as a hereditary caste, and civilians liable to serve in local militias, were harbingers of the Dark and Middle Ages.

The Romans were never enthusiastic sailors, and the needs of the army were always their highest priority. But when mastery of the sea became imperative in the struggle against Carthage, they not only constructed a fleet but emerged victorious in spite of their adversaries' long experience of naval warfare. Subsequently Pompey cleared the Mediterranean of pirates whose extensive operations made them a virtually independent power, and the fate of the Roman world was decided by battles at sea between Octavian and Pompey's son, Sextus Pompeius (Naulochus, 36 BC), and between Octavian and Mark Antony (Actium, 31 BC).

For military purposes the Romans employed the galley, powered by banks of oars. From the mid-2nd century BC many of their ships were built and manned by Greeks, who had a long experience of seafaring and had developed sophisticated manoeuvring and ramming techniques. Generally speaking the Romans took a simpler, less seamanlike approach, relying on their ability to produce ships in large numbers and use them

to board enemy vessels, leaving the *classiarii* (sea-trained or maritime legionaries) to do the rest. Significantly, Roman naval improvements were largely confined to grappling and boarding devices. The most famous was the *harpex*, developed by or for Octavian's master-general, Marcus Agrippa, which played a possibly decisive role in his victory at Actium; fired by a catapult, it smashed into the hull of the enemy ship, which was then reeled in like a fish and boarded.

Since the Mediterranean was effectively a vast inland sea within the Empire, its security was vital. At its height in the 2nd century AD the Roman imperial navy had fleets in many ports, with its command centre at Misenum on the Bay of Naples. Squadrons protected the grain routes from Egypt, North Africa and, far across the Black Sea, the Caucasus. Roman vessels patrolled the Danube, and during Agricola's governorship the British fleet made a rare contribution to geography, proving that the British Isles were indeed islands by sailing right round them. But the Roman navy deteriorated during the upheavals of the 3rd century AD, and by the 5th century, as the western empire fragmented, it ceased to be an effective force.

Opposite: medical orderlies treat the wounded while, above them on the relief, other legionaries carry the standards into battle; scene from Trajan's Column. Such support services were one of the strengths of the Roman army.

A soldier's tombstone, 1st century AD. Honouring Tiberius Calidius Severus, it includes a set of reliefs displaying his equipment. Whether conquering or upholding an empire, Roman soldiers found death in many far-away places.

4 RELIGION AND IDEAS

Minerva, goddess of wisdom; gilded bronze head of a statue found at Bath, England, where she was worshipped as Sulis Minerva. As usual, the Romans sought religious harmony by fusing their goddess with the local British deity.

THE PRIMITIVE RELIGION OF ROME WAS A RELIGION OF HARD-WORKING FARMERS, CONCERNED TO ENSURE THE GOODWILL OF THE SPIRITS (*NUMINA*) FELT TO BE ALL AROUND THEM. EACH STREAM, GLADE, COPSE OR OTHER NATURAL FEATURE HAD ITS *NUMEN*, TO WHICH IT WAS WISE TO MAKE OFFERINGS. THE HOUSEHOLD ITSELF HAD ITS *LARES* AND *PENATES*, SPIRITS OF WHOM CARVED FIGURES WOULD OFTEN BE BROUGHT TO THE TABLE SO THAT THEY COULD SHARE THE FAMILY MEAL; THE GODDESS VESTA GUARDED THE BLAZING HEARTH; AND THE *PATERFAMILIAS* HAD HIS OWN GUARDIAN SPIRIT OR GENIUS (A WORD WITH A LONG AND INTERESTING HISTORY). THE HOUSEHOLD SPIRITS WERE BENEVOLENT UNLESS OFFENDED, WHEREAS MOST OTHER FORCES NEEDED TO BE CAREFULLY HANDLED AND PROPITIATED, AMONG THEM THE *MANES* OR SPIRITS OF THE DEAD.

GODS AND SPIRITS OF OLD ROME

At an early date some *numina* acquired the wider powers and significance of gods, and Jupiter, Quirinus and Mars made their appearance on the Capitol. This triad apparently represented a coalition of Roman and Sabine divinities, later replaced, as Rome fell under the influence of Etruscan beliefs, by Jupiter, Juno and Minerva; these three – the sky god, his wife, and their daughter the goddess of wisdom – remained the principal Roman deities even when they were revamped to correspond to the Greek divinities who lived on Mount Olympus. The Greeks thought of their gods as irresistibly powerful and immortal, but essentially human in their tempers and appetites; by contrast, the Romans possessed a powerful capacity for abstraction, inventing a god for each of the forces of nature, for every conceivable function (Janus, two-faced god of gates; Terminus, god of boundaries) and even for qualities such as Virtue and Fortune; yet they abstained from giving their creations personalities or mythical adventures like the love affairs so characteristic of the Greek Zeus, king of the gods. The legalism so typical of the Romans manifested itself in the scrupulous care with which ceremonies were conducted and the curious lack of warmth in the relations between men and gods; instead of the hot-blooded deities of Greece, Jupiter and his family were thought of as exacting their rights with lawyer-like precision; and men behaved with equivalent nicety to win their favour.

The belief system that developed was a state religion, with a supreme pontiff, the *pontifex maximus*, who was a layman; Julius Caesar held the office, and it became in effect hereditary among the emperors. This combination of religious and political functions was typical of the Romans: magistrates performed religious ceremonies as part of their duties, and members of the priesthood were able to pursue political careers. There were a number of colleges of priests, including the *flamines* and the Vestal Virgins. Each of the 15 *flamines* was responsible for the sacrifices, ceremonies and processions appropriate to one of the major and minor Roman gods. The Vestal Virgins were particularly venerated; as priestesses of Vesta their task was to keep alive the sacred flame on the altar of the goddess's temple in the Forum. The *pontifex maximus* chose them by lot from girls of good family between six and ten years old; they served for 30 years, during which time any lapse from celibacy was punishable by death.

Despite abstractions and contracts, the Romans' gods were not entirely reasonable beings; otherwise it would not have been necessary to ponder every unusual event in case it proved to be an omen or portent, while seeking further information from the augurs, who studied the flights of birds and scrutinized the entrails of slaughtered animals for clues to the future. The conclusions drawn from such exercises might forward or delay the actions of Senate and consuls, which were already enmeshed in ritual; but although the formalism of Roman religion sometimes hindered effective action in an emergency, it also gave Roman society a cohesion and stability that the more volatile Greeks lacked. The link between religion and morality was curiously oblique (except for the morality of contracts, derived from religious oaths, which the Romans took with deadly seriousness); the *pietas* and *fides* of the family, and by extension of the state, formed almost a separate value-system from the elaborate propitiatory mechanisms of public religion.

The marriage of Venus, goddess of love, and Mars, god of war. They appear on the left-hand side of this wall painting from Pompeii; 1st century BC. Despite Mars' helmet and Cupid's wings, the ambience is curiously domestic.

OLYMPIANS AND PHILOSOPHERS

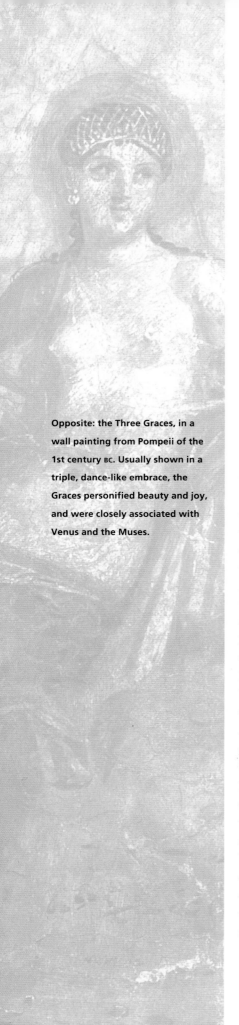

Opposite: the Three Graces, in a wall painting from Pompeii of the 1st century BC. Usually shown in a triple, dance-like embrace, the Graces personified beauty and joy, and were closely associated with Venus and the Muses.

Much has already been said about the impact of the Greeks on their Roman conquerors from the 2nd century BC. Some Greek influence was felt on religion even earlier, either through the Etruscans or from the Greek cities to the south of Rome. The famous Sibylline books – oracular pronouncements which the Romans consulted during great crises – were written in Greek verse and, according to legend, were brought to Rome from the Greek city of Cumae. The last king of Rome, Tarquinius Superbus, was said to have been offered twelve books by the Cumaean Sibyl. When he refused to pay the price she asked, the Sibyl burned three of the books and offered the remaining nine at the same price. This performance was played out twice more, until a chastened Tarquinius agreed to buy the remaining three books at the asking price.

The prestige of the Sibylline books probably encouraged the Romans to identify their gods with the gods of Greece: Jupiter came to be equated with Zeus, Juno with Hera, and Minerva with Athene. Gradually a Roman pantheon emerged that matched that of the Olympians: the war god Mars took on the attributes of Greek Aries, Venus became identified with Aphrodite, the Greek goddess of love, and similar accommodations were made between Diana and Artemis, Neptune and Poseidon, Vulcan and Hephaestus, Ceres and Demeter, Mercury and Hermes, and Eros and Cupid. Gaps were filled by directly bringing in a few Greek deities, notably Heracles (re-named Hercules by the Romans), Apollo and Asclepius (Roman Aesculapius). The gods acquired human characteristics and Greek myth became the common possession of the Greco-Roman world; this constituted an immense fund of stories about the doings of the gods and also of the heroes who took part in Jason's expedition to recover the Golden Fleece, or in the fabled Trojan War; these acquisitions enriched the Roman literary sensibility, even if they were less obviously of benefit to Roman religious and moral convictions. By contrast, the Romans had few myths of their own beyond the pseudo-history of Romulus

and Remus and the early kings; even the foundation myth of Aeneas represented a development of the Greek Trojan War stories. The culminating Greek triumph occurred when the Romans, shaken to the core by Hannibal's victories, sent a special embassy to Delphi for the oracle's advice. However, the older traditions were not abandoned: most Romans also continued to honour the *lares* and *penates*, and to seek the help of Fortune and other abstract deities.

In the last centuries of the Republic, Rome conquered much of the known world and made peace with its peoples and their gods. In most respects the Romans were tolerant in matters of religion; they suppressed some British cults because they involved human sacrifice, but they generally left local customs undisturbed and, if possible, absorbed foreign deities into a nearly all-inclusive Roman pantheon. Under the Empire, Augustus and Livia even had offerings made in their names at the Temple in Jerusalem, despite the Jews' unshakeable conviction that theirs was the only true god, and that consequently all the Romans' gods were false.

By this time many educated Romans had come to feel that all temple gods embodied aspects of the divine; Augustus and Livia clearly believed something of the sort, or at any rate found such a conciliatory view politically convenient. Such an all-embracing attitude was bound to weaken faith in specific deities and myths, and certainly encouraged the more reflective Romans to turn from religion to philosophy.

Philosophy too was a Greek import, and one of the many that were regarded in republican Rome with a mixture of admiration and suspicion; from time to time philosophers were banished from the city but, like other Greek luxuries, they were always re-admitted in the end. The Greeks had effectively invented philosophy and had begun to explore most of its aspects from the nature of matter to the theory of perception. The Romans, characteristically practical in outlook, were mainly interested in two Greek philosophies that offered a rule to live by: Epicureanism and

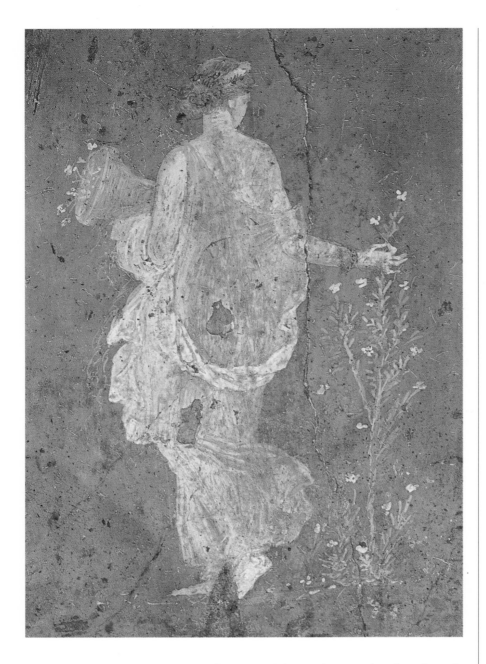

Flora, goddess of flowers and the spring. Thanks to the humanizing of divinities in the classical world, Flora appears in the most natural light, as a charming girl gathering flowers; wall painting from Stabiae, 1st century BC or AD.

bearing adversity without complaint and cultivating a self-sufficient happiness that could not be shaken by the blows of fate.

The Romans gave noble expression to Epicurean and Stoic attitudes, but added little to their substance. In a long philosophical poem, *On the Nature of Things*, Lucretius presented the most detailed and lucid exposition of Epicurean doctrine that has survived; but although Epicurus had followers, the prevailing philosophy among serious men in imperial times was Stoicism. One of its most influential exponents was a lecturer at Rome from the Greek East, the ex-slave Epictetus from Phrygia in Asia Minor; after his death (*c.* AD 135) his lectures were published, and among their readers was the Emperor Marcus Aurelius, whose own Stoic *Meditations* were jotted down in Greek in the midst of his campaigns on the Danube and in the East. Epictetus taught the Stoic doctrines of fortitude and self-sufficiency, placing particular emphasis on his conviction that a man might, if he chose, be 'happy on the rack'.

Although Epictetus also argued for a divine scheme of things and the brotherhood of man, these are even more strongly present in the writings of an earlier Stoic, Seneca, who has already been encountered as one of Nero's ministers and an enemy of the blood-saturated games. The brotherhood of man was a reasonable inference from the belief that men represented sparks from the divine flame, that inner control was the supreme achievement, and that a man's position in the world was an external accident to be dutifully ('stoically') endured, not praised or blamed: only the Sage was worthy of admiration, and there was no reason why an emperor, or a slave, or even a barbarian, should not become a Sage. This emphasis, in itself new to the more aristocratic form of Roman Stoicism, acquired a surprising emotional, even religious, force in Seneca's works. All men need the help of God, he says; but prayer is pointless: the divine spirit is 'near you; with you, within you'. In this life, the soul is in prison: a man resembles a soldier who has signed on for a term of years and must make the best of it, with the prospect of finer things to

Stoicism. Epicureanism taught that the sole worthwhile object of life was pleasure – but it was not 'epicurean' in the modern sense, since recklessly indulging desires only intensified cravings and ultimately brought unhappiness. The ideal existence was one of temperance and calm contentment, freed from ambition and fear of the gods, who were either non-existent or indifferent to human affairs. Stoicism recommended a more heroic course. The human soul was a spark from the cosmic fire, to which it would return if faithfully tended; this meant that the Stoic must do his duty out in the world, come – for Seneca sometimes appears to believe in a future life in which the individual will become part of the world-soul. Like other Stoics he preaches 'happiness in adversity', but in his case the austere Stoic ideal is modified by belief in the importance of human sympathy and mutual help.

Understandably he was later considered a proto-Christian, and for centuries a fake correspondence between Seneca and St Paul was in wide circulation. In life Seneca may have been less admirable. A Spaniard, he made a successful political career at Rome, tutored the young Nero, and in collaboration with the praetorian prefect Burrus ran the imperial government during the early ('good') years of Nero's reign; on the other hand he is said to have amassed an enormous fortune in government, and to have lent money at such extortionate rates that the British under Boudicca were provoked to revolt. When Nero began to take a hand in government, Seneca prudently retired, and even presented the emperor with his fortune to blunt his jealousy. However, after a conspiracy against Nero was discovered, the emperor believed (justly or otherwise) that the aged philosopher was implicated, and he was graciously permitted to kill himself.

Marked by thought and experience. This bust has traditionally been identified as the philosopher Seneca, who put his Stoic beliefs to the test as minister to the Emperor Nero; in fact it may well be a copy of a Greek work.

NEW IDEAS FROM THE EAST

The philosophical writings of Seneca showed that Stoicism was capable of inspiring strong feelings, comparable with the intensities of religious belief. Although Seneca was unusual in his own time, a century later the emotional-religious note was being sounded even more strongly, but with a new accent of melancholy that cast doubt upon the capacity of philosophy to satisfy the soul. In Marcus Aurelius' *Meditations* the emperor's world-weariness is much more apparent than any vestigial Stoic's pride in self-sufficiency; duty is joyless, the world has become the soul's prison indeed, and it longs to be away. Some of this reflects Aurelius' personal situation – that of a sensitive man tied by a sense of duty to camp life

and the slaughter of fellow creatures; but it also expresses a more general mood. In the 2nd century AD – the age that the historian Gibbon thought the happiest of all to live in – a sense of futility had begun to gain ground; there was a vague sense of dissatisfaction with life and its rewards, and a yearning towards some other-worldly state. It was not necessarily the mood of the majority, who continued to honour the old gods, whether from full-hearted belief or just because it was good form to do so – part of what it meant to be a Roman and a civic as much as a religious duty. In any case, such activities were not incompatible with new spiritual cravings: given the un-exclusive religious outlook of the

Ceremony of initiation: an intense scene from a long frieze painted on the walls of the 'Villa of the Mysteries' at Pompeii; a young woman is being whipped by a winged figure (out of the picture), while a naked woman dances in ecstasy.

Egyptian goddess in classical guise. The cult of Isis became very popular during the imperial period, but the style of this statue suggests that the goddess lost some of her distinctively Egyptian qualities in the process.

Romans, there was no reason why the doubtful should not hedge their bets by honouring the *lares* and *penates*, worshipping the Capitoline triad, and also taking part in one or more cults that promised exciting mystical experiences and a more fulfilling afterlife. The early 3rd-century emperor Severus Alexander was one Roman who took this policy to an extreme, filling his private chapel with cult figures of Jesus, Orpheus and other assorted sages and deities – a policy that did not, however, prevent him from coming to a sticky end.

In response to the new mood, cults and religions poured into Italy, almost exclusively from the East, whose sophisticated creations had an appeal for the Romans that the tribal rites of Celts and Germans were unlikely to match. Cybele, the non-Greek Great Mother, had been imported from Asia Minor as early as 205 BC; but her state recognition had been exceptional, reflecting the Romans' desperate casting-around for any forces that might help them in the struggle against Hannibal. A few years later Bacchus (the Roman version of the Greek god Dionysus) also became established, although the orgies associated with his worship were for a time regarded as dangerously subversive; the ritual of initiation, culminating in flagellation, is portrayed in superb paintings on the walls of a room in the Villa of the Mysteries at Pompeii.

But it was in the imperial period that a bewildering variety of non-state cults emerged and achieved respectability. Temples of Isis, for example, were erected at Rome itself and at Pompeii, where the steps still lead up to an altar area now exposed to the sky and surrounded by broken walls and columns. The Egyptian goddess Isis became a popular deity all round the Mediterranean, claiming a more exclusive allegiance than most, yet remaining thoroughly Egyptian in the priests she employed and the Nile water prescribed for her ceremonies. Although associated with her husband Osiris and their son Horus in an Egyptian 'trinity' concerned with death and rebirth, outside her native land Isis seems often to have achieved a superior or independent status. She was also linked with a composite god, Serapis, who combined elements of the Egyptian bull cult dedicated to Osiris with attributes belonging to Zeus and other Greek deities. Both Isis and Serapis frequently presided over what were in effect mystery religions – that is, cults offering personal salvation through secret knowledge; their ultimate truths were revealed in full only to initiates who had passed through one or more stages of ritual purification.

Among the most popular mystery religions were several that originated in Greece, notably the Eleusinian mysteries and the Orphic cults. The sacred site of Eleusis was famous all over the Greco-Roman world, and every year devotees fasted and walked in a great procession from Athens to the hall of mysteries; there, where the corn goddess Persephone was said to have emerged from her captivity in the underworld, a spectacle was staged in which darkness again gave way to light and the initiates, like the goddess and her crop, were reborn.

Such ceremonies had a great appeal, satisfying the growing craving for magic, secrets,

Mithras sacrificing a bull. Many versions of this scene have been found in territories once ruled by Rome. In these the hero-god, wearing a cap and with cloak flaring, is almost always shown in the very act of sacrifice.

miracles, salvation and immortality. One of the more touching indications of a belief in personal immortality is the great increase in the number of sarcophagi made during the 2nd century AD: whatever their precise religious allegiance, people who hoped for resurrection in the body abandoned cremation, presumably anxious not to overtax the powers of their deity.

Belief in magic and mystery drove out belief in reason; the process, visible in the stable world of the Antonines, accelerated in the disordered 3rd century. Even philosophy took on a mystical hue: the outstanding figure was Plotinus, an Egyptian-Greek who held that union with God was the aim of existence. Plotinus elaborated on the work of the much earlier Greek philosopher Plato (4th century BC), taking over Plato's concept of Forms or 'Ideas' – the perfect originals of which all existing things were imperfect copies – and arranging them into a hierarchy supposedly accessible to intellectual contemplation.

Neither mystery religions nor mysterious philosophies were likely to provide the basis for a new world religion, which would have to be accessible to the masses, easily understood, and equipped with a commanding moral or ethical code. A more likely candidate was the cult of the Unconquered Sun (Sol Invictus), with its immediate appeal as the ever-renewed source of light and life, and its easy identification with an emperor who was himself increasingly a godlike being in his own lifetime. In the 3rd century the main rival of Sol was Mithras, originally an import from Persia. He too was a god of light, and was represented as leading the struggle of good/light against evil/darkness. The bull was the potent symbolic animal of Mithraism, its sacrifice signifying the renewal of all things and the rebirth of those who participated in the ceremony. The whole tone of the religion was more sober and disciplined than that of most Eastern cults, a fact that may account for its popularity among Roman soldiers, who took it to the ends of the empire; British evidence of Mithraism includes the remains of a temple uncovered in the City of London some years ago.

With its notion of a struggle between good and evil, its shepherds worshipping the newborn Mithras child, and its communion service of bread and wine, Mithraism had important points in common with Christianity. In fact the ultimate victory of Christianity is easier to understand in the light of the myths and beliefs prevalent in late antiquity: virgin births; divine trinities; deaths and renewals; the divinity within; mutual love; and the promise of immortality. A doctrine incorporating such beliefs was likely to unite the Roman world if it was to be religiously united at all. Christianity had a hard fight of it, and was more liable to persecution than most of its rivals; but it possessed compensatory advantages, in terms of its broad appeal and its capacity to inspire loyalty, that brought about its final victory.

The Catacombs of Calixtus, which is among the best known of the many underground Christian cemeteries around Rome; 3rd century. The photograph shows a passageway with niches for bodies on both sides of it.

ROMAN CHRISTIANITY

In films and novels the Roman Empire is most often presented as the cruel persecutor of Christianity. This is only a partial truth: for almost two centuries Christianity was identified with Rome as the state religion of the western empire, and in the East the partnership lasted even longer. Moreover the entire early history of Christianity took place within the Empire, and Jesus, his disciples, and all the martyrs, saints and fathers of the early Church were citizens or subjects of Rome. The Roman-Christian relationship was crucial to the destiny of both.

Early Christianity was officially suspect or actually proscribed, and its 'underground' existence means that there is little evidence about the forms it took. It is seldom mentioned in surviving texts by Roman authors, and those who do notice it tend to dismiss it as a criminal conspiracy. The historian Tacitus asserts (possibly wrongly) that Nero put the blame for the great fire at Rome on the Christians

although it was his own doing – not that Tacitus was sorry for the Christians, who were 'the enemies of mankind'. It was rumoured that Christians indulged in orgies (perhaps a distorted view of early 'love feasts' or eucharistic banquets) and even incest and cannibalism. The non-violence and communistic tendencies of early Christians were probably more worrying, threatening military morale and the social order; an early 3rd-century Church Father, Tertullian, wrote 'We Christians hold everything in common except our wives'. And of course Christians insisted that theirs was the only true god and denied the emperor the pinch of incense, acknowledging his divinity, that was as much a civic duty as a religious act.

In the circumstances it is surprising that the persecutions were so sporadic and partial. Nero, and later Domitian, seem to have been persecutors, although the details are obscure. During the 2nd century Christianity remained illegal but Christians were usually left alone if they gave no trouble. The most ferocious assaults took place during the 3rd century, under the aegis of emperors – Decius in 250–1, Diocletian and Galerius in 303–13 – who were trying to shore up the beleaguered Roman state and believed that encouraging a revival of the traditional Roman religion would contribute to that end.

Meanwhile in the 1st century Christianity began to spread through the cities of the East and a small community was even established at Rome; the new religion remained so much an urban phenomenon that followers of rival creeds were eventually lumped together as pagans – that is, *pagani* or country people. A canon of sacred writings, mostly in Greek, was agreed, and Christian communities were guided by elders (later priests) and appointed leaders who would become known as bishops. Always potentially under pressure, Christians worshipped in private houses. Preferring to inter rather than cremate corpses, they established underground cemeteries, or catacombs, with recesses in the walls to hold bodies; the most celebrated and extensive examples are in the environs of Rome. Christians were still a minority when Constantine

Jesus as the Good Shepherd; wall painting from the Catacombs of St Priscilla, Rome. This image, not the bearded and crucified Christ, predominated in early Christian art; here the new faith is linked with the old pastoral tradition.

Christian mosaic found at Hinton St Mary in Dorset, England; 4th century AD. The beardless Jesus in the central roundel appears with an early symbol, the Chi-Rho, made up of the first two letters of the Greek word for Christ.

gave their faith an official status. State funding and tax privileges enriched the Church and made it possible to adapt older buildings or construct new ones as places of worship. Paganism displayed considerable vigour until it was forcibly suppressed, and Christian polemicists such as St Augustine developed formidable intellectual resources in defence of their beliefs. As a result, many long-held doctrines were defined during the Roman period, including Original Sin, the perpetual virginity of Mary and everlasting punishment in Hell. The ascetic strain in Christianity also became more pronounced, as hermits and monastic communities retreated to the Egyptian desert and sexual puritanism took hold.

The events of the 5th and 6th centuries had momentous consequences for the Christian Church. In the East, the political survival of the state ensured that the emperor continued to be the supreme authority in religious as well as secular matters. By contrast, the collapse of imperial authority in the West allowed the bishops of Rome (popes) to assert their independence. The role of the Church in general was greatly expanded, with bishops emerging as the leaders of local communities in their dealings with the new barbarian rulers. It was primarily the Church that organized the collection of taxes, provided relief for the poor, and succeeded in preserving elements of the old Roman culture including the Latin language. Many of the invaders, although Christians, were Arian heretics; but in time they were converted to orthodoxy, making their absorption into the local population easier; and as Roman, Christian and tribal inheritances fused, medieval Europe began to take shape.

LITERATURE

Roman literature has had an immense influence on the western mind, despite the loss of huge quantities of writing through time, war and neglect. Latin derived its alphabet from Greek, via the Romans' Etruscan neighbours, and almost all surviving Roman literature was shaped by much earlier Greek models from the epic poet Homer onwards. But, here as elsewhere, the Romans reinterpreted their Greek inheritance and produced works stamped with their own distinctive characteristics and qualities.

Although Latin verse is known to have existed from the late 3rd century BC, the first poet whose works survive in any quantity is Ennius (239–169 BC). He wrote an epic history of Rome in a verse metre taken over from Greece; the work is lost, but several hundred lines have been preserved because they were quoted admiringly by other authors. The earliest known verse dramas date from a generation earlier, when Plautus (254–184 BC) began to adapt Greek comedies, and the metres in which they were written, to Latin. He had worked in the theatre before becoming a playwright – interesting evidence that some sort of Roman drama existed from a very early date. He composed his vigorous if rough-hewn works at such a rate that he must have been driven by the need to make a living; of his 130 plays, 20 survive. Paradoxically, Plautus' successor, Terence, had more leisure to polish his work in spite having been born a slave. He found a patron in Scipio Africanus, the conqueror of Hannibal, who was an ardent enthusiast for Greek culture; consequently he was able to write six elegant plays in the Greek New Comedy style before his early death in 157 BC, at about the age of 26.

The political upheavals of the 1st century BC turned Roman poets away from public affairs and towards more personal concerns. The names of many of these 'new poets' are known; but only the names. The works of two great poets – not necessarily typical of the period – do survive. Lucretius wrote *Concerning the Nature of Things*, a scientific and philosophical treatise, extraordinary in its range, in the form of a 7,500-line poem; while advocating the Epicurean philosophy, it puts forward an atomic physical theory and speculates on the origins of life and sexuality. Sex was also much on the mind of Catullus, who led the brief, intense life (*c.* 85–53 BC) appropriate to a Romantic poet. A master of passionately tender and outrageously vituperative verse, he found occasions for both in his famous poems to the faithless 'Lesbia', believed to have been the fast-living Clodia, sister of the notorious street-politician Clodius, sometime henchman of Julius Caesar. In the absence of works by other 'new' poets, Catullus appears as a revolutionary force in Roman literature, restlessly experimental and direct and personal in expression.

Publius Vergilius Maro – Virgil – was a very different figure, able to express public and private sentiments in verse distinguished for its majestic rhythms and brilliant verbal effects. Born in Mantua in 70 BC, he belonged to the generation that experienced the civil wars and appreciated

Erato, the Muse of poetry and the lyre: detail from a mosaic floor at Thysdrus (El Djem) in Tunisia, 3rd century AD. The Nine Muses, originally an ancient Greek concept, were the deities of literature and the arts.

Prince of poets. Virgil is seated between the Muse of epic poetry, Calliope (on the left), and Melpomene, the Muse of tragedy, who carries a theatrical mask. The poet holds a scroll containing part of his *Aeneid*.

the peace and security brought by Octavian, later the Emperor Augustus. During the wars Virgil actually forfeited his property in 41 BC, presumably because of some real or supposed connection with Brutus and Cassius; its restoration by Octavian, and subsequent patronage by Maecenas, were reasons enough to be grateful, and if Virgil is in a sense the 'official' Augustan poet there is no reason to believe that his praise of the emperor was insincere.

Virgil's earlier works, the *Eclogues* and the *Georgics*, were on bucolic and agricultural themes, heavily influenced by Greek pastoral poetry. Then, at 40, he was in effect commissioned by Maecenas to write a great national epic. He spent 11 years on the *Aeneid*, reaching the end of his story but dying in 19 BC before he could revise and polish it. His deathbed wish was that his manuscript should be burned – presumably because of its imperfect state – but his friends were rightly convinced that it was a masterpiece, and preserved and published it.

The *Aeneid* is the story of Aeneas, the mythical Trojan leader whom the Romans regarded as their distant ancestor. In Virgil's epic Aeneas has been at sea for seven years after his flight from Troy, a great city captured and burned by the Greeks. Bound for Italy, he is blown off course and lands at Carthage, where he becomes the lover of the queen, Dido. When the god Mercury reminds him of his destiny he sets sail for Italy and the heartbroken Dido kills herself. The Trojans reach the mouth of the Tiber, where King Latinus betroths his daughter Lavinia to Aeneas. But the royal household is divided and Lavinia's former betrothed, Turnus, chief of the Rutulians, is hostile. After many fights and adventures the issue is decided by a single combat between Aeneas and Turnus.

The green room, the modern name for the place behind the stage where actors can unwind; in this Roman equivalent, theatrical masks are scattered about and one of the gathering plays the flute. Mosaic from Pompeii.

Such a summary cannot do justice to the complexity of the narrative, or to the parallels and echoes with which Virgil relates the Aeneid to the great Greek epic poems, The *Iliad* and The *Odyssey* of Homer. Aeneas himself is a heroic warrior like Homer's Achilles; but he is also a new type of man, with a Roman sense of duty and level-headedness that makes him superior to Achilles or to his own rival Turnus, both of whom are concerned only for their personal honour. Aeneas can also be identified with Augustus, whose achievements, and the concomitant imperial destiny of Rome, are triumphantly celebrated in Virgil's epic.

Other major poets were at work during the Augustan age. Horace, like Virgil, was dispossessed, having fought for the wrong side in the civil war; he worked as a clerk until rescued by Maecenas and enabled to compose skilfully wrought poems in praise of his Sabine farm or

pointed descriptions of the contemporary social scene. Propertius wrote melancholy love poetry, somewhat overshadowed by that of his flamboyant younger contemporary Ovid (43 BC–AD 18), whose *Love Poems* and *Art of Love* take a sophisticate's view of the subject that may have prejudiced Augustus towards him and influenced the emperor's eventual decision to send the poet into miserable exile on the shores of the Black Sea. Sweet, fluent and inventive, Ovid's verse is at its finest in the *Metamorphoses*, a treasure-house of mythical transformation stories. Later Roman poets often wrote with distinction, but only two satirists of the Antonine age, Martial and Juvenal, engage the modern reader with their frank and fierce descriptions of Roman manners.

The novel or romance flourished under the Empire, mainly in Greek hands and as escapist literature in which lovers are parted and, after various tribulations, reunited at the end. Only two known contributions to the form were made in Latin, but each broke new ground. Under Nero, Petronius wrote the *Satyricon*, celebrated for its satirical descriptions of new-rich vulgarity, but also notable as foreshadowing the picaresque novel which relates the low-life adventures of likeable rascals. Apuleius' *The Golden Ass*, written a century later, is a highly entertaining first-person narrative in which the author dabbles in magic, is changed into an ass, and experiences many aspects of Roman society before being restored to humanity.

The Romans distinguished themselves in many other prose forms. Cicero and the younger Pliny wrote letters of great historical as well as literary interest. Seneca was a philosopher and sensational tragedian. The prolific elder Pliny is now remembered for his 37-volume *Natural History* – and, of course, for his death while investigating the eruption of Vesuvius. But above all the Romans excelled as historians. Their poetry reveals the extent to which they were conscious of themselves as part of history, and they kept official records and compiled annals from an early date. The first substantial histories to survive, and certainly the first contemporary histories in Latin, were Julius Caesar's *Gallic War* and *Civil War*, describing his own campaigns; these apparently plain and straightforward third-person narratives have increasingly been recognized as superbly devised, subtly propagandist works. Subsequent historians included Sallust, master of the compressed rapid style, and the Augustan Livy, whose superb narrative skill and sense of drama make him the greatest storyteller among Roman historians; 35 books of his vast, 142-book *History of Rome* survive. Many later historical works have been lost, including those of the Emperor Claudius, but two important figures bridged the 1st and 2nd centuries AD: Tacitus, whose style is famously colourful, abrupt and often difficult, and the biographer Suetonius, whose *Twelve Caesars* is indiscriminate, gossipy, salacious and highly entertaining. Later historians – notably the 4th-century Ammianus Marcellinus – are informative and interesting, although all too much of their work has failed to survive.

Roman theatre at Orange in southern France; the city also has an imposing triumphal arch. The theatre is well-preserved, thanks to the fact that an economical later ruler incorporated its fabric into the new city wall.

5 ART AND ARCHITECTURE

THE ROMANS HAVE SOMETIMES BEEN DESCRIBED AS A PEOPLE OF LIMITED ARTISTIC GIFTS, IMITATIVE AND, ON OCCASION, FLORID AND VULGAR. THEY WERE CERTAINLY INDEBTED TO THE LONGER-ESTABLISHED CULTURE OF THE GREEKS, IMPORTING GREEK WORKS OF ART IN QUANTITIES AND BORROWING GREEK STYLES FOR USE IN THEIR OWN ART AND ARCHITECTURE; THE CLOSENESS OF THE RELATIONSHIP IS RECOGNIZED BY THE FREQUENT USE OF TERMS SUCH AS 'GRECO-ROMAN', 'CLASSICAL WORLD' AND 'CLASSICAL ANTIQUITY', ALL OF WHICH ASSUME THAT GREECE AND ROME WERE ESSENTIALLY PARTS OF THE SAME CIVILIZATION, AND ONE DISTINCT FROM THE CIVILIZATIONS OF EGYPT AND THE NEAR EAST. THIS GRECO-ROMAN CONNECTION IS INDISPUTABLE; BUT IT IS EASY TO UNDERESTIMATE THE CONTRIBUTION TO THE ARTS MADE BY THE ROMANS. ENDOWED WITH A GENIUS FOR LARGE-SCALE PLANNING AND ORGANIZATION, THEY CREATED ENGINEERING MARVELS, EMPLOYING THE ARCH, VAULT AND DOME TO CREATE STRUCTURES OF AN UNPRECEDENTED SIZE AND GRANDEUR. THE FINEST ROMAN SCULPTURE BRINGS A NEW REALISM TO THE CLASSICAL TRADITION, UTTERLY MATTER-OF-FACT IN ITS TRUTHFULNESS; WHILE THE PAINTINGS DISCOVERED AT POMPEII, HERCULANEUM AND A FEW OTHER SITES ARE EFFECTIVELY OUR ONLY WINDOW ON THE COLOUR AND VARIETY OF ANCIENT PICTORIAL ART, SUPPLEMENTED BY THE SPLENDID MOSAICS THAT ADORNED PUBLIC AND PRIVATE BUILDINGS ALL OVER THE EMPIRE.

The Pont du Gard, the modern name for the splendidly preserved Roman aqueduct that served the city of Nîmes in France. This spectacular feat of engineering dates from the 1st century BC; the water ran along a channel at the top.

BUILDINGS AND MONUMENTS

Roman feats of construction are their most visible and impressive artistic legacy. In the engineering works of their empire they created a functional art, employing all the technological resources of antiquity (some of their own devising) to build roads, bridges, aqueducts, sewers, great public buildings, arcades, theatres and amphitheatres, and a variety of monuments that included triumphal arches and commemorative columns. The roads, measured off with regular stones from the Golden Milestone in the Forum, linked the cities of the Empire from the Euphrates to Hadrian's Wall, promoting trade and travel as well as military and political control. The aqueducts are among the most majestic of all Roman remains, their arches and piers space-stepping over land and water; the finest surviving example is the late 1st-century BC aqueduct now known as the Pont du Gard, which supplied Nîmes, one of the great cities of Roman Gaul.

Structures of this kind could only have been built by exploiting the principle of the arch, which made it possible to span wide spaces safely and economically, without using impossibly heavy masses of masonry. The arch was known to the Greeks, but the Romans were the first people to use it on a large scale; theirs was the true arch, spanning two pillars in a curve by means of wedges neatly arranged so that their thinner ends formed a part-circle (as opposed to the type of arch made up of overlapping stones, used in many ancient cultures). The vault and dome are extensions of the same principle, and in combination with the Roman invention of concrete they were employed to span areas that had previously proved impossible to cover without the support of a forest of columns that darkened and crowded the interior spaces.

Roman methods of construction were fundamentally different from those of the Greeks, which were based on nothing more sophisticated than the use of pillars or columns to support horizontal beams. Nevertheless a number of visual discoveries and an exquisite sense of proportion enabled Greek architects to design some beautiful temples such as the Parthenon at Athens (5th century BC), surrounded by columns, with a distinctive triangular feature, the pediment, closing off the eaves at each end, and filled with relief and free-standing sculptures. Roman public buildings, like Roman houses, tended to be unspectacular outside; unlike Greek temples they were not decorated with paint and lavish sculptures. But the Romans did take over the pediment and the decorative styles employed by the Greeks in carving columns and the area immediately above them (including the frieze and cornice). These styles remained in use even after the Romans had developed techniques, based on the arch and dome, that produced structures very different from anything done by the Greeks; so that externally there is a certain appearance of 'classical' continuity between Greek and Roman buildings.

There were three of these decorative styles, or orders. The Doric column had a sturdy body, no base and a plain cushion capital (headpiece). Ionic was more ornate and slender, standing on a base; its capital had a distinctive double-scroll or

Decorative styles in Roman architecture. The middle three, Doric, Ionic and Corinthian, were Greek in origin; the Romans added variations of their own including Tuscan Doric (far left) and Composite (far right).

The Maison Carrée at Nîmes in France, probably built about 20 BC by Marcus Agrippa. By contrast with Greek temples, most of the surrounding columns in the Roman version are purely decorative, half-buried in load-bearing walls.

rows of Doric, Ionic and Corinthian columns. Finally the Romans devised their own super-ornate order, the Composite, furnished with a capital that combined the Ionic volute with the acanthus leaves of Corinthian; the column made its first appearance on the Arch of Titus (late 1st century AD) and from then onwards enjoyed considerable popularity.

Although the column remained an important element in their visual repertoire, the Romans' technological mastery eliminated its function as a support; strong walls and skilful distribution of stress turned it into a primarily decorative feature that could be partly sunk into the wall ('engaged') or even flattened against it to achieve a rectilinear effect. This development occurred quite early on, during the republican period. Relatively little republican architecture survives since, at Rome in particular, most older buildings were swept away during the city-development boom under the Empire. But a provincial temple, the Maison Carrée at Nîmes, still looks much as it did during the 1st century BC. It is a stolid Roman adaptation of the Greek temple style, raised on a podium and undecorated outside; but instead of a peristyle of free-standing columns surrounding the body of the temple, the walls are placed wider apart than they would have been on a Greek building and the columns are built into them except at the porch; unlike its double-ended Greek counter-parts, the Roman temple had a single entrance, clearly indicated by the steps leading up its high podium to the porch.

The 'Augustan' transformation of Rome actu-ally began with Julius Caesar; but it was Augustus who finished his uncle's projects, as well as building for himself on a larger scale and leaving the city, as he boasted, marble – or rather marble-faced, since the economical Romans habitually used brick and mortar as core materials beneath the more glamorous stone. Caesar, Augustus, the Flavians and the Antonines created great public squares (fora) to beautify Rome and relieve traffic congestion, as well as reconstruc-ting the original market place and civic centre, the Forum Romanum, which is often referred to simply as the Forum. The fallen grandeur of the Forum and the Palatine Hill, along with the

volute. The Corinthian order was still more ornate, with an intricately carved capital of acan-thus leaves. The Greeks had mainly favoured Doric and Ionic, but the Romans used the elabo-rate Corinthian order extensively and also two sober Italian variations on Doric, the Tuscan and Roman Doric orders. Roman builders were less strict than the Greeks in their employment of the orders, and as their confidence grew they varied or permutated them according to a taste that grew more florid (though not more certain) during imperial times. On occasion all three orders were used on a large building with, in ascending order, remains of Nero's Golden House, demonstrate the scale on which the Romans planned and built, although their state of decay makes it easier to appreciate them as romantic ruins than as works of architecture.

The most famous surviving Roman monuments date from the Flavian and Antonine periods. Among them are a number of triumphal arches and columns, intended to commemorate Roman victories, of which the best-known survivors are the Arch of Titus in the Forum, the Arch of Trajan at Beneventum, and the columns of Trajan and Marcus Aurelius, both in Rome. The triumph was an official honour granted to a victorious general, who rode laurel-wreathed through the city in the midst of a great procession of captives, soldiers, senators and magistrates; triumphal arches cannot have been built quickly enough to have been marched through by the procession, so their function must have been purely commemorative. This type of arch-cum-

building, decorated with architectural elements, sculptures and a large, boldly cut inscription, was to have a long history, for example re-appearing in Paris as Napoleon's Arc de Triomphe. Both arches and columns were also important as repositories of Roman sculpture.

The Flavians' greatest monument, and certainly the most famous of all Roman buildings, was the Colosseum; this was the name given by awe-struck medieval writers to what the Romans knew as the Flavian Amphitheatre. Finished in Titus' reign only nine years after it was begun, the Colosseum is among the most spectacular of all achievements in functional building – however nauseating the function may have been. It was at least as well planned as most modern sports stadiums, efficiently taking in and disgorging its 50,000 spectators through intelligently distributed entrances. There were quarters for large numbers of wild beasts beneath the amphitheatre, as well as store-rooms and an underground

The Colosseum, awe-inspiring even in its ruined state; it was begun in AD 72 under Vespasian and officially opened by his successor, Titus, in 80. A lake stood on the site until it was drained and filled with concrete.

passage to the chief gladiators' school in Rome. The building itself is a masterpiece of engineering in concrete, brick and travertine limestone. The outer wall rises in four tiers, three of arches and one solid level broken by small windows. The architectural orders are, as usual, engaged and decorative only – starting from below, Doric, Ionic and Corinthian, with a flattened Corinthian at the top. This was not mere vulgar display, for the verticals of the columns were visually important: in combination with the arches they lightened and lifted up a building that might otherwise have given an impression of being an intolerable dead weight. In hot, sunny weather a vast awning was raised on poles to protect the spectators, an operation so difficult that there has never been an entirely satisfactory explanation of how it was carried out.

Trajan, militarily the most successful of the Antonines, is commemorated by his column; its splendid, action-packed reliefs are better known than the Forum of Trajan in which the column stands, or than the vast nearby market built by the emperor. Such schemes were characteristic of the Romans, who were unlike most ancient peoples in lavishing more resources on secular than on religious buildings. It is ironic, then, that the best-preserved of all the great Roman buildings should be a temple to all the gods, the Pantheon, erected in Hadrian's reign to replace the Augustan original, which had burned down. Externally the Pantheon is a curious and not entirely successful combination of Roman engineering and Greek style – a domed circular building with a pedimented portico stuck on to the front of it. But the interior, with its enormous coffered dome and wide light-admitting 'eye' open to the heavens (the *oculus*, over 8 m [27 ft] across), is one of the Romans' great triumphs of spatial engineering.

By contrast, among the most impressive of all romantic ruins are those of Hadrian's villa at the resort of Tivoli outside Rome. The 'villa' was actually a great residential complex – a palatial country retreat where the most cultivated and philhellene of all the emperors assembled reproductions of the wonders he had seen on his journeys all over the Empire, including the Stoa at

Athens and the Serapeum at Alexandria in Egypt. Now, at any rate, it has an appropriately nostalgic quality, thanks to its long vistas of calm waters and broken stone.

Later emperors continued to build on a large scale and almost certainly in a competitive spirit. Roman skills in organizing space functionally and covering vast areas were displayed in one of the vital municipal services, the public baths, which were also masterpieces of hydraulic planning, incorporating both underfloor heating and supplies of hot and cold water via cisterns and pipes. The main block of the Baths of Caracalla in Rome is estimated to have been capable of holding some 1,600 bathers, but the baths built in the city by Diocletian were twice as capacious; a single hall, the *tepidarium*, sufficed to serve as a large church, Santa Maria degli Angeli, converted by the great Renaissance artist Michelangelo and still one of the sights of Rome.

The Basilica of Maxentius, built in AD 306–315, shows the Romans' ability to vault vast areas. It was the last great basilica in the pre-Christian sense (a hall for public business) erected in ancient Rome.

Opposite: the Baths of Caracalla in Rome, their great vaults and mosaic floors still evoking their original vastness and splendour. Built between AD 212 and 216, the baths were a gigantic leisure complex catering for most tastes.

BRONZE AND MARBLE

Roman sculpture was deeply influenced by Greek art, and might almost be described as one of the tributaries of its late, Hellenistic phase. As early as the 5th and 4th centuries BC, sculptures were fashioned in Athens and other small Greek city-states that combined naturalism with ideal beauty; this was later known as the Classical style. Then, as Greek culture spread all over the eastern Mediterranean and the Near East, many different centres produced sculptures in the Hellenistic style, or styles, exploiting a great many genres from brutal realism to extremes of sentimentality and pathos. Greek sculptors, like Greek architects, created masterpieces that rank among the greatest works of art in history, so it is understandable that the Romans should have fallen

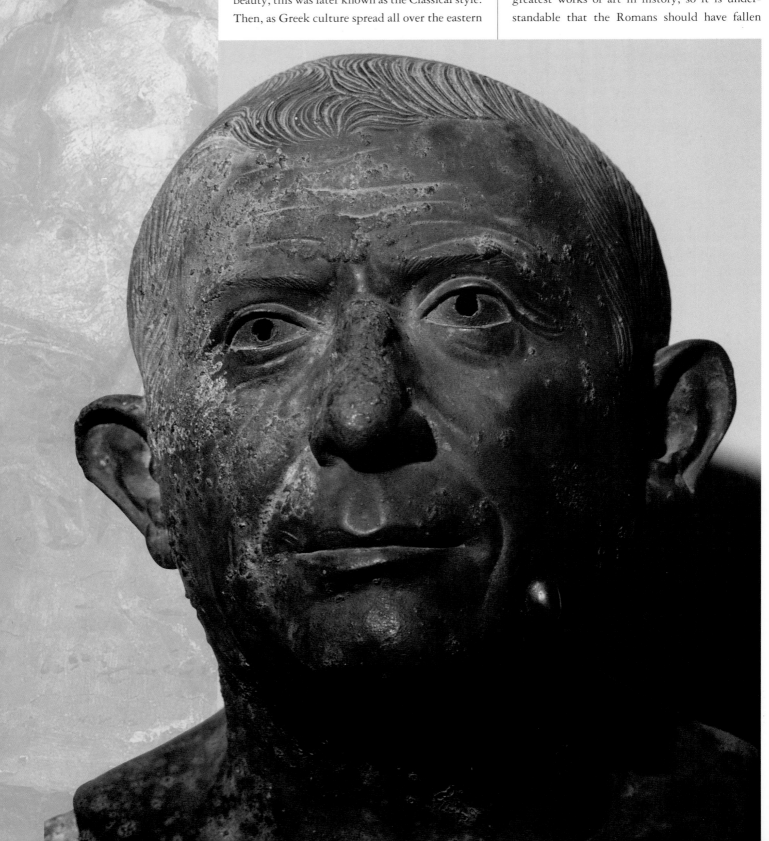

under their spell; if anything, it is surprising that they were so successful in making Hellenistic art a vehicle for their own distinctive qualities.

The Romans' artistic reputation has suffered because of the way in which they acquired much of their Greek culture: by fighting and plundering. Works of art began to flood into Rome in 210 BC, after the capture of the Greek city of Syracuse in Sicily, and as conquest followed conquest, more and more was carried off; to give only a single example, after defeating Macedon in 167 BC, Aemilius Paulinus came away with some 250 wagonloads of aesthetic loot. In Rome, collecting Greek sculpture became all the rage, not always conducted with much taste or discretion: in his letters the orator Cicero pestered a friend who lived at Athens to send him statuary from the city so that he could decorate his new house, seemingly confident that, as long as the works were Greek, they were bound to impress. For much of their history the Romans commissioned sculptors (a good many of them probably imported Greek craftsmen) to create works 'in the Greek style', and on occasion Roman portrait heads were even fitted on to specially manufactured bodies that had been cast or copied from Greek originals of athletes, gods or heroes. Roman patrons also bought copies of older Greek sculptures that had become recognized as classics; in fact Romans were such enthusiastic purchasers that copying became a skilled industry, with the unexpected result that many Greek masterpieces such as the Discus Thrower are now only known in Roman copies. This is especially the case where the original was made of bronze, a metal that later generations were liable to melt down and re-use (often for weaponry); the Roman habit of making copies in marble, however deplorable, accounts for their survival more or less intact.

The sublimity of Greek sculpture may have had an inhibiting effect on the Romans, who never sought to surpass the images of gods and god-like men created by the older culture. But an alternative explanation is that the Roman attitude towards the gods — less inclined to view them as larger-than-life humans — was different from that of the Greeks. Temperamentally, too, the Romans were more down-to-earth — curious

about real people and the real world, and impelled to document at least some aspects of them. They were probably encouraged by the realistic tendencies that also existed in the art of the contemporary Hellenistic world; but Roman realism has a sober, literal look that refuses emotion or exaggeration, and this makes it quite distinct from the sensationalism that is never far away in Hellenistic works. Roman taste was expressed, and influenced, by the portrait busts of ancestors that were customarily displayed in the house. These were intended as records of people as they had been known and remembered, not of mythologized heroes; and there is evidence that many of the busts were made directly after the death-masks that had been cast from the faces of the deceased. With such a precedent, the Romans went on to reproduce plain and truthful portraits of emperors, commanders, farmers, freedmen and slaves, on busts, statues, coins, sarcophagi and memorials. Except for a few periods of glamorizing 'official' art, even emperors and victorious generals allowed their jug-ears, stubbled or doubled chins, warts and other defects to be included in portraits of suitably Roman *gravitas*.

Realistic observation of animals, plants and everyday life also occurred, especially on reliefs of the imperial period. However, during the

Opposite: Roman realism. Greek art profoundly influenced the Romans. But where the Greeks generalized, creating ideal types, the Romans remained attached to specifics, including individualized 'warts and all' portraits like this one.

Augustan classicism: marble relief from the Ara Pacis in Rome, with a crowned goddess and a young man. The idealized figures are partly Greek-inspired, but are also propagandist, intended to emphasize the peace and harmony brought by the Empire.

Hadrian as a benevolently god-like figure; appropriately, this bronze bust of the widely travelled emperor was found far from Rome, in Israel. A lover of all things Greek, Hadrian sponsored a classical revival in the arts.

Antonines by a softening romantic tendency, sometimes with retrospectively disconcerting effects: the odious Commodus, sporting the lion's skin and club of Hercules, looks a benign and soft-featured individual, with glamorous curly locks and beard. Sometimes the way in which an individual was portrayed varied over time; images of Marcus Aurelius in the Capitoline Museum at Rome, for example, show him impossibly youthful-smooth and beautiful, and then nobly middle-aged; finally, on his column in Rome, he is trouble-scarred and disillusioned at the end of his life. An outstanding feature of Antonine portrait sculpture in marble was the treatment of hair; by carving and drilling the sculptors achieved virtuoso effects that successfully captured the wild and wavy fashions of the time.

The Romans disliked empty surfaces, and consequently huge numbers of reliefs were cast or carved on walls, altars, gates, tombstones, sarcophagi and other objects. The largest were on the great marble monuments of the Flavians and Antonines, where they served a vital propagandist purpose. They are particularly satisfying because, unlike many other reliefs, they can be viewed in the setting for which they were intended. The Arch of Titus in the Forum celebrates the victories of Vespasian and his son in Judea; among the reliefs is one showing Roman soldiers carrying off the seven-branched candelabrum from the Temple in Jerusalem. By contrast with these scenes, tucked away inside the arch, Trajan's column is florid and boastful. The reliefs wind round and round the column from bottom to top in a continuous scroll, and the style too is less restrained: instead of action shown realistically, Trajan's soldiers and their enemies are arranged in registers, one above the other, as if on a slope, filling up the available space vertically as well as laterally. This is not a failure but a conscious device: at the expense of photographic realism, the column provides a continuous, crowded, thrilling narrative, in 150 episodes featuring 2,500 figures. In its details it is highly realistic, giving graphic pictures of throwing a pontoon across a river, setting up a camp, and other operations involving the Romans' military engineering skills.

Augustan age a distinctive style of official sculpture was developed which gave a noble or idealized turn to realistic portrayals, no doubt for conscious propagandist reasons. The famous statue of Augustus from Livia's villa, his arm extended in an oratorical gesture resembling a benediction, is the portrait of a real man, but very much the real man seen in the most favourable light, as the bringer of universal peace. The reliefs on the almost exactly contemporary Altar of Peace (*Ara Pacis*) are consciously 'classical' in style, featuring a dedicatory procession that echoes Greek reliefs on the Parthenon in Athens. Although the carving is technically very assured, and animals and plants are closely observed, the overall effect is a little bland. Augustus himself is ever-youthful in his portraits, as befits the saviour-figure if not the human being.

Flavian portraits went back to the realistic tradition, but this was modified under the

The column of Marcus Aurelius, erected 80 years later under his son Commodus, obviously derives from Trajan's column and has the same subject: imperial campaigns against northern barbarians. But its spirit is different: the figures, deeply cut, are more emotionally expressive: instead of the smooth Trajanic narrative of victories, their horrors blunted by a kind of serene assurance that emanates from the emperor and his troops, the Aurelian column is discontinuous and violent, as if designed to turn men against war. The late-Antonine sense of unease, manifested even in these scenes of triumph, is also visible in the famous equestrian statue of Marcus Aurelius – a bronze that survived the Middle Ages only because it was wrongly believed to represent Constantine, the first Christian emperor, and was therefore an object of veneration. Although on horseback, the traditional image of human majesty and mastery, the emperor is thought-oppressed, and his raised hand gives him a gloomily prophetic rather than military air. The art of this period already hints at great changes to come.

Equestrian statue of Marcus Aurelius, c. AD 165, which stood on the Capitol in Rome until recent times, when it was taken for protection to a nearby museum and replaced by a replica. It survived the centuries, unlike many triumphal images, because it was believed to represent the Christian emperor Constantine.

PAINTINGS AND MOSAICS

Painting gives us a pleasantly different view of the Roman world, which is otherwise known almost exclusively through restricted media such as mosaic, or from the hard, uncoloured volumes of bronze, brick and stone that comprise the sculptural and architectural record. The surviving Roman paintings provide a more sprightly and colourful view of Roman life, although there are too few of them to encourage generalizations. All are wall paintings, and were probably regarded as decorative rather than 'serious' works, unlike those intended for galleries; the Romans certainly had both public and private galleries, and almost certainly followed the Greeks in filling them with the works they considered to be masterpieces. These have vanished, and what remains is a small selection (random, not qualitative) of room decorations intended to be lived with and difficult to evaluate in terms of a now largely non-existent tradition. Scholars have, however, categorized the largest group of murals, from buried Pompeii, into four distinct styles, depending on their subject-matter and the extent to which the style is illusionistic (painted realistically enough to deceive the eye). Illusionism was certainly popular, since it appeared to enlarge the room by turning the wall into a lovely landscape or creating false windows that looked out on mock-architectural features; and the inclusion of masks and theatre architecture in a number of these paintings suggests a preoccupation with the interplay between reality and illusion such as occurred in the Baroque art of 17th-century Europe. Although the quality of the surviving works is uneven, the best painters had a grasp of most perspective effects and foreshortening, and an ability to render the play of light – skills that were later to fall into disuse in Europe until the 14th century AD.

The strongest impression given by Roman wall painting when seen on the spot at Pompeii is of an unexpected lavishness. After the reserve of the street facade, the painted interiors had a palatial air, all the more striking for the sparseness of the furnishings; and beyond, in the courtyard, more bright, bold scenes and decorations stretched round the walls behind the colonnade; although now broken and faded, these must have been splendidly effective when fresh and seen in combination with garden, fountains, statuary, sunlight and people.

A second impression is of the all-pervading nature of myth. The paintings at Pompeii confirm that the imaginative and emotional life of the Roman was saturated by myths, despite the fact that so many of them were not native creations but had been imported from Greece. At its most serious, in the Villa of the Mysteries, the myth embodied religious truth: the marriage of Bacchus and Ariadne and the initiation scenes in the house were part of the same visionary experience. Elsewhere, in a painting from a house on the Esquiline Hill in Rome itself, the spectator looks between painted pillars at a wall-filling enchanted landscape whose misty romanticism turns out on a closer examination to be devoted to the adventures of Odysseus. On a more ordinary level of pictorial anecdote Thisbe

Part of a Roman picture gallery in the atrium of the House of the Vettii at Pompeii. The house was owned by two wealthy merchants who filled it with paintings that were only a few years old when Pompeii was destroyed in AD 79.

discovers Pyramus self-slain, Pentheus is torn apart by women in a Dionysian frenzy, and the infant Hercules reveals his potential by strangling serpents. The use of myth for anecdotal painting is understandable, but the Romans seem to have been reluctant to abandon the mythical convention even where it was manifestly unnecessary (much as Italian Renaissance painters put forward every picture of a fetching young woman with a baby as the Madonna and Christ Child). Even a subject from ordinary life such as women playing knuckle-bones – a stunningly beautiful drawing on a marble plaque from Herculaneum – is translated into Niobe with her daughters, of whom she was so proud that jealous deities struck them down.

Roman love of nature, expressed with an apparently spontaneous art in the 'garden room' of the Villa of Livia at Prima Porta, near Rome; 1st century BC. The delightful painted garden runs round all four walls.

A rather self-conscious sea-god Neptune drives over the waters in a chariot drawn by two horses with fishy tails. The mosaicist's technique is of a high order, highlighting surfaces and capturing a range of textures.

A number of paintings show the extent of the Romans' interest in nature and everyday life. Many decorative or symbolic compositions have a few details drawn from the natural world and closely observed – blossoms, an eagle, birds and snakes, a crab being ridden by a cupid, a dog chasing a stag, foliage shading a dreamy Narcissus beside the fatal pool (he saw his own image in the water, fell in love with it and pined away). Pure landscape is found in a large and lovely painting from the villa of Livia in Rome – a garden-orchard with trees, blossoms and birds enveloped in a nostalgic-seeming blue-green atmosphere. Everyday life appears whimsically on a frieze in the House of the Vettii at Pompeii, where a row of cupids are working as goldsmiths, wine merchants and flower sellers, while elsewhere an official or baker hands out loaves to eager customers. There are also portraits – of the rather solemn young lawyer Terentius Neo and his wife, and of a pretty 'sappho' who holds her stylus to her lips while, lost in thought, she looks straight through the spectator.

Just enough Roman painting survives to tantalize and provoke speculation. Mosaics, less easily destroyed and less vulnerable to variations in climate and temperature, can still be seen in reasonable numbers over most of the once-Roman world. This was another art invented by the Greeks (who began by using coloured pebbles) and taken up with enthusiasm by the Romans. Greek and Hellenistic mosaics were relatively small pictures with borders, inviting the kind of scrutiny given to works of art in spite of the fact that they were laid out on the floor. The Romans, characteristically lavish, covered entire floors with mosaic, although for a long time designs restricted to black and white were preferred in Italy; more colourful mosaics, both abstract and figurative, appeared in the western provinces, and particularly in North Africa, which has yielded some of the finest and best-preserved examples of the art.

The basic technique was to set *tesserae* (black-and-white or coloured pieces of stone) into a bed of mortar, so that they formed a pattern or picture. At their most refined the *tesserae* might be tiny, specially manufactured cubes of coloured glass; in skilful hands these could give highly naturalistic effects, even extending to gradations of tone. However, surviving mosaics show very wide differences of style and quality; inferior examples can be poorly drawn as well as carried out on the cheap with large, labour-saving *tesserae*. Wall mosaics were also popular, as excavations at Pompeii and Herculaneum have revealed; perhaps some people favoured them because they were less likely to depreciate than paintings, thus reducing the owner's bills for redecoration. Mosaics were particularly effective as ornaments for the fountain-niches in Pompeian houses, often featuring intricate, colourful, bead-like designs reminiscent of Eastern and later Byzantine styles. By contrast, the famous Alexander Mosaic from Pompeii is a splendid battle-scene showing the youthful Macedonian conqueror, Alexander the Great, confronting his Persian quarry, King Darius; while a lively naturalism appears in the grand Nilotic scenes on Alexandrian mosaics, teeming with watery plant and animal life and including loving portraits of hippopotamuses and crocodiles, carefully labelled in Greek for the benefit of the uninformed. Finally, to support the contention that there is nothing new under the sun, some Roman mosaics are so patterned that they shift, contract and expand under the gaze, very much in the style of 1960s Op Art.

Although the Empire contained many peoples, provincial art styles tended to be variations on the dominant Hellenistic-Roman mode. This was even true of Egypt which, more than any other country, figured as a land of mystery in the Roman imagination, never yielding herself wholly to outside influences; a striking example of the funerary exoticism she inspired in Romans is the pyramid-tomb of Cestius at Rome, close to the Porta San Paolo. The Egyptians returned Cestius' compliment by adapting Hellenistic portraiture to their own ancient burial customs, which entailed drying out, embalming and bandaging the corpse so that it would last for ever as the physical home of the dead person's soul. During the Roman period the Egyptians took to inserting vividly realistic painted portraits of the dead among the wrappings of mummies; they were painted on wood or canvas, using powdered colours mixed with hot wax, and are consequently known as encaustic paintings. Their quality is staggering and the effect they produce is almost eerie; these painted men, women and children are astonishingly, insistently lifelike, looking straight out at the spectator as if to communicate their sad consciousness of transience and mortality.

Intensely alive, though gone before. This portrait of a young woman is one of the beautiful and vivid encaustic paintings placed among the wrappings of mummies in Roman Egypt; 1st century AD, from the city of Antinoöpolis.

OBJECTS OF LUXURY AND UTILITY

Many ornamented domestic items and *objets d'art* have survived from the Roman world, their numbers greatly increased by intentional and accidental burials; the eruption of Vesuvius in AD 79 was of course the most spectacular, saving Pompeii and its neighbours from centuries of plundering, melting down of metals, and destruction through use. As a result it is possible to appreciate the sophisticated skills of Roman craftsmen, whose creations often carried on traditions already well-established in the Hellenistic East.

Many of these craft works were for use or display in the houses of affluent Romans. Their residences were more than places of security and comfort: since the role of patronage played such a large part in Roman life, regular visits by his clients made it essential for a patron to decorate his public rooms in a suitably impressive style. Wall paintings, mosaics, busts and statues demonstrated his wealth and good taste, but the general effect was enhanced by the presence of elegant figurines and sumptuous utilitarian objects. This partly (though only partly) explains the Romans' reluctance to leave any surface undecorated; but whereas the result is sometimes oppressive in large-scale works, it is often charming when applied to everyday objects. Typical of this taste are oil lamps covered with reliefs or fashioned as dogs' heads, or phalluses, or dolphins ridden by cupids; and pieces of furniture with horse's-head terminals and supported by sphinxes and paw feet. In much of their public art the Romans sought to commemorate historical events or glorify emperors; in private they were more likely to indulge a preference for mythical narrative, theatrical or erotic scenes, or images of the natural world. They drew on a wide decorative repertoire that comprised scrolls and fluting, cupids and sea monsters, floral borders and leaves, and many other motifs. At their most luxurious the works of Roman craftsmen might be made of precious metals and brilliantly bejewelled or enriched by a great variety of techniques including fretting, beading, layering, colouring, engraving and inlaying.

However, humbler materials were also used to good effect. Terracotta (unpainted and unglazed pottery) was a great all-purpose material, mass-produced from moulds as oil lamps, figurines, tiles, spouts, roof ornaments and small plaques. The oil lamps were made in many ingenious shapes as well as in the standard 'boat' form with a relief on the top. The relief plaques were originally intended as external decoration but soon moved indoors and were usually embedded in the walls. Now known as Campana reliefs (after the pioneering collector-scholar who first studied them), they mainly feature mythological scenes in a consciously 'classical' style, and were perhaps popular because they were cheaper than marble reliefs, and cheaper and also more durable than wall paintings, especially where climatic conditions were unsuitable. The same considerations may account for the widespread use of plaster (stucco) reliefs in baths, where wall paintings

Opposite: terracotta oil lamp: an everyday object for the discerning customer, with an interesting shape and a surprising amount of decorative detail. As a bonus, there are two little mould-made scenes on the top that are very much to the Roman taste.

Magical craftsmanship. This bronze hand was evidently intended to be a potent object. It is shown in an attitude of benediction and was evidently intended to exercise a considerable occult influence, since it is festooned with charms.

British treasure: a spectacularly large silver dish, 61 cm (24 ins) across; from a silver hoard found at Mildenhall in Suffolk, England. It is thoroughly pagan in its revels and its exceptionally sinuous figures; mid-4th century AD.

about AD 100 Arretine ware had been driven from the market by cheaper *terra sigillata* made in Gaul; and later still Gallic wares were in turn displaced by North African products.

Pottery often served as a relatively inexpensive substitute for materials such as bronze, silver and glass. Although most large-scale works in bronze were melted down from late antiquity onwards, craft artefacts have fared better. Bronze was used to make oil lamps, a variety of dishes, vessels and pails, mirrors, furniture fittings, caskets, votive and decorative figures and arms and armour. The huge scale of military operations probably did much to stimulate Roman bronze technology. Advanced solid- and hollow-casting techniques had been developed by the Greeks, but the Romans devised new methods of prefabricating parts and greatly improved soldering, welding and other assembly techniques; consequently they were able to mass-produce bronze objects of all kinds for civilian as well as military consumption.

Silver was a softer, and therefore less workaday, metal than bronze; but it was also more valuable. Wealthy Romans used it for elaborately worked cast plate rather than jewellery, although those who could afford them bought silver rather than bronze mirrors. The prestige of silver plate was such that, on their accession and on other occasions for celebration, emperors habitually presented large, splendidly decorated examples to high officials and other favoured individuals. Like most objects made of precious metals, Roman silver has only survived through being lost and discovered centuries later – for example at Boscoreale near Vesuvius, which shared the fate of Pompeii and Herculaneum, and at Hildesheim, where the hoard may have come from the baggage of the unlucky Varus, whose legions the Germans destroyed. Even more discoveries have been made of hoards that were almost certainly buried by people who found themselves in danger and vainly hoped they would be able to dig up their valuables when better times returned; this situation occurred all too often from the 3rd century AD, and the many hoards unearthed include a famous late Romano-British cache at Mildenhall in Suffolk, England.

would have deteriorated rapidly; and in fact some stucco reliefs are believed to have served as reproductions of famous paintings.

The Greek tradition of painting pottery vessels with figures and scenes disappeared as early as the 3rd century BC, and the main Roman type was *terra sigillata*, 'stamped clay', so called because it was often signed by the maker. Sometimes also known as Samian ware, it was a red-gloss pottery made in moulds, usually with relief decoration (also moulded); because of the absence of colouring to distinguish the relief from the red ground, it makes a rather subdued impression, but the designs are often reminiscent of the classical Greek or Augustan style in their clean-cut elegance. The history of *terra sigillata* shows Roman industrial production at its most cosmopolitan. The ware originated in the eastern Mediterranean, reaching Italy during the 1st century BC. There the main centre of production was Arretium (modern Arezzo); but by

Glass was made plain for everyday use and also in more sophisticated forms. The material was cast in moulds until about the mid-1st century BC, when glass-blowing techniques were developed. Blown glass was favoured because it was so much quicker and cheaper to produce, but reliefs and other effects could only be achieved by using moulds. Eventually, in the 1st century AD, the techniques were combined and the glass was blown into moulds. Roman taste tended towards the florid and highly coloured, but their preference in drinking vessels was for colourless, translucent glass. But there were also set-pieces, cut with extraordinary virtuosity, such as the famous Portland Vase from the Augustan period, made in two layers (itself a feat) with blue glass within white; by cutting away most of the white glass to leave only figures and objects, the craftsman created a white relief on a blue ground. Equally spectacular and much stranger, 4th-century 'cage cups' were so deeply cut that the end result was a vessel surrounded by a fragile set of glass rings that were barely attached to the body.

Roman taste in personal adornment was not characterized by restraint. Gold was the preferred metal, worked in a variety of well-established techniques to make hair ornaments, pendants, pins, rings, and mounts for precious and semi-precious stones. Gem-cutting was highly skilled and, to judge from the craftsmen's names that have been recorded, mainly practised by Greeks. Designs might be cut so that they appeared beneath the surface of the gem (intaglio) or so that they stood out as reliefs. Stones such as sardonyx, in which there were layers of more than one colour, could be carved into cameos, with the relief subject standing out against a background in a different colour, as in the Gemma Augustea, a celebration of the Augustan *Pax Romana* that is as impressive in its way as the monumental *Ara Pacis*.

A cameo fit for an emperor, cut from a sardonyx in the 1st century AD; the gold and enamel setting was added in the 18th century. The subject of this beautiful piece is the Emperor Claudius and his infamous wife, Messalina.

THE ART OF LATE ANTIQUITY

For several centuries the mainstream of Roman art was based on naturalism, or fidelity to physical appearances. In late antiquity this Greek-influenced 'classical' tradition gradually gave way to an art of symbol and pattern, designed to convey a message rather than identify an individual or tell a story. The change took place very slowly and not at all smoothly: despite the general trend away from naturalism, classical elements reappeared in the visual arts at various times and places over a long period, even outlasting the Roman Empire in the West.

The otherworldly message of Christianity found an effective vehicle in the new art, but did not initiate it; here as elsewhere, Christianity began by employing or adapting the existing Roman culture. The earliest surviving Christian works are paintings, most of them done on the walls and ceilings of the catacombs outside Rome where believers were buried. Some do include symbols which served as codes for Christian phrases, notably the cross, the fish and the Chi Rho, a device that combined the Greek letters X and P as an abbreviation of *Christos*, Christ. But

The Good Shepherd, from a mosaic in the Mausoleum of Galla Placidia in Ravenna; mid-5th century AD. Despite the tendency towards a more patterned, symbolic art, naturalistic detail persisted for a surprisingly long time.

the figure-style of the paintings was based on classical practice and the subjects were often reworkings of episodes from classical myth, which were treated as allegories of Christian truths. The un-classical subject of the crucifixion rarely appeared, and the most popular image of Jesus was as the Good Shepherd, a being with familiar associations thanks to the pastoral conventions of classical literature and art.

Meanwhile new tendencies were appearing in official sculpture. They are particularly easy to identify on the Arch of Constantine. Erected to celebrate the exploits of the first Christian emperor, the arch is traditional in form but unusual in incorporating carvings from imperial monuments dedicated to Trajan, Hadrian and Marcus Aurelius alongside contemporary reliefs featuring Constantine; presumably the intention was to portray Constantine as the most recent of the 'good' emperors. But aesthetically the contrast between the works of the two eras is very striking: the older scenes are naturalistic, achieving a sense of movement and depth, and the individuals and groups shown in them interact with one another; whereas a relief such as one that shows Constantine giving money is emphatically non-classical: stylized, flattened and static, with the figure of the emperor enlarged and centrally placed to emphasize his supremacy and the foreground of the panel crammed with a row of near-identical suppliant figures.

Constantine's patronage made it possible for Christians to build special places of worship, and the earliest churches were adaptations of existing Roman buildings. Pagan temples were not designed to hold large congregations, so a type of municipal hall, the basilica, became the model for early Christian churches; it consisted of a large oblong hall, with aisles created by colonnades and a semi-circular apse at the end. Constantine built many basilican churches; none survive in their original form, but there are examples of interiors in Rome from the 5th century, including Santa Sabina and Santa Maria Maggiore.

The opulent decorations of Santa Maria Maggiore (completed in 440) display the wealth and confidence of the now-established Christian Church. By this time mosaic was

Solemn, frontal, hieratic: the Emperor Theodosius I is shown at a ceremony commemorated on a large silver dish of AD 388. Although it is skilfully made, the emperor appears as majesty personified rather than a recognisable individual.

becoming the chief form of decoration, spreading over ever-larger surfaces and creating dazzling colour effects. Here, too, naturalism was progressively abandoned and figures were simply lined up in frontal poses, staring ahead so that they communicated, if at all, only with the spectator; the most famous examples of all are the groups showing the Emperor Justinian and his empress, Theodora, with their retinues in the church of San Vitale, Ravenna. Similar effects are seen in imperial groups featuring the late 4th-century Emperor Theodosius on a silver plate and on a relief added to an Egyptian obelisk. A medium with points in common with mosaic, *opus sectile*, also became popular during the late imperial period. It consisted of large pieces of coloured marble fitted together into a scene or pattern; the effect, anti-naturalistic but rich and striking, is seen in examples from the 4th-century Basilica of Junius Bassus.

Ravenna was an outpost of the East Roman Empire, and the church of San Vitale belonged to a new architectural style being developed at Constantinople whose masterwork was the church of St Sophia, based on raising a central dome on square walls. Though far from being a complete break with classical principles, it too belonged essentially to a new age.

6 THE ROMAN LEGACY

BY THE END OF THE 5TH CENTURY AD THE ROMAN EMPIRE IN THE WEST LAY IN RUINS AND NEW PEOPLES AND KINGDOMS WERE BUSY OCCUPYING ITS FORMER TERRITORIES. BUT ROMAN CIVILIZATION LIVED ON, BOTH MATERIALLY AND SPIRITUALLY. IN THE EAST, EMPERORS CONTINUED TO HOLD COURT IN CONSTANTINOPLE; BUT THE EAST ROMAN EMPIRE INCREASINGLY TOOK ON A GREEK AND MEDIEVAL CHARACTER THAT MADE IT VERY DIFFERENT FROM ANCIENT ROME – A FACT THAT HISTORIANS HAVE ACKNOWLEDGED BY RENAMING IT THE BYZANTINE EMPIRE. IN THIS FORM IT DEEPLY INFLUENCED THE NEIGHBOURING SLAV PEOPLES AND EVOLVED A CHRISTIAN IDENTITY THAT EVENTUALLY SEPARATED ITS CHURCH FROM THE LATIN (ROMAN CATHOLIC) CHURCH IN THE WEST. MEANWHILE NEW AND VIGOROUS SOCIETIES AROSE IN WESTERN EUROPE. THEY POSSESSED VALUES, CUSTOMS AND ARTS OF THEIR OWN, YET THEY REMAINED OVERAWED BY THE ACHIEVEMENTS OF THE ROMANS, REPEATEDLY LOOKED BACK AND SOUGHT TO LEARN FROM THEM, AND VIEWED MANY OF THEIR OWN GREAT MOVEMENTS AS PARTLY INVOLVING A RETURN TO CLASSICAL VALUES. EVEN THE MODERN MIND, HOWEVER CULTURALLY INDEPENDENT, IS SATURATED BY WORDS, THOUGHTS AND IMAGES THAT ORIGINATED WITH THE EXTRAORDINARY CIVILIZATION OF ANCIENT ROME.

THE BYZANTINE EMPIRE

Catastrophes aside, there are few clean-cut endings in history. The last emperor in the West was forcibly retired in AD 476, but in the East the Roman Empire went on without Rome. However, these East Romans who spoke Greek are not the people we normally mean when we talk of the ancient Greeks and Romans; and historians have generally agreed to distinguish between the East Roman Empire of late antiquity and what is now known as the Byzantine Empire, which belongs to the history of the Middle Ages. The reign of Justinian (527–565) makes a convenient watershed, although some historians defer the transition from Roman to Byzantine until the disastrous 7th century, when the Arabs, inspired by the doctrines of Islam, swept out of the Arabian peninsula and conquered the Near Eastern and North African provinces, which became part of a huge new Muslim empire that stretched from Spain to India.

From this time onwards the heartland of the Byzantine Empire was Anatolia (Asia Minor), with more or less precarious extensions in the Balkans and Italy. The empire was beset from west and east by Slavic and Islamic enemies, and much of its subsequent history represents a struggle for survival. Even so, Byzantine wealth, luxury and culture were the astonishment of barbarians, both west-European and Slav: the wonders of Constantinople, the size and splendour of its palaces and churches, and its mechanical and military marvels (including the famous Greek fire, a sort of Molotov cocktail) had a great deal to do with the conversion of the Slavs to Christianity. Unwilling to defer to a 'barbarian' Rome, Byzantine Christianity asserted its independence, ultimately emerging as the Eastern Orthodox Church, which still commands the allegiance of most Slav and Greek Christians. Byzantium produced a flourishing Greek literature, a Greek version of Roman legal codes, and a splendid and opulent art which found expression in illuminated manuscripts, wall paintings, mosaics, ivories, metalwork and enamelling.

From the 9th to the 11th century the empire was at its height; but then disaster struck. The Normans expelled the Byzantines from Southern Italy; and in 1071 the Byzantine army – prudently nurtured and conserved for centuries by a limited-risk strategy – was shattered at the battle of Manzikert by a new people, the Seljuk Turks. Manzikert, and the loss of Anatolia, were blows from which the Byzantines never properly recovered. Help arrived from western Europe in the form of crusaders, but 'Latins' and 'Greeks' got on badly, and during the Fourth Crusade (1204) it was the crusader Latins, not the Turks, who stormed and took Constantinople for the first time in its history. Within half a century most of the Latins had been driven out, but the empire was now visibly in decline. A new Turkish people, the Ottomans, surged into Asia Minor and on to the Balkans, bypassing a beleaguered Constantinople, and during its last years Byzantium was little more than an Ottoman vassal state. The storming of Constantinople in 1453 – nominally the end of one of the great epochs of world history – was almost an anticlimax. However, as events in the West were already demonstrating, the heritage of ancient Greece and Rome lived on.

Byzantine forces drive back the Bulgars; 11th-century miniature. The Byzantine Empire survived many onslaughts before falling to the Ottoman Turks in 1453. It preserved and passed on important elements of Greco-Roman culture.

ROMAN HERITAGE

The posthumous influence of ancient Rome has no parallel in history. The barbarians who had almost unintentionally brought down the Empire wondered at its works and imitated it as well as they could; and for centuries any advance in western civilization was equated with a restoration of Roman institutions, styles and values. In AD 800 the Frankish king Charlemagne crossed the Alps and was crowned emperor by the pope; in effect Charlemagne was perceived as a new 'Roman' emperor, and the central European Holy Roman Empire (however un-Roman in reality) remained on the map for the next thousand years. The uneasy relationship between Holy Roman Emperors and popes was a central issue of medieval politics. As bishop of Rome the pope was also a successor to the Roman emperors, deriving part of his authority from his position in the old world capital; and, of course, as *pontifex maximus*, he inherited his title from pagan Rome.

Struggling to recreate civilization, men like Charlemagne could think of nothing better than to imitate antiquity – sometimes in a literal reproduction like Aachen Cathedral, which is San Vitale, Ravenna, with some refinements absent. Rulers in the Dark Ages continued to use the main Roman unit of currency, the solidus, and copied it when they became confident enough to mint their own coins. The literature and learning of the ancient world was largely preserved through the

Rome revived. In this painting by J. L. David, Napoleon distributes eagle standards in a consciously Roman-imperial setting. Napoleon went from First Consul to Emperor, building triumphal arches and much else in Roman style.

efforts of monks, who wished to preserve the heritage of civilization despite their suspicion of pagan authors' morals and messages; and the earliest attempt to create a Christian drama was undertaken by a Saxon nun who produced sanitized versions of Terence's comedies for convent use.

The first great European style of architecture betrays its affinities in its name: Romanesque. In its 12th-century successor, Gothic, Europeans at last produced a great style that owed little to the classical past; but intellectually they were still dependent on Roman and Greek authorities (the latter mainly in Latin versions). Everywhere in the medieval West, Latin was the language of learning, law, theology, diplomacy and debate, although long since 'dead' as the vernacular of a people.

Remarkably, when new intellectual and artistic preoccupations appeared with the Renaissance, they were mainly expressed in terms of a renewed cult of antiquity. Petrarch, like the Roman poets, was laurel-crowned on the Capitol. The Dutch satirist Erasmus polished his Latin style through the study of Cicero. Architects studied the Roman author Vitruvius and built domed churches and country villas. Artists like Michelangelo were inspired by Roman copies of Greek masterpieces. Beginning in Italy, the Renaissance spread out over Europe, taking various forms; its promotion of Latin literature influenced everything from poetic metre to the four-act play, and made Virgil and Ovid major influences on European writers from Dante to Shakespeare and beyond.

In the 16th and 17th centuries the vocabulary of art remained classical, although the Mannerist and Baroque movements put it to uses that would have outraged the Greeks and Romans. The 18th century brought the first extensive discoveries at Pompeii and Herculaneum, inspiring a new version of the antique, Neo-Classicism, which transformed interior decoration and placed a little temple in the grounds of every country house or Palladian (that is, Roman-style) villa.

At the end of the 18th century the hold of antiquity seemed as strong as ever. Rousseau's *Du Contrat Social*, often regarded as the textbook of the French revolutionaries, discussed political problems almost entirely in terms of Greek and

Roman history. The revolutionaries themselves, partly inspired by Neo-Classical painting, aped Brutus and Cato; while their ladies (once things had relaxed a little) dressed in sexy dampened 'classical' shifts. Napoleon, First Consul and Emperor, with his legion of honour, Arc de Triomphe and eagles, was even more conscious of playing a heroic-antique role.

Even the replacement of Latin by vernacular languages, the rise of science and the advent of the Industrial Revolution failed to shake the hold of classical antiquity on the western mind. For better or worse, in the 19th century Greek and Latin remained central to upper-class education, and classicism in art and architecture came to represent a rejection of the new. Consequently the reaction against Victorianism also affected attitudes towards the classical past; some people still think of it as dull, although 'blockbuster' films have done a great deal to cure that. Now, technology and Post-Modernism may – arguably – have made the Roman heritage 'irrelevant'; but it remains obstinately embedded in contemporary language and ideas. Senates, capitols and dictators are still with us, and in our time *Apollo* has landed on the moon and Mars beckons.

Rome revived, 20th-century style, in this instance as a gargantuan American consumer fantasy at Las Vegas. It remains to be seen whether any more meaningful Roman revival will prove possible in the course of the 21st century.

INDEX

PHOTOGRAPHIC
ACKNOWLEDGEMENTS

In source order

AKG, London 7 Centre, 10 insert, 26 insert, 49, 51, 85, 97, 110 Main Picture, 112 Bottom, 136 insert, 161, 162 Main Picture/Archaeological Museum, El Djem/Gilles Mermet 7 Bottom Centre, 98, 112, 158 Main Picture, 174/Bibliotheque Nationale, Paris/Erich Lessing 179/Chateau de Versailles, Musee Historique 7 Centre Right, 184 Main Picture/Coll. Archiv fuer Kunst und Geschichte Berlin 3 Background, 7 Background, 13 Background, 18 Background, 30 insert, 181 Background/Deutsches Archaologisches Institut, Rome 144/Hilbich 21, 81, 135, 140 Main Picture/Karthago Museum/Erich Lessing 16/Kunsthistorisches Museum, Wien 40, 142, 145, 154 /Erich Lessing 7 Top Left, 44, 65, 66, 87 Bottom, 94, 115, 155, 156 Main Picture, 164, 170, 180 Main Picture/Gilles Mermet 64, 84/Museo Capitolino, Rome 11, 25/Musee de la Civilisation Gallo Romaine, Lyon 7 Bottom Left, 112/Musee D'Art et d'Historique, Metz 101/Musee du Bardo, Tunis 159/Musee du Louvre, Paris 37, 68-69, 109, 151/Museo Archeologico, Florence, Italy 12/Museo Nazionale Romano del Terme 173/National Museum of Archaeology, Naples 8 insert, 17, 18, 27, 79 Bottom, 102, 139, 160/Rheinisches Landesmuseum, Trier/Erich Lessing 71/Joerg Sorgen 171/Staatliche Antikensammlung, Munich 24 /Erich Lessing 13/Vatican Museum, Rome 34, 36, 62-63
Ancient Art and Architecture Collection 54/Donald Sheridan 74
Bridgeman Art Library, London/New York 57/Agrigento, Sicily/Peter Willi 14/Ashmolean Museum, Oxford, UK 131 Top Right/John Bethell 48/Bode-Museum, Germany/Bildarchiv Steffens 175/British Museum, London, UK 58, 157, 177 178/David Lees, Florence 46/El Palatino,Italy/Index 172 insert/Fitzwilliam Museum, University of Cambridge, UK 107/Forum, Rome, Italy 132 Main Picture/Galleria e Museo Estense, Modena, Italy 100/Herculaneum, Campania, Italy/Index 75/Kunsthistorisches Museum, Vienna 35/Kunsthistorisches Museum, Vienna, Austria 42/Leptis Magna, Lybia 83/Lourvre, Paris, France/Index 138/Louvre, Paris, France 93, 96, 143/Metropolitan Museum of Art, New York, USA 22, 105/Museo Archeologico Nazionale, Naples, Italy 8-9 Background, 10 Background, 14 Background, 20 Background, 26 Background, 30 Background, 32, 36 Background, 43, 44 Background, 46 Background, 52 Background, 54 Background, 56 Background, 58 Background, 62-63 Background, 68 Background, 74 Background, 76 Background, 78, 80, 84 Background, 86 Background, 94 Background, 98 Background, 102 Background, 104 Main Picture, 104 Background, 108, 110 Background, 114 Background, 116 Background, 118 Background, 118 Main Picture, 120 Background, 122 Background, 124 Background, 128 Background, 132 Background, 136-137, 140 Background, 146-147 Background, 148 Background, 149, 150, 152 Background, 156 Background, 158 Background, 162-163 Background, 168 Background, 172 Background, 176 Background, 180 Background, 182-183 Background184 Background/Museo della Civilita Romana, Rome, Italy/Roger-Viollet, Paris 90, 99, 128 Main Picture/Museo Ostiense, Ostia Antica, Rome, Italy/Roger-Viollet, Paris 117/Museum of Antiquities, Newcastle upon Tyne, UK 29/Naqsh-e Rustam, Iran 53 Bottom/National Museum of Scotland, UK 125/Pinacoteca Capitolina, Palazzo Conservatori, Rome, Italy 1, 9/Privat Collection 41, 163 Main Picture/Privat Collection, Accademia Italiana, London, UK 106/Roman Baths Museum, Bath, Avon, UK 127/Rome, Italy/Index 141/Somerset County Museum Taunton Castle, UK 15/Staatliches Museum, Berlin, Germany 52/Verulamium Museum, St Albans, Hertfordshire, UK 103, 129/Villa Medici, Rome, Italy 169
Corbis UK Ltd/Archivo Iconografico 2, 72, 137, 176 Main Picture/Gianni Dagli 130/Werner Foreman 82, 168 Main Picture/Christel Gerstenberg 134/Angelo Hornac 59/Mimmo Jodice 3 insert, 6-7, 77, 89, 131 Bottom, 147, 153/David Lees 88, 167/Araldo de Luca 67, 166/Michael S. Yamashita 38/Joel W. Rogers 185/Mark L. Stevenson 61/Vanni Archive 53 Top, 76/Adam Woolfitt 6, 126, 146 Main Picture/Roger Wood 31, 92/Yann Arthus-Bertrand 80-81
Image Bank/Andrea Pistolesi 124 insert/Guido Rossi 60
Werner Forman Archive 7 Top Right, 19, 33, 45, 50, 55, 63, 114 Main Picture, 116 Main Picture, 119, 122 Main Picture, 133, 152 Main Picture, 165/Academia de la Historia, Madrid 181/Biblioteca Nacional, Madrid 182 insert/British Museum, London 28, 47, 79 Top, 95Pinacoteca Capitolina, Rome 56/Paul Getty Museum, Malibu, USA 87 Top/Museo Gregoriano Profano, Vatican, Rome 91/Museo Nazionale Romano, Rome 39/Museo Archeologico Nazionale, Naples 73/Scavi di Ostia 70